WindowFrames

WindowFrames

Learning the Art of Gestalt Play Therapy the Oaklander Way

Peter Mortola, PhD

A GestaltPress Book

published and distributed by
The Analytic Press
Mahwah, NJ

Copyright 2006 by   The GestaltPress
127 Abby Court
Santa Cruz, CA 95062

and   165 Route 6A
Orleans, MA 02653

email gestaltpress@aol.com, gestaltpress@comcast.net

Distributed by   The Analytic Press, Inc.
10 Industrial Avenue
Mahwah, NJ 07430

Library of Congress Cataloging-in-Publishing Data

ISBN: 0-88163-463-8

"All of us, from cradle to grave,
are happiest when life is organized
as a series of excursions,
long or short,
from a secure base..."
Bowlby, 1988

This book is dedicated to
Liz, Noah, and Violet

CONTENTS

12 Afterword

List of Figures and Tables

Foreword
by Violet Oaklander, PhD

It is my great pleasure to write these supportive words for this most welcome book. Can you imagine what it is like to have someone so interested in your work that he spends years participating in it, analyzing it, and writing about it? I sometimes think of Peter Mortola as a guardian angel of sorts.

I have been doing this two-week intensive training program that Peter writes about every year since 1981, and for six years I offered two of them. The work is joyful, very intense, exhausting, and sometimes lonely. I think that I sometimes lose sight of its overall value and spend too much time focusing on the work it takes just to make it happen. Yes, I know people come from all over the world. Yes, I am aware that there is nothing else like it around and the need for learning about good work with children is vast. And yes, people seem very enthusiastic about it. But when it's over, they leave, I clean up, put the supplies and equipment away (no easy task), and that's that. Occasionally, I hear from someone about how the training helped them in working with children, but I am already back to my regular life. During those two weeks, I come alive, it seems, and then when it's over, I'm back to my everyday way of being. Then Peter came along.

I met Peter when I first moved to Santa Barbara in 1987. He had read my book in the Confluent Education graduate program at the University of California at Santa Barbara. He heard I was here and asked to meet with me to talk about a manual he was writing for actress Jane Fonda's performing arts camp for children and adolescents. From the first time we met, it seems as if we have never stopped talking. Even though he moved to Portland, Oregon, six years ago to join the faculty in the Counseling Psychology program at Lewis and Clark College, we still talk. Besides continuing our work in the summer training program each year, we have also traveled to New York, Cleveland, and (amazingly) South Africa to present and do workshops together.

Peter's interest in my work sparked new energy in me. He decided at one point that he wanted to write about what I was doing and eventually that work became his dissertation. He has attended the training program each summer for ten years. At first he was a participant, then a helper and a documenter, and finally, for the last five years, he has been my co-presenter. Instead of being alone in this work, I now had someone to talk to about it, to share what was happening, and to get the kind of feedback that can only come from someone as deeply interested and involved in this work as I have been.

Besides the pleasure I have had from working and laughing with Peter, there is more. Peter has the ability to look at the work and tell me what I am doing from a fresh perspective. Peter has seen patterns in my work that I never knew existed. He has also linked my approach to other writing and research, such as narrative work, for example, in ways I hadn't previously considered. By his endless questions and interviews with me,

Peter has forced me to really think. I found myself explaining aspects of my approach in ways I had never done so before. Since so much of what I do is intuitive, it surprised me that my brain was also able to conceptualize the work.

Peter and I are also a great working team. At the training, he has taken the role of providing an overview of the work's structure and offering his analysis and synthesis to the participants as we go along. Peter has enriched the two weeks more than I can say. From the evaluations we receive, I know that the attendees feel this way too. Peter and I also bounce our ideas and feelings off each other after each day—something I never had an opportunity to do before he came along. This, in and of itself, is a tremendous aid in presenting the very best experience possible to the participants.

There is another aspect to this as well. Peter has not only written about my approach, he has also been an integral part of it. He has lived it and he believes in it. Needless to say, time has a way of continuing on and taking me along with it. I'm probably well past the age when most people retire, and there are times when I feel that I have done enough and now I just want to sit back and rest, and, of course, write. I don't think I could continue doing the training program if it weren't for Peter. There is a lot of administrative work, a lot of planning, and plenty of schlepping. The training program is important, I know that. Peter knows this, too, and is willing to do whatever he can to keep it going. And he knows this program in a way that I have never been able to describe to anyone else. He knows it from many viewpoints: participant, observer, schlepper, schedule planner, teacher.

Thank you, Peter, for writing this book. I hope those of you who read it will gain from it an appreciation of what it takes to create and run such a training program, as well as insights into the complexity of teaching adults to learn how to work with children and adolescents in a vital and effective way.

Violet Oaklander

Santa Barbara, CA

August, 2004

Introduction

About this book

This book is about two, related things. First, it is a book about Dr. Violet Oaklander's particular approach to doing therapy with children and adolescents. Second, it is a book about her methods of training adults to do that kind of therapy with the children and adolescents with whom they work. These two things are related in that Dr. Oaklander's methods of doing therapy with children and her methods of training adults share important parallels. These parallels are explored throughout the book, and the result is a text that should be of interest to anyone involved in or interested in working with children or adolescents in the counseling, therapeutic, or educational contexts. Essentially, I believe this book will be of interest to anyone who wrestles with a fundamental question that has captured my ongoing attention: how does one come to understand and work effectively with children?

About Violet Oaklander's theory and practice

Dr. Violet Oaklander is a pioneer of child and adolescent therapy. Her 1978 text *Windows to our Children: A Gestalt Therapy Approach to Children and Adolescents* presented a model of working with children and adolescents in the therapeutic setting that has since influenced practitioners worldwide. Presently, this text is published in ten languages – English, Spanish, Portuguese, Italian, Serbo-Croatian, Croatian, Russian, Chinese, Hebrew, and German. Work is underway to translate the book into Korean and Czech as well. *Windows to our Children* is also a popular textbook used in counseling programs at universities and colleges around the world, including Australia, New Zealand, South Africa, Brazil, Israel, Canada, the United States, and many countries in Europe. Despite her worldwide reputation as an eminent trainer, psychotherapist, and scholar, one of the keys to Dr. Oaklander's success is the personal, relational style that she brings to all her interactions and her writing as well. To honor this relational approach to her work, for the rest of this text Dr. Oaklander will be called by the name most everybody uses when referring to her or her work: Violet.

After twenty-five years of maintaining a private practice working therapeutically with children and adolescents in California, Violet is currently supervising and consulting with therapists who work with children and adolescents as well as working on a follow-up to her first book. Additionally, Violet is regularly invited to give presentations both nationally and internationally. In April of 2000, for example, nearly 500 mental health workers attended trainings that Violet was invited to give in three South African cities. Recently, Violet has been the keynote speaker at three major international child therapy conferences held in Cork, Ireland; Graz, Austria; and Mexico City, Mexico.

Violet offers a two-week intensive summer training each year in Santa Barbara, California for mental health professionals working with children and adolescents. It is that summer program that is the focus of this book. As I write these words in the Spring of 2005, the summer training scheduled for July is already fully booked and has been since early February. As usual, there is a waiting list, and also as usual there are participants coming to the training this year from all over the globe, including Mexico, South Africa, Ireland, Italy, Saudi Arabia, and Hong Kong.

So what is it about Violet's work that appeals to mental health practitioners in so many diverse cultural settings around the globe? What can be learned from a close study of her therapeutic methods with children and her training methods with adults? These are the questions that I became interested in over ten years ago when I first learned about Violet's work, read her book, and began attending her workshops and trainings. It will take me the bulk of this book to fully address these two questions. In this brief introduction, however, I would like to touch on two things that I think serve as the foundation not only for Violet's vast popularity with practitioners and but also to her rich contribution to the field of child therapy at large. First, Violet holds a unique theoretical perspective for therapeutic work with children and adolescents that makes sense to practitioners. Second, she is able to put that theoretical stance into seemingly effortless action in way that practitioners can understand. Put succinctly, Violet has a good talk, and she knows how to walk it.

The unique theoretical orientation that Violet holds in regard to her therapeutic work with children and adolescents is grounded in Gestalt therapy theory (Perls, et al., 1951). Although many mental health practitioners have had a cursory introduction to Gestalt therapy theory in their own training (watching a videotape of Fritz Perls' confrontational work with Gloria, for example), most have never connected a Gestalt therapy approach to working with children and adolescents. Moreover, Gestalt therapeutic work is stereotypically thought of as a set of tricks or techniques (using "the empty chair," for example) and not as theoretical orientation with any depth or breadth (Perls, L., 1992). Once practitioners have read *Windows to our Children* (Oaklander, 1978), however, or attended one of Violet's trainings, they begin to understand the richness and uniqueness that her Gestalt orientation has to offer.

One way that Violet's Gestalt-based theoretical approach is unique in the field is in the way that she holds a deep and abiding belief in the central role that authentic relationship plays in the therapeutic process. Without what Violet calls a "thread of a relationship" being established between the child and the therapist, no therapeutic work can happen. Violet's stance about the therapeutic value of relationship is based in Martin Buber's (1958) description of the "I/Thou" relationship in which two individuals come into a relationship as equals and remain open to what the encounter may bring. As Buber states, "All real living is meeting."

Violet's theoretical stance regarding authentic relationship offers both a challenge and an invitation to practitioners interested in her approach to therapy. The challenge is that the therapist must meet the child or adolescent in the therapeutic encounter in an authentic way (Latner, 1973). From a Gestalt therapy theory perspective, assuming the role of an "expert" or an "authority" or a clichéd therapist will not be helpful (Polster and Polster, 1973). A therapist must bring his or her authentic self to the therapeutic encounter in a way that encourages children to also engage authentically as well. But how does one do this within the responsible and healthy boundaries that must exist in a therapeutic relationship with children? Throughout this text, we will see how Violet negotiates this issue in multiple settings.

Though this kind of authenticity in a therapeutic relationship can be a challenge, Violet's relational approach also offers an invitation and a rare sense of permission to practitioners. Her approach invites practitioners to be themselves in their work, to let go of artificial roles that do not fit or make sense to them (Nevis, 1992). I stress this idea of the unique invitation to be authentic because so many of the dominant models of working with children (both therapeutically and educationally) emphasize the taking on of specific, prepackaged roles — and the personal distance that results with such professional role-playing. There are many variations: practitioners are taught to identify children's problems and assume an expert stance in telling children how to solve them; practitioners are taught to observe a child's play, keep their distance, and make only reflective statements about what they see; practitioners are taught to interpret a child's drawings and design interventions based on those professional interpretations; or, practitioners are taught how to manipulate behavior and other variables to bring about desired results with children. In none of these approaches is an authentic, non-hierarchical relationship between the child client and the adult therapist considered central to what might happen therapeutically.

In contrast, Violet has represented, written about, and embodied a unique theoretical perspective that puts the relationship between the therapist and the child at the center of the therapeutic process. This theoretical stance allows Violet to address and work with what is happening relationally with the child at the moment it is happening. For example, if Violet is working with a child who is struggling with attentional issues, she may sit with that child on the floor and work with him using clay to help him to make sustained contact not only with the clay project at hand but also with her as a therapist. In this way, Violet uses her theoretical approach based in a relational way of working as both a diagnostic and a therapeutic guide, as a way to both identify problems and intervene with them. Throughout this text, Violet repeatedly emphasizes that if a child has difficulty building a relationship, then that is where the work must start. Examples of Violet doing such relational work are woven into many of the chapters that follow.

The brief description I just gave regarding Violet working with a child with clay speaks to what it is about her work that makes so much sense to practitioners: Violet has a theoretical stance rich in ideas about what troubles children as well as rich in ideas about how to help them. In other words, Violet's work answers the troubling concern many practitioners have regarding what to actually *do* with a child or adolescent in therapy (*Windows to our Children* was in fact originally entitled *What Do I Do with the Kid?* when it was in the pre-publication stage).

What you do with children in therapy, Violet shows throughout this book, is to establish an authentic relationship with them and to help them to be in healthy contact with both themselves and their environment so they can work to get their needs met and continue developing in productive ways. Children get pushed off the path of healthy development when they are met with relationships that are not supportive and when they are cut off from healthy contact with themselves and the world around them. Violet believes that experiencing a healthy relationship and good contact in the therapeutic context is restorative for an injured child. From Violet's Gestalt therapy perspective, this lived experience of relationship and contact offers support to the self-regulating capacities of the children with whom she works. Violet works to "strengthen the self," as she describes it, not to control or manipulate it. In this way, Violet's approach reflects, as Wheeler (2005) describes, "a deep faith in each person's innate striving for growth and wholeness." In our present social climate where our work with children is more rooted in the defensiveness of behavioral medications and anger management, Violet's optimistic and gentle approach to child therapy offers a clear and unique alternative.

Part of the reason for this introduction of the theoretical richness and complexity behind Violet's therapeutic approach is that her work can look deceptively simple. The elegance with which she puts her theory into action with both children in therapy and adults in the training can obscure the deep theoretical base that grounds her work. At its root, her theoretical approach addresses the most foundational philosophical concerns regarding how children learn and grow. Epistemologically, her Gestalt-based approach both describes and demonstrates how children construct knowledge about themselves and their world through their relationships with others. Deeper still, Violet's approach demonstrates, ontologically speaking, how children come to be who they are through their relationships with others and through contact with the environment in which they live. Importantly, Violet's theoretical orientation to working with adults in the training also gives us a parallel demonstration of how adults learn and develop through such a relational, constructivist approach.

A close reading of the following chapters will reveal not only pragmatic ideas about how to work with both children and adults, but also how these practical methods are deeply rooted in a theoretical orientation based on Gestalt therapy theory as it has evolved and developed over the past fifty years. Although I cover some aspects of this theory in the chapters that follow, I refer the reader who is interested in a deeper grasp of this topic to the rich body of literature that exists regarding Gestalt therapy theory (e.g., Latner, 1973; Nevis, 1992; Oaklander, 1999; Perls, et al., 1951; Perls, L., 1992: Polster and Polster, 1973; Wheeler, 1991, 2000, to mention only a few authors).

About the structure of this book

The form of this book mimics the form of Violet's two-week summer training program. Thus, each of the first ten chapters of the book describes and highlights the events of one day of her two-week summer training. Additionally, these first ten chapters each conclude with a section entitled "reflective notes" in which I reflect on and analyze these daily events as well as discuss them in relation to broader context of the two-week training as a whole. These reflective notes highlight the more structural and directive aspects of Violet's work and, in that way, are complementary and contrapuntal to her seemingly fluid and non-directive approach to therapy and training. Hopefully, these reflective notes will contribute to a more complete understanding of her work.

The eleventh chapter of this book, a kind of epilogue, follows Violet to South Africa to explore cross-culturally relevant aspects of her approach through the voices of child therapy practitioners in that country half a globe away from her home. In the twelfth and final chapter of this book, I describe in more detail the background and methodologies that underpin my long-term research project of Violet's work that enabled me to collect and analyze the data that formed the basis of these chapters.

Briefly, the bulk of the data for this book was collected in the summer of 1997 as part of what has become an ongoing research project for me (1996-2005). The book as a whole primarily reflects that particular training as it unfolded over the ten-day period of July 14-25, 1997. However, since Violet's training methods have necessarily changed and been modified over time, I have added some elements from later trainings (1998-2004) that help the book more truly reflect the summer training as it has evolved over time. Even though this book is then in some ways a hybrid of Violet's ongoing summer trainings, anyone who has experienced the training and reads this book will recognize it in large part. Anyone who has not experienced Violet's summer intensive training will be able to understand through reading these chapters the basic forms and lessons that these trainings over the years have contained.

This book is meant to serve as a kind of bridge in a number of ways. First, I link descriptive observation and reflective analysis of Violet's work in the construction of each of the chapters that I have just described. Second, I show connections and parallels between Violet's work with adults in training and her work with children and adolescents in therapy. Lastly, by beginning the book in Santa Barbara and ending it in South Africa, I show that Violet's approach serves as a bridge for diverse professionals working with children and adolescents in varied cultural contexts. By making these connections explicit, I strive to offer in this book not only a clear "window" into Violet's methods of therapy and training, but also a kind of "frame" or helpful way of looking at her approach. Violet's ground-breaking book, *Windows to our Children,* was written to help adults gain a better view into the emotional lives of children and adolescents. The central intent of this book is to help the reader gain a helpful view — a well-framed window — into Violet's methods of training adults to do that kind of therapy with children and adolescents.

Acknowledgements

Because this book is essentially about the human processes of struggle, change and learning, I could not have written the following chapters if many individuals had not been willing to have their own moments of struggle, growth and change described in these pages. For this reason, I sincerely thank each of the training participants and the child guests that were willing to let me write about their sometimes very personal experiences in the training.

My heartfelt thanks also to Jeffrey Fletcher, Robert Lee, Jon Snyder, Elizabeth Stephens, and Gordon Wheeler for your support and encouragement in the writing of this text. My biggest thanks, of course, go to Violet who opened up her trainings, her mind, and her heart to me over the years with sincere trust and friendship. It has been a truly inspiring gift to see the essential helpfulness of your approach in so many diverse settings and with so many individuals and groups.

WindowFrames

1

Day One: Monday
Building a Relationship

"Let's get started"

People from all over the world are coming in the door of the conference room. Marisa has come from Brazil. Dawn is from New Zealand, and Juan Carlos says he is from a beautiful city on the outskirts of Mexico City. I can hear the lilting sound of Portuguese mixing with the sweet twang of English as it is spoken in southern Mississippi. It is the first day of Violet Oaklander's "Intensive Summer Training" on a mid-July, Monday morning in Santa Barbara, California, and, as in years past, it is an international affair.

This diverse group of twenty-four participants put on name tags, pick up binders full of handouts, and then each finds a place to sit, either around the perimeter of the room or on the floor in low-slung chairs. As the participants settle into their seats, Violet turns down the quiet music that has been playing on the CD player and calls everyone's attention to the front of the room where she is sitting. "Okay," she says, "Let's get started."

In contrast to her reputation as a world-renowned therapist and trainer, Violet's manner is casual and comforting. She wears a t-shirt with a colorful drawing and words that state "my head is full of children." She says something funny as she looks for her glasses, laughs a little, and a good number of the participants laugh along with her. She welcomes all the participants, tells them she is excited they have all made the effort to come, and states matter-of-factly that she has some business to take care of. She starts going down a long list of items ranging from "taking care of one's own coffee cup" to how she will "control the feedback" when she works with volunteer participants in front of the group.

Even though I have participated in numerous summer trainings and workshops led by Violet, I am always a bit nervous at the beginning of them. I imagine I am not alone with this feeling, as we are all new members of a brand new group. I look around the room and notice a number of shy smiles and a few awkward glances, but I also sense a general excitement that we have brought with us into this room that we all will share for the better part of the next two weeks.

Even with our collective "opening day jitters," I am once again surprised how quickly I notice any anxiety in the room dissipating. There are a number of things that Violet does to help set a comfortable opening tone to the training. First, she jumps right into dealing with the details. Somehow it is comforting to see her go around the room and respectfully check with each participant to make sure names and addresses are correct on the roster that she has provided. Second, she asks each of the participants to introduce themselves, telling a bit about where they are from, what brought them here, and what they would like to get out of the training. It is fascinating to hear the participants speak, some with English that is tinted by an Irish, Spanish, or New Zealand accent.

Two of this year's participants are from Mexico, two are from Ireland, one is from Brazil, and one is from New Zealand. Seven participants come from a wide range of states across the U.S. including Mississippi, Texas, Montana, Oregon, and Ohio. Most of this year's participants include in their introductions how they have a number of years experience in the practice of psychotherapy or counseling with children and adolescents, though the settings widely vary — from community mental health centers to schools, foster care organizations, and hospitals. Of this year's participants, 21 are female and 3 (not counting me) are male. There are 4 participants with Ph.D.s and 3 who are psychologists. The rest of the group members have Masters degrees in Psychology or Education. Generally speaking, this group is fairly representative of the mix of participants in the training over the years in terms of gender, professional orientation, and international participation.

During the opening introductions, the sixth participant to speak references "the bible" when referring to Violet's book *Windows to our Children*. Joan, a Social Worker from Mississippi, says, "Your book is like the bible to me, I keep it by my bedside at night and look at it when I need to feel inspired about my work." There are plenty of nods and smiles after this comment, and it is referenced and reinforced by others in the group as the introductions continue.

In prior years, I have teased Violet privately about such

biblical references to her book, especially in light of the fact that she was raised in a Jewish family by parents who were very politically progressive and atheists to boot. It has become a kind of "inside joke" for us each year to wait and see who will be the first to utter such a comment. When they do, I can't help but smile inwardly. At the same time, I have learned to respect the deep feeling her book has engendered in the participants who speak so glowingly and with the deepest sincerity about the impact it has had on them in their therapeutic practice with children and adolescents. In fact, it is this reverence of her text and work from practitioners world-wide that first got me interested in finding out just what she does in her trainings and practice that speaks so powerfully to such a diverse set of participants. What I found will be explored at the heart of the chapters that follow.

After the participants have completed their introductions, and just after a fifteen-minute morning break, Violet leads everyone in an exercise that further helps this diverse group to "arrive" and relax into the training.

"Draw yourself as a child"

During her opening comments, Violet had mentioned that each day of the training will generally follow the same pattern: we will begin at nine in the morning and go until four-thirty in the afternoon, with short morning and afternoon breaks, and a longer break at lunch. On this first day, just as participants are getting resettled in their seats after the morning break, Violet announces "All right. Now we're going to do a drawing." Spread out on the floor in front of her are large sheets of drawing paper, piles of sturdy drawing boards, large containers of many-colored pastels, crayons, and markers, and small plastic bowls to hold a handful of these drawing implements. Violet introduces this drawing exercise with the following directions:

We're going to begin with an experience now. What I'd like you to do is just to get as comfortable as you can in the place you're sitting. I'd like you to close your eyes. I always start these experiences with a little relaxation exercise. I do the exact same exercise with the kids that I work with. All ages. So just kind of go inside yourself and see how you feel. Notice if you have any aches or pains. Just notice it. Notice how your legs are placed, how your arms are placed, and feel free to move at anytime. If you want to change your position it's okay. Feel the pressure of the chair and the floor against your body. Wiggle your toes. Notice how you breathe. What I'd like you to do is take a deep breath. Hold it, and then let it out. Do that again. Take a deep breath, hold it, and let it out. Let's do it once more. Notice when you let it out your shoulders generally drop. Try that again. Take a deep breath and then let it out.

I'm going to make a sound. I'd like you to listen to the sound for as long as you can [she rings a small chime twice]. What I'd like you to do is to go back to a time in your childhood, some memory of your childhood that suddenly pops into your mind when I say that. It could be a happy memory, it could be a sad memory, it could be an angry memory, or a mixed memory. Go back to a time...it could be way back, or it could be in the middle years, or it could be as a teenager. Pick a time. Pick a memory. You don't have to have this memory in great detail. It could be a vague memory. Go back to this memory and notice what's happening to you in that memory. Where are you? What surrounds you? Who is with you, if anyone? Maybe you're not with anyone.

And then notice how you feel in this particular memory. Get a sense of what it was like for you to be this child. I'm going to ask you in a minute to draw this. Always remember, I won't have to understand your drawing. You can use colors, lines, shapes, scribbles... whatever. You can use color or no color. However you want to do it. You might want to draw the feelings in colors, lines, and shapes. You might want to draw stick figures to make it easy. It doesn't have to be a wonderful drawing. I'm not grading you on the drawing. It's just for you to set down this memory.

So when you are ready, you can open your eyes and, without any talking, I'd like you to get a drawing board and a piece of paper. Take a handful of pastels or markers and put them in a bowl. You can stay in the room; you can go outside; you can go in the hospitality room or out on the patio. You'll have about 10 minutes to do this drawing. You don't have time to do a great drawing. So when you're ready, I'd like you to do that. You can take a handful of pastels, and if you don't get the color you want, you can always come back and find the color you need.

As participants slowly open their eyes and quietly start collecting materials with which to draw, I notice how the atmosphere in the room shifts. Now, instead of the "surface level" expressions and connections one is used to making in a new group composed of professionals who are mostly strangers to each other, suddenly there is a relaxed silence where participants are focusing on their own memories and on choices related to color, form, and the kind of physical and emotional expression that is allowed through the simple act of drawing. After doing my own drawing about being a sixth-grader home from the hospital and being visited by friends, I jot down the following notes in the margins of my drawing:

> People are sitting around on the floor, using pastels, quietly drawing. Violet sits and watches. I draw from childhood, too, and it is relaxing to draw. First to do the relaxation, then to draw, and to be quiet with a group, engaged in a non-verbal activity. (July 14th, 10:45 a.m.)

Later in the evening of that first day, I wrote more about this activity in my reflective notes for the day:

> I had such a strong sensation and my feelings changed when the room went from the somewhat formal, verbal, legs crossed and notebooks on laps, early-morning activity – to when I looked around the room after doing my first drawing and saw intense, silent, non-verbal

activity that filled the room with color – I felt excited, engaged, and relaxed. (July 14th, 9:26 p.m.)

After about ten minutes of drawing time, Violet asks participants to "begin to finish." About a minute later, when they are done, she asks them to break up into groups of five to share their drawings. She stresses that we are to share the pictures "as a way of getting to know each other" and that we should avoid analyzing them. Having moved from personal reflection to silent expression, the participants now describe their drawings to each other in small groups. After approximately 20 minutes, when everyone has been regrouped by Violet, she asks for general comments on the activity. One participant comments about the "childlike medium" of the crayons and pastels and how important they were for her "expression of childhood experience" that Violet had requested.

Another participant comments on the difference between the crayons and the pastels, remarking that the pastels "were harder to use, but loosened you up a little." This comment was echoed in my own small group discussion by Siobhan, a child therapist from Ireland, who said that the "messy pastels helped her draw more like a child would." When Siobhan said this, I remembered that when Violet and I were getting the drawing supplies ready the night before, Violet had purposely chosen more pastels than crayons or markers, wanting to encourage this type of expressive exploration. She had also made a comment regarding how the real purpose of the drawing was for the participants to remember their own experience as children: "You can't do this kind of work and not remember what it's like to be a child."

"Why kids come into therapy"

After participants have had a chance to make comments on the first drawing exercise, Violet says that she would like to talk about "what brings kids into therapy." Having just had a rich sensorial experience themselves, participants now hear Violet state that the two main reasons children come into therapy are related to sensorial experience or lack of it. The first basic problem is related to what Violet calls "an inability to make good contact," or, as she defines it, "the ability to be fully present in a situation using all the modalities and senses of the organism to do so: looking, touching, tasting, seeing, listening, smelling." The second basic problem related to contact is "a diminished sense of self" that is caused by blocking one's emotional and sensorial experience. Violet describes:

> Anything that you can name that brings a child into therapy has something to do with cutting themselves off in some way. When I say that kids cut off, I mean that they get cut off from their own ability to make contact with both their own needs and the resources in the world around them to get those needs met.

Given the framing of these two fundamental problems that bring children into therapy, Violet states that the "job of therapists is to unblock emotions and help children get back in contact with their own emotions, bodies, and their natural ability to cope with life." As Violet describes,

This is based on the theoretical idea from Gestalt therapy theory called "organismic self-regulation." To understand this concept you need to see the way the human organism constantly works to regulate itself, to find homeostasis, to find balance. It tells us when to eat, when to sleep, when to go to the bathroom, and when to drink water [she sips from glass]. And if we don't listen it will make things much worse. If I didn't listen to my thirst, eventually I wouldn't be able to talk. It tells us what we need, and when we meet that need then there's balance. This is the process of living. The same thing is true for all the aspects of the self: psychologically, emotionally, intellectually, and spiritually. We constantly have new needs that we have to look at because we are always in a different place in life. Children have a lot of trouble recognizing and meeting their needs because they are changing all the time.

Violet states that organismic self-regulation is the natural ability of the organism to maintain equilibrium by becoming aware of and addressing its own needs. Such self-regulation, she explains, "makes you feel relaxed — like how you feel after a good cry." She goes on to say that this self-regulating process in children can be interrupted when they begin to restrict or block themselves, their emotions, and the awareness of their needs. Children end up in therapy when they have lost contact with their own self-regulating abilities, she explains. Therapists can help children in therapy to make better contact with their own self-regulating process by first getting them back in touch with all the aspects of their organism — their senses, their emotions, and their thoughts. By getting back in touch with themselves and their own self-regulating process, children also are able to make better contact with the therapist and the rest of the world in order to work to get their needs met. Through this experience of making good contact with themselves and others, children are also able to gain a more definite and affirmative sense of themselves and their capabilities.

The House, Tree, Person drawing

To demonstrate how a supportive and nurturing therapeutic relationship with the therapist is fundamental and primary in this therapeutic process of helping a child make better contact with themselves and the world, Violet next leads the participants through a variation of the House, Tree, Person drawing (Jolles, 1964) just after the afternoon break. Violet often uses this drawing at the beginning of her therapeutic work with a child, she states, for three reasons: 1) to help the child enter the therapeutic process easily through an artistic, sensorial exercise; 2) to help build and strengthen the relationship with the therapist, and 3) to help both the child and the therapist begin to construct a "window" to the child's world and needs.

"For this drawing," Violet says to the training participants, "we are not going to close our eyes. I just want you to draw some scene, any scene you like, as long as it has in it at least one house, one tree, and one person." For the second time on this opening day of the workshop, participants are hard at work silently spreading colors over their sheets of paper. Only the sounds of tearing paper and scratching pastels can be heard while visually the "color quotient" in the room rises dramatically once again.

After about ten minutes, when the participants have finished their drawings, Violet describes the way that she uses these drawings with children. She frames this exercise as something she does with children to help them make "statements that define themselves." In this way, this exercise is in alignment with the theoretical issue she discussed earlier about developing a strong "sense of self." Violet describes how she helps her client make "self statements" by saying to the child or adolescent, "Your drawing may tell me something about you, and I will try and figure that out. But I need you to tell me whether I am right or not, okay?"

Violet goes on to describe how she makes statements about what she notices about the drawing and what it says to her and then she asks the child to confirm or disconfirm these statements. She then writes down what the child says on back of the drawing and, in doing so, demonstrates that what the children say about their own drawings is more important than how the manual or the therapist interprets the children's drawings.

After this brief introduction to the participants, Violet begins to move around the conference room, making statements about each of the drawings that the participants have made and asking the participants to confirm or refute the validity of her statements. She does this with the tone of a playful guessing game and with a general sense of lightness and fun. To Elizabeth, who has drawn a house with many large windows, Violet says,

"This drawing, with all these large windows, tells me that you might be a very open person." Elizabeth responds: "This is true, there are times when I feel very open, but there are also other times when I do not feel open." Violet then says that if this exchange took place with a child client of hers, she would write down this information on the back of the drawing, along with other things she learns about the child through their discussion. The object, she emphasizes, is not to interpret the drawing, but rather to build a relationship and help children make statements about themselves:

> At this point in the therapy, we don't delve deeper. Because we are making a relationship, there is a lot of material that will show itself. But to address that material now before the relationship gets stronger would scare children and make them defensive.

As Violet moves around the room on this first Monday afternoon, I write the following in my notes:

> She spends a lot of time doing this, moving in and out of the "audience space" (warming up the crowd?). By doing this she is actually modeling the introductory work she does with kids to build a helpful relationship...and she is doing it with us too. It is interesting that she goes "in and out" in this exercise. She describes what she would do with a child (e.g. "I would write that on the back") and then she goes back in again as if she were talking to a child (e.g. "I would say, 'You'll have to tell me because I

could be totally wrong, but I think you feel rushed in your life. This person in the drawing looks so relaxed reading a book under that tree. To me that often means that this is a wish, and that maybe you don't have enough time in your life to relax like this. That's why I said you might feel rushed. Is that true?'")

As Violet makes her way around the room, demonstrating how she would use these House, Tree, Person drawings with children, the adult participants in the group also end up learning quite a bit more about each other. One participant agrees with Violet that she loves her home and gardens (Violet had guessed that "Home is important to you. I say this because in the drawing the person is standing in the doorway of a big house.") Another participant, though, says that the long walkway to the house in her drawing does not mean, as Violet guessed, that she "is a fairly private person." Instead, the participant says that she is a "pretty open person, just a little shy at first when I meet new people." This is a good example, Violet says, of the kind of "self statement" that she hopes children will make, some kind of statement that will help children define themselves on their own terms, thereby strengthening themselves as well as the relationship with the therapist.

More than one participant in the group has drawn a tree laden with fruit standing beside the house. Violet shares a good laugh with the group when she quotes from a version of an interpretive manual for the House, Tree, Person drawing that states, "pregnant women or those desiring of children often draw apple trees" (Jolles, 1964). Violet also shares how the manual states that a child who draws an animal peeking from a hole in the tree may have, "and, I quote, 'regressive yearnings for a withdrawn, warm protective uterine existence.'" This type of adult, clinical interpretation of a child's projective drawing is the opposite of her approach, Violet states. Instead, she says that her work is based on children deriving their own meanings from their own drawings:

> As you will see in the many projective-expressive exercises we do in the next two weeks, I don't find it helpful to interpret. I try to help children identify and own the projections in their drawings, sand trays, clay pieces, whatever. The work is in helping them identify and own what parts of their drawings make sense for them, not in me telling them what their work means.

The closest she gets to interpretation, Violet goes on to state, is when she playfully takes a stab at what the House, Tree, Person picture might tell her about the person who drew it. But she always waits to see if her guess is accepted or not by the individual who drew it.

At 4:35 p.m., Violet closes the day by saying that tomorrow morning she will bring in examples of House, Tree, Person drawings to show how she has done this same exercise with children and adolescents. She also assures the participants as they leave that in the days that follow, her "non-interpretive" approach to expressive, projective exercises will become clearer.

Reflective notes for day one

In this first set of reflective notes, I will highlight an important theme that emerges on this first day of Violet's training. That is, that Violet conducts the workshop for adults in ways that are deeply parallel to the ways that she conducts the therapeutic process with children. These parallels run throughout the two weeks of the training and will be noted throughout this book. In this opening section of reflective notes, I will highlight two foundational parallels that exist between Violet's work in training adults and in doing therapy with children and adolescents. First, I will highlight the ways in which she emphasizes the role of relationship in both the training and therapeutic contexts, and, second, I will highlight the ways in which she emphasizes the role of experience in her work with both adults and children.

The role of relationship

One of the most notable themes that emerges early in Violet's training and that continues throughout the two weeks is the importance of the kind and quality of relationship that she establishes in her work with both children and adults. Tomorrow, on the second day of the training, Violet will spend a significant amount of the morning talking about the importance of creating a non-hierarchical relationship with her child and adolescent clients. In a parallel way, she has spent much of the first day working to build a similar kind of relationship with the adults in the training: a relationship that is non-hierarchical, yet containing clear boundaries, and a relationship that will serve as a "secure base" from which the participants can take risks in their learning.

Even though many of the participants come into the training already putting Violet and her work "on a pedestal," she immediately levels the playing field and sets them at ease in a number of ways: she dresses casually, makes jokes at her own expense, sits in a chair as part of the circle of participants (and not behind a podium), and generally does not allow herself to be put in a "one up" relationship. In this way, she works to create a more comfortable environment wherein the adult participants will be willing to take risks in their learning just as she hopes children will do in the therapeutic setting when she meets them using the same respectful and non-authoritarian approach.

Even though Violet presents herself in a non-authoritarian manner, this does not mean she is a pushover. One of the precepts of Gestalt therapy theory is that we can help others establish good personal and professional boundaries by making our own limits clear. In this way, Violet is congruent in her approach with both adults in training and children in therapy in that she does not set an overly-permissive atmosphere with either population. She sets clear limits and boundaries with the adult participants in multiple ways on this first day. One small example can be seen in the way she discusses "cleaning out your own cup" within the first 10 minutes of the training. A larger example can be seen in the way she describes the way that she will "control the feedback" when she works with volunteers in front of the group. In short, Violet is warm and welcoming with both adults and children, but she also lets them know very clearly that boundaries are important, both for her and for the participants.

Violet also parallels the therapeutic process with children and adolescents on the first day of the training with adults in the way that she moves slowly into exercises and activities that provide the adult participants with a sense of support, even as they are asked to take small risks. Yes, she has the participants taking the risk of drawing pictures with pastels in a group of professional colleagues, but the first picture they draw is of themselves as children. In this way, their first drawing helps the adult participants bring more of themselves into the training by literally drawing on their own experience. As Violet describes, children need a "strong sense of self" to function well in the world and, in a parallel way, she is helping the adults in the training strengthen their own sense of self on this first day as well.

The second drawing that the adult participants do in the afternoon of the first day is the House, Tree, Person drawing. Violet states explicitly that she uses this drawing with children early in the therapeutic process to "begin to build a relationship," and it serves the same purpose in the training with the adults. Instead of taking the authoritative position and interpreting what the adult participants' drawings mean, she lets them tell her if her guesses are correct or not. Thus, she demonstrates in the adult training the same stance she takes with children in therapy: it is a stance that invites active participation in safely, measured steps, all within the supportive context of a respectful and developing relationship.

The role of experience

Violet sets the tone early on in the training that the adult participants will be encouraged to take an active and experiential stance toward their learning. On the first day of the training, participants have already gotten their hands messy twice with oil and chalk pastels, markers, and crayons as they created two drawings and then used them in exercises with Violet and the other participants. Although there has been much note-taking and many scholarly issues discussed, Violet has stressed two experiential themes on this first day of the training. First, she makes clear her expectations that participants be able to bring into awareness, experience and discussion their own experience of childhood (as with the "draw yourself as a child" experience). Second, Violet makes it clear that the adult participants not only need to remember their own childhoods, but also to be experientially familiar with the same tools and practices that they will ask children to use in therapy. Violet stresses that adults doing this type of work with children must be comfortable involving themselves in the same types of experiences that they will ask of the children with whom they work. By the end of the training, participants will have engaged in many rich experiences involving their imagination and senses using clay, music, sand, and other expressive media, all of which they can apply directly to their work with children and adolescents in therapy.

In addition to having the adult participants engage in the same media of expression that children will be expected to use in the therapeutic process, Violet sets up the training so that the adult participants experience the therapeutic benefits of the work as well. For example, on the morning of this first day, Violet introduced two ideas involving the importance a child's ability to make good "contact" with themselves and others as well as the ability to have a strong "sense of self." Through engaging in the drawing activities of the first day, the participants have themselves already had an experience of making good contact with themselves and with others in the training, and, in so doing, strengthened their own sense of self at the beginning of this two-week adventure.

Additionally, throughout the training, the participants will not only make drawings and work with clay and other materials, but will also have opportunities to process these experiences at varying depths and dimensions. On this first day, participants briefly shared their childhood drawings and responded to Violet's guesses about their House, Tree, Person drawings. In this way, they have been able to "test the waters" of this training environment without risking too much. Within the next two weeks, however, participants will have more extensive opportunities to participate in the experiences and in the processing of the activities that Violet guides them through. On the third day of the training, for example, they will have 20 minutes each to process their experience working with clay and, during the next two weeks, about an hour each to process their experiential efforts during both the sand tray and the practicum experiences. In these numerous ways, Violet clearly signals the importance of an experiential approach to both learning and therapy, whether she is working with children or adults.

The two themes I have explored in this first reflective notes section, relationship and experience, serve as foundational pieces that underlie the entire two-week training to follow. In both therapy and training, the kind of relationship that Violet constructs with those with whom she works serves as the secure foundation from which risky experiences can be beneficially and successfully negotiated, leading to learning and growth for both children and adults.

24

2

Day Two: Tuesday
Making Contact

Child examples:
The House, Tree, Person drawing

At 9:03 a.m. on this second day of the training, after the participants have settled in place in chairs and on the floor with their coffee cups and notebooks, Violet greets everyone and wonders aloud, "So what did you all do last night?" After hearing some responses ("walked on the beach," "went to a restaurant with others," "went to bed early to recover from jet lag"), Violet encourages the group to spend time together outside the training and to be inclusive of those who are here alone. She then jumps right in to work by stating, "To finish from yesterday, I'll show you a few of the House, Tree, Person drawings from children that I have worked with."

Restating a point that she had made yesterday about the House, Tree, Person drawings, Violet reminds the participants that, "I don't use this as an interpretive tool. I'm really using it to make a connection." With that comment, she holds up a drawing from nine-year-old Adam that has a tower-like house and a line of little "garages" arranged in front, but no trees or people. (See figure 1 below.)

Figure 1: Illustration of Adam's HTP Drawing

Violet comments that some children won't follow the instructions to draw each of the requested items of a house, a tree and a person, and Adam is such an example. A participant, looking intently at the drawing, suggests that all the separate "garages" in the drawing make her wonder to what extent the child "compartmentalizes" aspects of his own life. But before she is able to finish this line of thought, Violet gently interrupts her to reiterate what she had said earlier:

> The purpose of these drawings from my point of view is to get the child to begin communicating with me. I don't use these as an interpretive tool. I'm really using this to make a connection. For example, I said to this boy, "This

drawing tells me that you like cars." And he said, "Oh, I love cars." So right away we have a connection. Sometimes other things will come up that they will tell me, and those to me are much more important than what I could interpret about the drawing. If I see something very unusual, I might think about it and see if it comes out in other work that they do to see if there is a theme there.

Another participant raises the question: "Do you also pay attention to the process of the child doing the drawing?" To which Violet responds, "Oh, thank you. That's very important!" She then goes on to tell the following story from her own practice:

Usually I'll say to the children, "Do you mind if I just sit over here and watch you draw?" Most kids tell me it's okay. I do truly love to watch kids draw. It's so fascinating to me. And I'll say to them that I really like to watch all kids draw. So I sit and watch them, and I watch their process.

An example of this is a twelve-year-old boy who put bricks on his house. And then he took a marker and he started coloring in each brick, which is really difficult with markers. And I could see if we waited he would never finish it on time. So I said to him, "Let's say we'll know that the house is covered with bricks. Why don't you do the rest of the drawing?" And when it was time to process it, I said, "I think you are somebody who tries really hard, who works really hard on things. But sometimes you set a goal that is too much, and then it's hard to finish it, and maybe some people get mad at you for that." And he started to cry. It's like I had gone right to the core of his problem, because everybody in this child's life complained. They thought he was lazy, that he didn't do his work, and that he didn't study. It wasn't that he was lazy, it was that he was wanting to do too much. He set the standards way too high.

So it was from his process of drawing that I got that. And sometimes you see kids who draw very quickly. It's like they can't make a connection. It tells me that might have they trouble with contact. They have to protect themselves.

Another participant asks the question, "What if you get a child who can't tolerate the amount of contact in discussing his picture?" Violet responds, "That's why we would stop. If I sense that they're getting very uncomfortable, I'll say, 'Okay, I think that's enough. Let me just read back to you what I wrote and then we can do something else now.'" This is related, Violet explains, to the Gestalt concept of "contact and withdrawal." All organisms have periods of needing to reach out to their environment to satisfy the needs they have, she says, but they also have the need to withdraw from contact. This is reflected in the pattern of waking and sleeping as well as in the pattern of needing both social contact and solitude. Violet says she tries to respect this subtle pattern in the counseling session as well, not pushing children to encounter issues they are not ready for.

Another theoretical concept that is central to Violet's practical work of doing therapy with children is that of "projection." Violet discusses this concept in answer to another participant's question, "Can you speak about the child that will just give you stylized drawings. Ones of, you know, Batman or a cartoon character." In response, Violet says:

Yes, and I certainly have kids who do that, especially boys about eleven or twelve [laughs]. That's fine. My philosophy is that everything is a projection. You hear me talking and you put your own experience to my words. I don't even know if you hear what I say. In other words, you take my words and put them into your own experience, which is good because you are trying to apply it to your own lives. I think that kids who are interested in those images are telling us that those images are touching something important in them. Like being the hero or being the all-powerful thing. So we just use that. I might say, "I think that you might like to feel more powerful, or maybe you already feel powerful in your life. Which one would it be?" And then they'll choose one.

This fundamental concept of projection will play a central role in many of the activities and exercises in Violet's training. The underlying idea being that given a chance to playfully draw or create something from imagination, both adults and children will "project" something meaningful from their own experience into what they create. Violet states that the work of "re-owning and re-integrating" projections is central to her approach, but that in order for such work to take place, a strong relationship needs to be developed between the therapist and the child.

"The working relationship"

Having spent the first part of the morning emphasizing the importance of making an early "connection" with the child through the HTP drawings, Violet says, at 9:33 a.m., "I want to talk about the therapeutic relationship." She points out to the participants that they have a hand-out in their binders on the "I/Thou Relationship" and asks them to look at it. She states that these ideas, fundamental to a Gestalt approach and to her own work, are based on the philosophy of Martin Buber (1958). She describes his philosophy in the following way: "Two people come together as equals. I'm not a better person in my role as therapist. I have that attitude and I meet them with that stance. It's very subtle and yet kids pick it up almost immediately...My presence in the relationship..."

In one succinct passage from the hand-out, clear references are made to the issue of "contact" that Violet discussed yesterday, as well as the issue of "relationship" that is being discussed today:

I have the responsibility to meet the child at her level (abstractly and concretely), to respect her rhythm, to be present and contactful, to be genuine and congruent (not manipulative and phony or playing a role), to honor and respect the child and the parents as entitled, worthy human beings (and not be judgmental or feel superior),

to respect my own boundaries and limits and put them
out clearly.

Also included on this sheet are the statements: "I am willing
to be affected and moved by the client. I can endure the pain of
not being able to make this client's life better — I can separate
myself from this pain." In reference to these statements, one of
the participants asks the question "Should you cry with a client?"
Violet responds to this question by telling the story of her own
efforts to seek competent counseling during the agonizing
process of watching her teen-aged son die of a rare form of
Lupus. She relates how both the first and second therapists she
went to see were overwhelmed by the sadness of the situation
("They turned to jelly") and ended up crying in front of her. The
third therapist she went to see wanted to give her medication.
Since none of these approaches were helpful to her, a friend
recommended that she go to Esalen to meet with Jim Simkin,
one of the founders of the Gestalt therapy approach. True to the
vision of the "I/Thou relationship," Simkin was moved by the
sadness of Violet losing her son, but also was separate enough
from the pain to help her "do the work" necessary to move
through the grieving process.

This experience was so significant in her own life, Violet
relates, that she pursued training as a Gestalt therapist,
ultimately incorporating this approach with what she had
learned about working with emotionally disturbed children in
her previous career as a special education teacher. In reference
to the importance of being "affected" by the client's pain and yet
also "separating from the pain," Violet states: "People ask how I

can work with people who have had such awful experiences and yet have fun?" She does not answer this posed query, yet the theme of "being able to play with that which is painful" will emerge as a central theme as the training develops.

"The first three minutes"

A playful activity that the participants move into immediately after this discussion is described by Violet as the "first three minutes exercise." She asks participants to practice the "I/Thou" approach by breaking up into pairs and taking turns pretending to be themselves as a child entering a new counseling relationship with an adult therapist. She asks participants to "watch what happens in the first three minutes alone with a child. Just begin the relationship and assess the level of contact you are able to make with the child without using any games, drawings, etc."

Soon there are pairs of participants spread out around the room and out on the porch, taking on their imaginary roles, each getting to know the other in the first three minutes of a counseling session. After about 15 minutes, the whole group is back together again to respond to Violet's question of "How was it?" A long discussion follows regarding what participants said they liked and didn't like as the child clients. Central to this discussion are issues of control and power when dealing with resistant children. "It's sooo slow, trying to get going," says one participant. To which Violet responds:

It's true. But you are working first on the relationship and then on contact. Some children are so injured emotionally that they have trouble making a relationship. So that becomes the focus of the therapy—finding creative ways to make the connection.

Another participant mentions: "As I child, I was aware of how fast I could tell if the therapist was being authentic with me or just playing the role." Violet confirms that children are a lot more sensitive to that than we imagine as adults.

As the noon hour approaches, Violet mentions that after lunch she will talk more about "contact" and that, later in the afternoon, the group will again be using the drawing materials that have been sitting unused in the middle of the floor all morning.

"Contact and the relationship"

Violet starts off the after-lunch session by stating, "I want to say a couple of words about contact which is an integral part of the counseling relationship." Although the topic of "contact" was introduced on Monday in her presentation of "what brings a child into counseling," Violet elaborates on the concept of contact today in the following way: "Ideal contact is having all of yourself present in a situation: your senses, body, emotions, intellect." Through making good contact, she says, we are able to use all these aspects of the self to meet the environment and get our needs met. Conversely, when we are cut off from our own senses, body, emotions and intellect, we are not able to make good contact with the environment and do not have the "self-support" necessary to address our own needs. She goes on to say:

> Self-support means that I feel strong enough to face inner or outer difficulty and assertive enough to work through conflict. Self-support is necessary for the child to go forward in the work of continuing to make good contact as more difficult issues come up in therapy. When it's not there the child will close down – and you can see contact is breaking. Children open and then close down throughout the therapeutic process. In this way, the work is done in small segments with children.

Thus, the therapist must respect the ebb and flow of both contact and withdrawal in developing a relationship with a child. Resistance in a child is not to be "overcome," but respected as a normal part of the process of developing an intimate and helpful relationship. Violet draws an image on the white-board that reflects how ideal contact includes both intimacy and withdrawal from intimacy (Figure 2). Too much withdrawal leads to isolation, but too much intimacy leads to confluence or enmeshment.

In this way, the child's relationship with the therapist is a kind of dance in which the child moves closer to the therapist, then backs away. It is this dance of relationship that helps the child learn both support of self and support by others in a healthy way. Through this healthy contact with a therapist, children are helped to have three powerful experiences: first, they are helped to get better in touch with the totality of themselves

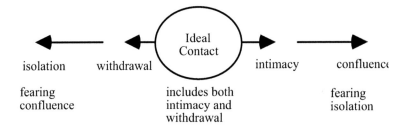

Figure 2: Ideal Contact

including their senses, feelings, and thoughts. Second, they are helped to make healthy contact with others, in the person of the therapist. Third, by making healthy contact with both themselves and the therapist, they are engaged in having positive experiences at the contact boundary, the place where the self and the world meet and the place where all important needs of the self must be negotiated.

Toward the end of this discussion of contact and relationship, Violet tells the participants that she would now like them to do a drawing that she calls "the Safe Place drawing." Violet describes that this drawing is an example of an exercise that can be used early in the therapeutic process when the relationship, trust, and good contact are still being developed. She says, "This exercise is not heavy, and it appeals to kids. It's non-threatening, but it goes a little bit deeper." She also states that even though she uses both the Safe Place drawing and the House, Tree, Person drawing early in the therapeutic process, both of these drawings can be used again later in the counseling process as well.

The Safe Place drawing

After a few moments in which the participants put down their notes and get re-settled in their seats, Violet gives the following prompt for the safe place drawing. She gives the prompt in a calm and slightly quieted voice, speaking slowly and gently. As with the House, Tree, Person drawing, Violet leads the participants through the Safe Place drawing exercise while also describing how she uses it with children:

> What I would like you to do is get as comfortable as you can where you are, and let yourself get as relaxed as you can. Close your eyes. I don't know if I've said this, but I always close my eyes when I tell children to close their eyes because usually they don't close their eyes, and yet if I don't close my eyes we're both sitting there looking at each other! [Laughter]. So I close my eyes, because, of course, they're either peeking or squinting, and if they see me with my eyes closed they feel safer to close their eyes. So they eventually do. How do I know that? Because I'm peeking [laughter]. But I'm not going to peek at you...
>
> So just close your eyes and go into yourself, see how you're feeling, see if you have any aches or pains anywhere. Just notice it. Notice how your arms are placed, and your legs are placed. Know that you can move any time you want to. Listen to any sounds that you hear outside the room. Listen to them. Notice your

breath. Again let's take a deep breath, hold it, then let it go. Notice that when you let your breath go, your shoulders tend to fall. Let's do that again. It's okay to make a sound when you let your breath out...

Let's imagine that you have a balloon and you blow up the balloon and you shove all the thoughts in your head into the balloon and tie it up and then you let it go, and you watch it just float away through the ceiling magically, or out the door, to balloon-land...

I'm going to make a sound with this small chime, listen to the sound as long as you can [she rings chime twice].

I want you to imagine that you can go to a safe place, whatever safe means for you. Now this place could be some place you remember from your childhood that comes to you, or a place in your life now, or a place you make up. You could make up this safe place. It could even be on the moon. It could be any kind of place, or it could be a place that you know and that you add things to and make even better for yourself. It could be inside or outside. So what I'd like you to do is go to this place...[10 second pause]...If you can't think of a place, I'd like you to make one up right now. Make up a place. It doesn't have to be a perfect place. Just choose a safe place, and go there, and look around, notice the colors, the light, and the shadow of the place. Listen for any sounds in your place. Maybe there are some particular smells to your place. Allow yourself to touch various things in your place to feel texture and temperature. Of course if you happen to be barefoot, have your feet do this too. Notice what you do in your safe place: are you doing something or are you just sitting?

And what I'm going to ask you to do soon is to draw this place, and I want to remind you that I don't have to understand your drawing, no one has to. It's your drawing. It can be any way you want it to be. If you need to draw something that you don't know how to draw, it could be just a shape, and you'll know what it is. It could be abstract, or it could be as concrete as you want it to be. It could be any way. It could be a mixture. You might have the feeling of the place around the colors, lines, and shapes. Just draw it any way that you want to. So when you're ready, get a leaning board, a piece of paper, and a handful of pastels. You can always go back and get the colors you didn't get, so don't worry about that. You can go anywhere. You can stay here or go out, just find a place to do your Safe Place drawing...

When Violet began this prompt, there was a significant shift in activity in the room. Just before the exercise began, participants were sitting around in upright chairs or on leaning chairs on the floor. Many of them had their binders open on their laps, listening, asking questions, taking notes, and processing the theoretical information from the discussion. Once the prompt began, however, participants relaxed their postures in their seats, closed their eyes, and remained quiet for the duration of the prompt. My notes from that day just after the prompt reflect my interest in this shift:

> I again am reflecting on...what? Ritual space? Changing the environment by changing to a focus on the senses? Last time I focused on how color changed the room, this time I notice what it's like to have my eyes closed, in silence, a quiet preparation to draw, to engage in another sensory experience – I almost want to have the tape recorder on to record the little quiet sounds, the sighs, the whispers, paper tearing off the pad, crayons rustling in small plastic trays, the subtle scratch of pastels on paper, the fan...

Approximately twenty minutes after she started the prompt, Violet asks participants to finish up their drawings and then to share them with other participants in groups of three or four. After another thirty minutes, Violet says that she will work with a volunteer after the break.

Adult demonstration:
Safe Place drawing with Lydia

Hands shoot up after the break when Violet asks for somebody to work with her as a demonstration of what to do with the Safe Place drawing. Violet asks for someone who will not mind the demonstration being recorded on audio tape. She chooses Lydia, whose hand was up first. Lydia, an MFCC intern from New York, is one of only two participants still in their twenties in the training (the average age of training participants is generally between 40-50 years old). Lydia sits down next to Violet, who asks her first to hold up her Safe Place drawing for all to see; then Lydia places it on the floor. My notes from this moment in the workshop describe her drawing and the scene in the following way:

> They sit gazing at the picture on the floor between them – a picture of a yellow, fluffy bed with a big, brown headboard and a green tray in the center of the bed with what looks like chocolate-chip cookies on it. The bed looks soft – it has yellow, green and pink swirls and ruffles.

For the next twenty minutes, Violet and Lydia use the picture of the fluffy bed and the tray of cookies to engage in a conversation about where and how Lydia finds comfort and safety in her life. A central theme of their discussion is Lydia's surprise about the way the drawing itself turned out. She hadn't started with any particular image of a safe place when she began drawing, just with an idea about using "yellow and pink swirls." She thought these images might turn out to be a sun and was surprised when the image of her stepmother's bed began to take shape for her. Lydia describes how she became quite detailed with her drawing after the image of the bed first emerged. She added the tray of cookies, for example, and the carpet that is rolled up behind the bed because in her stepmother's house, the carpet is too long for the room. Realizing that her stepmother's bed was very much a safe place for her, Lydia describes how her drawing "brought up a lot of emotions for me, because this is where we would sit and really talk." The demonstration session with Violet becomes an "acknowledgment" for Lydia as to the importance of this safe place and her stepmother's supportiveness in her life.

Violet's manner is soft and gentle in her conversation with Lydia, asking her first simply to describe the drawing and some of the details it contains. In what will become a recurring theme throughout the workshop, Violet asks Lydia at different moments to "be" parts of the drawing, to talk "as if" she were that character or object in the scene. In interviews Violet has described how this process of pretending allows one to "own" the projections that are in the drawing. At first, Violet only asks Lydia to be "on the bed" as if she were in the drawing, and describe what it is like. Then she asks her to "talk to" her stepmother Tonia who is also imagined to be in the scene. Finally, Violet asks Lydia to actually "be the bed," and, ironically, Lydia becomes most emotional while pretending to be this inanimate object. A brief excerpt from the transcript of their conversation follows:

Violet: Well, what I'd like you to do is be the bed. Say "I'm this bed..."

Lydia: I'm this bed, and I'm big, fluffy, and cushioned and supportive [6 second pause]. I'm made of feathers, and I'm soft...I give a lot of support underneath you, and I'm always here [14 second pause]...I have these tears for some reason...

Violet: [softly] Could you stay with the tears? Stay with them...Stay with that feeling and see what might emerge in that [6 second pause]...

Lydia: Maybe it's Tonia and that she's always there for me...

Violet: And what does that mean to you, that she's always there for you? Tell her...

Lydia: It means the world to me, that you're always there for me...and always have been [voice cracks...11 second pause]...And it's very unconditional [10 second pause]...

Through my experience of attending numerous trainings held by Violet over the years, it is no longer a surprise to see participants express such intense and personal emotions, even in front of the whole group. The participants themselves, however, often do remark that they are surprised by their own emotions and what they become aware of through a simple drawing or some other piece they have created:

Violet: Hm, mm. You said you were not sure about the tears...

Lydia: I think it's that I didn't really know it was there before...

Violet: That what was there?

Lydia: That she was really there for me

Violet: Oh...

Lydia: So it's more of a, more of an acknowledgment, you know?

Violet: Hm, mm

Lydia: It's weird how it just changed into a bed... Because I really didn't expect it to be that...

Asking Lydia to stay beside her in front of the room after they have ended the demonstration, Violet asks for comments and questions from the other participants. Violet specifically asks them to comment on their own experience in watching the demonstration or to raise questions about her approach as a therapist. She reminds the participants that she might interrupt them if the comments focus on the particulars of Lydia's own issues that were brought up in the demonstration. One participant asks about Violet giving Lydia tissues in the middle of the demonstration session and if that might have interrupted Lydia's tears. Violet states that from her experience clients with runny noses have more of a problem getting distracted. Another asks what was going on in the back of Violet's mind while working with Lydia, and Violet responds that she was just trying to go with what Lydia was presenting her.

Much of the following discussion focuses on the meaning-making process that Lydia described when the "yellow squiggles" became the "safe place" of her stepmother's bed. One participant mentions that Lydia's process is a nice example of Gestalt theory: the process of making meaningful "wholes" or gestalts out of ambiguous sensory stimuli. Later in the discussion, another participant mentions she was struck by how much time was spent looking at the drawing and how it was "out there" and constantly available as a non-verbal prompt to begin or continue their conversation and work together.

Child examples: The Safe Place drawing

Toward the end of this processing discussion, a participant asks,

"If this had been a child, would you later reference this drawing?" To which Violet responds, "That brings me right into showing you some children's Safe Place drawings." Violet then thanks Lydia for working with her and, picking up some laminated examples of children's drawings, states:

> I need to emphasize that children do not say, "Well, my safe place is a bed with my stepmother and it is soft and cozy." They will say, "My safe place is a forest." Period. So we begin a dialogue. And it is the dialogue that begins to build the story, the metaphor, whatever it is. Sometimes it takes a lot of prompting and questions from me.

Violet holds up a picture that one of her clients, a thirteen-year-old adolescent girl, has drawn. Violet explains that, early in her practice, she used black-and-white Polaroid photos of the children and then let them cut out their own images and include it in their Safe Place drawing. In this teenager's drawing, the girl's photographic image is included to make it look as if she is sitting on a beach with no other people around her, literally projecting herself into the drawing. Violet reads one of the statements that the girl made about her drawing which Violet had written down on the back of it. In reference to being alone on the beach, it says, "No one can bother me there." Violet comments that many of her child and adolescent clients do Safe Place drawings in which they are alone, stating, "It's nice for them to know that they can, in their imagination, be away from all that bothers them."

Violet tells case stories from her practice with children and shows other Safe Place drawings until 4:40 p.m. She then says:

> Tomorrow I will show you how to move a bit further into the therapeutic process with children. We'll be exploring what I call "self-work," which continues to build the relationship, contact, and self-support that we have been talking about.

Reflective notes for day two

In this chapter's reflective notes, I will highlight two linked themes from day two of the training. The first theme has to do with the role of play in Violet's therapeutic work with children and adolescents as well as in her training work with adults. The second theme has to do with how Violet's approach to working with both adults and children consistently employs what I call a "conversation piece."

The role of play

In the reflective notes at the end of chapter one, I discussed how Violet works in parallel ways with both adults and children (e.g. the roles of relationship and experience). Another parallel aspect of her work with adults and children is how she facilitates playful experiences with both adults in the training as well as children in the therapeutic context. She does this in a number of ways.

First, she sets a relaxed tone where fun and laughter are welcome guests. Violet has the uncanny ability to be utterly serious about the importance of her work while not taking herself too seriously. She has told me that if the adults and children with whom she works can be relaxed enough to laugh at something funny she might say, then she knows she's on the right track.

Second, she creates an environment that is safe but one that encourages playful risk-taking. As Bowlby states, "All of us, from cradle to grave, are happiest when life is organized as a series of excursions, long or short, from a secure base provided by our attachment figures." (1988, p. 62). Violet's work with both children and adults is centered around a series of playful excursions that take place within the safe and supportive environment that she creates through her relationship with them. For example, she encourages the training participants on day two to take the risk of drawing a safe place, but not to worry too much about the quality of the drawing. I have heard many adults express that this permission to "just draw lines and shapes if you want to" allows them to loosen up a bit and get more playful and expressive with the medium at hand. It is also important to note that the activity itself, consciously placed at this point in the training, contains both risk and safety (i.e. they take the chance to create a piece of art, but the drawing itself is about a safe place).

Third, the media themselves are playful. On the first two days of the training, Violet has had participants work with pastels and crayons to create images that they then discuss and share with each other. Later in the training, this palette of playful media will be broadened to include clay, sand and sand tray toys, puppets, musical instruments, and pantomime activities. On the first and second day of the training, the participants get their hands smudged with oil pastels, but by the fourth day they will have pottery clay smeared all over their hands and lodged under their fingernails.

This increasing sensory immersion has a playful and imaginative aspect to it. In fact, Violet explicitly deconstructs the formal rules of many of the media to emphasize the playfulness and expressiveness of the activities. "I don't have to understand your drawing," she says, "Just draw shapes and lines and colors if you want to." On Friday, Violet will also have the participants use musical instruments in a similarly playful way. She will set the rule that the flutes, drums, whistles, shakers and numerous other instruments cannot be played with any sustained rhythm or melody. The participants will then be free to focus on the playful act of making sounds and expressing feelings without the fear of making any "wrong notes" or musical mistakes.

A fourth way in which Violet encourages play with both children and adults is in the way she works with the objects that they have created. Violet has a very particular and consistent way in which she works with the drawings, the sand trays scenes, or the clay pieces that she helps others create. In the example of Violet working with Lydia and her Safe Place drawing, Violet invited Lydia to speak "as if" she were the soft yellow bed with cookies on it. In taking on the voice of this bed ("I'm big, fluffy, and cushioned and supportive"), Lydia moves into the world of pretend. Having first encouraged Lydia to work playfully with pastels in a kind of silent, sensory play-state, Violet now verbally pulls Lydia into a deeper and more involved play-state of imagination and pretend. Violet often speaks of this part of the work as "building the story or the metaphor." In Lydia's case, the story and metaphor that emerge are rich and detailed, involving home, safety, comfort, relationship and a very special physical place and presence in her life.

Paradoxically, Lydia sheds tears and describes significant details from her real life while "pretending" she is the bed and other objects in her drawing. In Violet's work with both children and adults, this is not unusual. The four ways in which Violet encourages play in her work (setting a tone, creating a playfully risk-taking environment, using playful media, working in a playful manner) serve the surprisingly paradoxical function of making the work she does with both adults and children very real. For example, what begins as a playful move into speaking "as if" she were a bed gets Lydia in touch with some very real emotions of significance from her own life experience.

In this way, Violet's playful approach somehow allows things to get real. I think this has something to do with the indirect support that her playful approach offers. If she were to ask Lydia, for example, to directly and verbally describe the most important examples of safety and comfort in her life, it is likely Lydia would stay at a somewhat superficial and cognitive description of people and relationships in her life. Instead, by entering such an exploration of her safe place through play — sensorially, metaphorically, and imaginatively — Lydia seems to access more of her own experience and what that experience means to her, as well as being able to identify and describe these findings in poetic, emotional, and personal terms. Thus, Lydia's work with

Violet is a nice example of Violet's assertion that being more in touch with one's own self creates the self-support necessary to move into deeper realms of experience with the therapist.

Another way to look at what Violet is doing through these playful approaches is that she is fostering both expression and integration of the sensorial, imaginative, and emotional aspects of the self. Such expression and integration are not easily supported when approached through words only, without a rich experiential context or foundation first being laid. Through her playful and experiential approach, Violet encourages those with whom she works to bring more of themselves to the present moment in a safe way. The result of such an approach often involves surprise: "I didn't really expect it to be that!" states Lydia. The surprise often involves learning something new or bringing something into awareness that has been forgotten about oneself or one's world, like Lydia remembering how important her stepmother is in helping her feel safe and comforted.

Violet's sense of play mimics what play theorists (Piaget, 1962; Vygotsky, 1934; Sutton-Smith, 1979) write about as being central to the experience of play: it involves a courageous willingness to step into an "as if" experience (e.g. "draw a safe place"), play by a new set of rules that are different than ordinary reality (e.g., "now speak as if you were the bed"), and be open to an uncertain result (e.g. "I didn't really expect it to be that!"). The positive outcome of this courageous willingness to step into play, however, can be the experience of an "expanded sense of self," as Csizkzentmihalyi (1991) writes about in his work on Flow theory. This experience of gaining an "expanded sense of self" is akin to what Violet describes as gaining feelings of "self-support". Maybe one way to describe Violet's role in both therapy and training is as a master coach who knows the playful game of self-discovery so well that she can lead others through the somewhat risky but ultimately rewarding steps of that process.

Violet not only uses play to coach the adults in the training about how to do therapy with children. She also uses play in the training to teach the adults something about play itself. By coaxing the adults in the training into many experiences they would not participate in without some normal, "grown up" reservations (such as drawing with pastels or pretending to speak "as if" they were a bed, for example), Violet teaches adults to take play as seriously as children do: "If you are going to do this kind of work," she says, "you need to experience what it is you are asking children to do."

So the participants leave day two with a working knowledge of the Safe Place drawing, but they also leave with a little more experiential knowledge and perhaps memory of what it is like to play, and what it is like to discover new things through play. On day one, Violet asked them to draw a picture of themselves as children so they could remember their own experience of childhood. On day two, Violet helps them all remember a bit more about that birthright of childhood that is too easily forgotten or dismissed by serious-minded adults: the experiential, integrating, richly textured world of sensory and pretend play.

The conversation piece

Most of us have experienced how much easier it is to talk with someone new when there is a shared point of interest to discuss. That shared point of interest may be a book we have both read or a small sculpture from Africa sitting on the fireplace mantel. A discussion about a book can turn into a revealing conversation about our personal likes and dislikes. The small sculpture on the mantel can spark a series of stories about how we came to travel to distant places and why. Paradoxically, we seem to be willing to say more about ourselves when we are talking about something other than ourselves. The same principle holds true in Violet's work with both children in therapy and adults in training: young or old, we seem more willing to enter the risky "play state" if we can do so by talking through a "conversation piece" rather than directly about ourselves.

During the Safe Place demonstration on day two, I sketched an image of Violet working with Lydia. In this moment, both Violet and Lydia are sitting in chairs, but they are not facing one another directly. They sit at a forty-five degree angle to each other and they look at each other only occasionally (Figure 3). More often than not, Violet and Lydia are looking down on the floor at the picture that Lydia has drawn. They point to it, touch it in different places, discuss its colors, and explore it. Lydia pretends "as if" she is the bed. She imagines what her experience would be like as that bed and that plate of cookies, and she voices what she would say to her stepmother if she were present. Through this playful exploration, Lydia gets choked up when she realizes how much of the drawing represents her warm and supportive relationship with her stepmother.

Figure 3: Lydia, Violet and the Safe Place Drawing

Yet, through all of this, Lydia has really been having more of a conversation with and about her drawing than she has had with Violet directly. Lydia and Violet spend the majority of their time looking at the drawing and discussing it and they spend very little time talking "face to face" with each other. In this way, the "conversation piece" really becomes the focus of attention for both Lydia and Violet. And yet, the result of this indirect focus is a very personal disclosure and significant learning on Lydia's part.

I am no longer surprised when a drawing of a yellow bed with cookies on it becomes a poignant visualization of love and support in a person's life. I am also no longer surprised when Violet coaxes that kind of revelation from someone with whom she has never really had a close conversation. To me, it now seems perfectly natural that, given the opportunity to talk about a "conversation piece," and not about themselves directly, both adults and children will open up in surprising ways. Part of Violet's genius seems to be her insight into the importance of providing the opportunity for individuals to speak indirectly about themselves. In this way, the "conversation piece" becomes a kind of mediating device, a kind of "scaffolding" (Vygotsky, 1978) by which the individual is able to feel supported and strengthened. By not confronting the individuals with whom she works head on and face to face, Violet provides the safety that can allow individuals to stick their necks out and take a few self-disclosing risks.

When Violet and I visited South Africa in 2000 and held workshops in three cities, we were told an important piece of cross-cultural information that also highlights the importance of these "conversation pieces" in that context. A participant of a workshop there described how most black, South African children learn from an early age that it is disrespectful to look directly at an adult when they are speaking with them. In this way, the "conversation piece" helps de-emphasize the power differential inherent in any child/adult relationship by focusing instead on an inanimate object as the point of discussion. The child does not need to look up at the more imposing figure of the therapist, nor does the therapist need to look down at the child. Instead, they both are gazing at a third object that the child has created and the therapist is interested in.

Additionally, it is also important to note the particular way in which Violet encourages the adults and children with whom she works to "speak through" the conversation piece. First, she helps them make one (by asking them to create a drawing or, as we will see later, a work in clay, music, sand, or puppets). She then pulls adults or children "into" the drawing or object and into a deeper involvement with it through having them speak "as if" they were that conversation piece or parts of it. Paradoxically, as the focus gets pulled away from the individual with whom Violet is working and moves deeper into the conversation piece, that individual seems to be willing to reveal more about him or herself than they would in a "face to face" discussion.

As will be discussed further in the next chapter, the "conversation piece" also helps children enter the therapeutic relationship from a position of comfort and confidence because they have drawn upon their developmental strengths in order to create it. That is, children use their non-verbal, imaginative and sensori-motor based skills to create something of both visual and tactile interest. In chapter three, we will see how Violet uses a different sensory medium – clay – in the same process of facilitating a playful, therapeutic experience through the use of a conversation piece.

3

Day Three: Wednesday
Experiencing the Self

"Self work"

Violet had ended Tuesday afternoon's session by showing participants examples of children's Safe Place drawings from her own practice. This morning, just before she jumps into "self-work," a participant asks her to say more about the difference between working with children and working with adults. Violet replies:

> Working with children is different than working with adults. They don't say, for example, "I know what I need to work on." Sometimes I lead and sometimes they do. It's basically give and take. You can't just say to a child, "Okay, express your feelings." In fact, I will often say "What are you thinking?" rather than "What are you feeling?" Kids will often tell me more about their feelings when I don't ask them directly.

After a brief discussion on the differences between adult and child therapeutic work that follows, Violet writes on the flip chart "Self-Work" and says, "We're going to be talking about working with the self." During the next few minutes, Violet refers to the concepts of "contact" and "sense of self" that were discussed on Monday and Tuesday. Here, she elaborates on what it actually means to do therapeutic work that "enhances the sense of self." She states that this is accomplished through experiences that involve the senses, the body, mastery, choices, self-statements, and issues regarding power and control. These ideas are written on the flip chart under the heading of "Self-Work" (Figure 4).

Self Work
Senses
Body
Mastery
Choices
Self-statements
Power/control

Figure 4: Self Work

Violet goes on to describe that her ideas about "self-work" are intimately connected to the ideas she already presented involving a child's ability to make contact and have a strong sense of self. Violet says that yesterday she defined the self as the totality of the aspects of the organism: the body, the senses, the ability to feel and express emotions, the intricate workings of the mind. In this way, the self is defined as the ecology of the organism that enables it to self-regulate, grow, and develop in healthy ways. From this point of view, Violet says, to help a child therapeutically is to strengthen and enhance all the aspects that make up the self and, therefore, assist that child in this process of organismic self-regulation. By addressing these aspects of the self directly, she describes, children become more aware of themselves and how all their distinct aspects work as a whole. This awareness, she argues, leads to a greater sense of integration and, therefore, a strengthening of the self.

In order to demonstrate some examples of "self-work", Violet drags a large black suitcase to the center of the room and begins pulling things from it. Each of the many objects that she pulls from the bag relates in some way to helping children be more aware of their sensorial experiences. There are small textured pillows and soft brushes for the sense of touch (she says she usually doesn't touch the child, but simply lets the child play with the objects) as well as the bubbles on packing plastic to pop. There are periscopes, kaleidoscopes, and "Where's Waldo" (Handford, 1997) books to enhance the sense of sight. There are cotton balls to blow across the table top, balloons to blow up, and harmonicas to play for children who have shallow or restricted breathing. There are also scented marking pens and a game called "Guess that scent" to enhance the sense of smell. And there are also gongs to ring and little plastic bottles filled with different things to shake (e.g. sand, pebbles, coins...) in order to enhance a child's sense of hearing. Violet also pulls out an authentic stethoscope and remarks that it's a big hit with kids. There are "oohs" and "aahs" from the participants as these items are displayed and some are passed around. Participants also laugh as a toy hammer that makes the sound of shattering glass accidentally "goes off" repeatedly as Violet rummages through the bag, pulling out other items.

When partial calm has returned to the room, Violet announces, "There's a book I want to read to you that involves all the senses." She proceeds to read aloud a book entitled, "Everybody Needs a Rock" (Baylor, 1974). This book details a little girl's account of why it is important for everyone to own a rock that fits "just right" in the palm of your hand and how one can go about finding one. Violet ends this reading with what she calls a homework assignment: "I expect each of you in the next few days to report on your own rock-finding activities."

Moving on to topics concerning the body, the breath, and the voice, Violet says, "one of the best ways to enhance the body is through pantomime because it involves all the senses." She then leads participants in a game of pantomime that entails using small hand movements to act out a simple gesture that can be recognized by others. Soon, participants are fully engaged in silently acting out small gestures: petting a cat, eating a watermelon, sewing on a button, and opening a can of soda, to name a few. Violet, clearly an expert in this area, pantomimes the process of discovering and smelling dog poop on the bottom of her shoe: "another big hit with the kids," she says.

"Another important aspect of self-work is the ability to make self- statements," says Violet as she displays a collection of therapeutic tools for this purpose. Self-statements, she says, are statements that the child or adolescent makes in terms of things that they like or that they don't like. Self-statements, she says, can also be made in terms of things that the child identifies with or things that they don't identify with. Such statements, Violet describes, help children to verbally strengthen their sense of self and identity: "Yes, I am a person who likes to swim" or "No, I don't like sports." Violet says that in her experience, adolescents will answer a question from a book more easily than a question from a person. Therefore, she has found the "Book of Questions" (Stock, 1987) helpful in having children and teenagers make statements about themselves in answering such questions as, "Would you rather have more time, or more money?"

In the same creative way that she adapted the use of the House, Tree, Person drawing, Violet also uses other published, psychological tests to help children make affirmative statements about themselves. With the Thematic Apperception Test (Murray, 1943), children are usually asked to "tell a story" about pictures they are shown. Violet has children or adolescents tell a story about a picture, but she reads aloud the interpretations of their responses from the manual and asks them to confirm or disconfirm these "official" statements. Violet describes how she also uses the "Luscher Color Test" (Luscher, 1980), "Linda Goodman's Sun Signs" (Goodman, 1985), and "The Hand Test" (Young and Wagner, 1999) to help children or adolescents make self-statements that define the view they have of themselves (e.g., "The book says Virgos are neat and tidy, are you like that?").

Violet explains that the essence of self-work has to do with children learning about and integrating more of themselves, and increasing their sense of self in the process. This results in children being able to make better contact with others and their environment. "A greater sense of self helps the child expand their boundaries," she says. Helping children strengthen their sense of self can also be accomplished by helping children identify things they have mastery of (e.g. reading books, playing volleyball, or making friends) and the things they can make choices about (e.g. the friends they make, the groups they join, etc.).

A therapist can also help children increase their sense of self, Violet explains, by giving them some sense of power or control within the session. Oftentimes, children feel powerless and by allowing them to make choices within a session, she says, the therapist can help the child experience a sense of control. This can be accomplished, she explains, through a child choosing to work with clay over doing a drawing or being the director of a puppet show in which the therapist is also engaged. The goals of self work, Violet says, are to "provide children with a greater sense of their own efficacy and the ability to meet their own needs."

By noon on Wednesday, when it is time to break for lunch, the floor is strewn with games, toys, books, and boxes of tests, these therapeutic tools having taken "center stage" from the drawing materials that were used yesterday. Before the participants break for lunch, Violet says that they will be working with clay in the afternoon, "another sensual and playful medium that helps children develop a stronger sense of self, but which is also helpful for emotional expression." Violet then points out to the participants that the steps of the work that they have been exposed to thus far align with the steps in her therapeutic process (Oaklander, 1978). She directs the participants to a hand-out in their reading packet, Figure 5, that outlines the following steps of this process that she has constructed over the years of working therapeutically with children and adolescents.

The Therapeutic Process

Establishing a relationship

Working with contact

Strengthening the self (self-work)

Aggressive energy work

Emotional expression

Self-nurturing work

Addressing persistent problems

Closing and termination

Figure 5: Oaklander's Therapeutic Process

Violet goes on to describe how in the training thus far, she has covered and given examples of the first three steps of the therapeutic process and how the remainder of the training will build on those steps and add others. In particular, the rest of the day today and all of tomorrow will be devoted to the challenging but important aspects of working with emotional expression, aggressive energy, and anger work.

"Working with clay"

After the lunch break, some of the participants are laughing as they re-gather in the conference room. Stella, a child therapist from Brazil, tells Violet that a few of them were practicing "self-work" by swimming in the pool and basking in the sun. Violet laughs with Stella as she continues handing out hunks of gray and red pottery clay that are about the size of a small loaf of bread. Each participant also receives a thin board about sixteen-inches square on which to place the clay. Before long, the hum of the group has died down and most of the group sits quietly touching and caressing the clay in front of them as Violet begins to speak. In the following transcription, Violet describes the many therapeutic uses and benefits of working with clay:

> Okay, so you all have your clay. Don't worry about making a mess with it. It's actually the cleanest material next to water. It washes easily. It comes right off your clothes. Many times I actually wear black just to show you that by the end of the day, it has turned to dust and fallen right off of me. Even on a rug, when it dries you just vacuum it right up. The only problem comes when you try to sponge it up when it's still wet. I even worked with a group of kids in my own living room for two years using red clay all the time, and they never made a mess.

It's much cleaner than Playdoh™ which sticks to stuff. Even Plasticine™ gets on your hands. I always put a bucket of water out, like we have here, for kids who are a little unsure about the messiness of it. They see that when they put their hands in the water and take them out, their hands are clean. I don't even take off my jewelry. You can even put it on your face and give yourself a facial! It's a natural material. It comes out of the ground. And clay is the most versatile of all the materials we use. You can do more with clay than with anything else. I'll give you a few examples.

Clay is good for kids who are very hyper because it's soothing. It's focusing. It's calming. Clay is good for kids who are insecure: you cannot make a mistake with clay. There's just no way. I could make a little animal here [Violet makes a rough animal figure and holds it up]...and you see this in a museum [laughter]. You can fix it and you can change it. And clay is good for kids who are angry. You can really get a lot of feelings out in the clay [she grimaces and pounds the clay on her board with her fists]. Clay is not expensive. I keep it in a plastic bag and put water on it when it starts to dry out. You can use it almost forever.

In my work we don't use clay as an art lesson. We use it as a therapeutic tool. So the kids usually put the clay back after they are finished. Once in a while children will make something they just have to keep and then I give it to them. It usually takes about a week to dry and even then it is very fragile.

Let's see...It's good for kids who are sexually curious because it's a sensuous material. Of course, eight-year-old boys will make feces [laughter]. It's good for one-on-one work, it's good for group work, and it's good for family work. It's good for couples. There are just so many things you can do with clay. You can use it with any age whatsoever...it's ageless...

One of the things I'll do when siblings or families come in is just leave clay out on the table. And we'll sit around and we won't do anything specific with the clay, but they'll do what we are doing now, just touching and playing with the clay. It helps them relax, be open, and start talking. It's just the most relaxing material and it seems to open up both adults and kids.

One thing I forgot to mention is that clay provides a tremendous contact experience, because clay almost has a life of its own. You have to push it for it to go this way [she pushes her clay around on the board] or that way. It's not like water, there's a real give and take. It's a great experience in that way. It's a very tactile experience. It provides a kinesthetic experience. You really have to use your arms and your shoulders and your body to work with clay in this way.

With kids I will usually have water, and they can put water on the clay. Or we'll use a spray bottle when the clay starts to dry out a little just so they can see how that feels. We have water available here, too, in those two buckets on either side of the room. There are towels available, too, for you to clean up with. So clay has different consistencies. Sometimes it's a little harder, sometimes when it gets wet it's a little sticky, but it's all interesting!

During the ten minutes or so that Violet has been talking, all twenty-four participants have been almost entirely quiet. Most of them are sitting on the floor with the clay on a board in front of them, their hands busy but seemingly relaxed as they knead and work the cool hunks of clay. Many of them gaze at their clay as Violet speaks, but some occasionally look up and smile when she makes a particularly emphatic point or demonstration.

After her brief introductory talk about the uses of clay, Violet then leads the participants through the first of two exercises: "Experimenting with the clay." In this first clay exercise, Violet has the participants try out all the things they can do with clay as an expressive medium rather than as an artistic medium, thus playfully deconstructing the expected uses of the clay:

Okay, now we're going to do two exercises. They're in my book, so you don't have to worry about taking notes. In the first exercise, we're going to do a variety of things with the clay like poking, squeezing, or pinching it. And we'll see how it feels to do those things. Most kids think that you are supposed to make bowls or use the slab method or the coil method. But they don't really understand all the things you can do with clay. That's one of the reasons we do all these things, so they can see how versatile it is.

Okay, so I want to see how you're going to feel about some of the things we're going to do. Some of the things you might not like, but try and go with it. I'm going to do all of them, too, with the clay I have here. Okay, let's try squeeeezing the clay, just squeeeeeeeze it, and squeeeeeze it. All right, let's try pinching the clay, piiinnching the clay. Okay, let's try poking the clay. Poke it! Use both hands, and you can bore a hole actually. Just take one finger and keep turning it around and around, and then you can actually see through it [she holds it up and looks at a few of the participants, laughing]...And let's feel the inside of that hole. It starts to feel different because of the moisture there [pause]...

Okay, let's tear the clay! Tear it! Just tear it all up! All right, there are big tears and little tears...tear it apart! [she does this with gusto and with a grimacing expression] All right, the thing that's beautiful about clay, is that unlike Humpty Dumpty, you can put it back together again. So put it back together [lots of pounding from all the participants]. Okay, let's punch it; punch it with both hands, different hands, your knuckles, [lots of pounding and thudding sounds in the room, some laughter]. Now, I want you to THROW IT! [she stands up and hurls her clay down on the board]. THROW IT! [Loud pounding and banging, laughter, comments: "Oh, I like that!!" "That's great, throwing it that way!" deep breaths being taken, more laughter]. You can make faces;

you can make sounds when you throw it! Arrrrgghh! [Now lots of growls and grunts in addition to the pounding. It sounds like a bookcase full of books falling down the stairs to the accompaniment of riotous laughter]...

Now, pick your clay up off the board and turn it over and you'll notice that by throwing it you've created a soft side, it gets flat on one side. Feel that [gently spoken as she strokes it]...You can stroke it; you can even make a groove and stroke it. [She speaks with a calming, cooing voice...very quiet in room now]. And you sort-of pat it [she lightly taps the clay]...and you sort of slap it! [She slaps it harder as do others in the room...SLAP! SLAP! SLAP! SLAP! SLAP!...a sound like applause in a large audience...then like the sound of a drum beat...finally it dies down after about 30 seconds.]

The feeling akin to a "calm after the storm" lingers in the room as this first exercise with the clay draws to a close. A few of the participants spontaneously take in and let out deep breaths, almost as if the group has done a kind of workout together. Shoulders drop and faces look relaxed as Violet begins the next clay exercise, which she calls "Making something with the clay:"

Okay, now I want you to make a lump, just a lump, and put it in front of you...put your hands over it. And what I'd like you to do is close your eyes and feel the temperature of the clay with the palm of your hands. Take a deep breath and when you exhale, imagine the air going down your arms, down through your fingers, into the clay. Do that a few times [deep breathing and exhaling sounds fill the room].

I want you to try an experiment, feel the clay with the palms of your hands with your eyes closed. Now open your eyes and feel the clay with the palms of your hands. Then close your eyes again. Did anybody notice a change? [A few participants nod their heads in agreement]. I think you can actually feel the clay more with your eyes closed. It's almost like your eyes take some of your energy away from it or something.

Okay, I'd like you to close your eyes again and keep your hands on your clay. Now, your clay has a lot of your energy in it, it's even warm where you've been touching it. I'd like you to begin to form something. Now just let the clay go where it wants to go, and then sometimes let your fingers tell the clay where to go. This might be just an abstract shape. It might be that you want to make some kind of an object or an animal or a figure of some kind. Just try, with your eyes closed, just try to make something, but don't look at it yet. Don't worry about what you are making, just continue working...[45 second pause]...

And then any time you feel like opening your eyes, just go ahead and look at your piece, but just keep working on it. At some point you'll want to open your eyes and just look at it and see it from all sides and see if you want to fix it or anything. Don't really change it... [63 second pause]. At this point you should all open your eyes if they are not open and just put any finishing touches onto what you've made...[30 second pause]. See if you're surprised at what you did...[14 second pause]. One of the things about this is that there's no real finishing place. You could sort of keep working and keep working at it, and so you have to say, "Okay, I'll stop now"...

Adult demonstration:
Clay work with Sabina

As the participants finish up their clay pieces, Violet says that she would like to work with a volunteer and his or her clay piece. Of the several hands that are raised, Violet chooses Sabina, a director of a mental health counseling clinic in Texas. She is a large woman, with a warm smile, and has been one of the most verbal participants in the workshop thus far. Sabina moves her chair next to Violet's and sits with her clay and board on her lap. At the start of their work together, Sabina follows Violet's request that she speak "as if" she were her creation in clay and describes herself as a kind of baseball glove with an imperfect crack in it:

> I'm this piece of clay. I'm curled with an indentation.
> Kind of heavy, massive. And I'm not perfect right here.
> It's kind of broken here. But there's a strong foundation,
> that I have. And I kind of resemble a baseball glove.

After more dialogue in which Sabina speaks "as if" she were the piece of clay, Sabina asks Violet if she could hit a different piece of clay. Violet encourages her to do this, and while striking the second piece of clay, Sabina says, "It's fun doing this. I don't remember ever punching things in my life." Soon after this interchange, Violet asks Sabina once more to "be the baseball mitt" and another opportunity for Sabina to punch the clay comes up:

Violet: Well, be the baseball mitt then. Come back to that... "I'm a baseball mitt..."

Sabina: I'm a baseball mitt. I catch things and I'm big...Which fits for me right now [patting her own hips], I'm big and I hate it...

Violet: That's something you could punch right now...say "I hate it!" and punch the clay...

Sabina: I hate it! [softly punching]

Violet: Punch the clay harder when you say that...

Sabina: [punching harder, loudly] I hate it! [punch!] I hate being big! [punch! punch! punch!] I want you to disappear...[pause]

Ultimately, the "heavy, massive" baseball mitt becomes a meaningful metaphor that Sabina uses to talk about her struggles to keep weight off since her adolescence and to express some of her difficult and conflicting emotions around this issue. During the 34 minutes that she and Violet work together, participants sit very quietly, some taking notes, observing and taking in the public demonstration that includes very personal issues. When the demonstration is over, Violet asks Sabina, like Lydia before her, to stay with her in front of the room as participants have a chance to comment on what they have seen. One participant comments on how it was to observe such intimate work:

> What you have been talking about a lot in the work is making a safe place. And I felt at first a little awkward. I felt like "Gee, I don't think we should be here!" But you were somehow able to expand, both of you, expand the container enough so that it felt okay. I felt very much a part of her work. I did not feel like a voyeur. I felt very fortunate to be part of it.

Many of the comments from the participants include both questions and statements about the technique as well as comments of appreciation for Sabina for being so willing to be vulnerable in her work with Violet. After Sabina takes her seat, Violet describes how the rest of the participants will now pair off and work with each other. In reference to the work she has just done with Sabina, she offers both a caution and a focus for the work to be done in pairs. As usual, there is a bit of humor thrown in as well:

> I don't expect that you would go into such deep places or deep work. Mostly just being the piece and talking about it. And with your partner guiding you into any place in terms of owning the projections that would emerge from your piece. Don't expect to really get into a deep, deep

place. If anybody needs a mallet for hitting though, I do have several here [Laughs]. You're ready to do that, huh? [Said to an eager participant]. Sometimes one does their own work! [Laughter]. And so what we'll do is you can take a break and get a partner. You'll each have fifteen minutes to work.

After the break and the half hour in which pairs of participants work together on the floor of the conference room, out on the patio, or even down by the hotel pool, everyone has re-gathered in the conference room and Violet once again asks, "Is there any feedback here? Anything you'd like to say to us here on your experience?" Many participants are eager to share their experience, with many noting surprise at what emerged in the work, both in their roles as therapist and as client. The following three comments are representative of a number of such comments made during this discussion:

I'm just really struck by what emerges from the clay, by what emerged for me from the clay. And part of it was very much issues that I am presently feeling, that I had no idea that I was holding! And it just took a life of its own. I was not at all in my head." It was a powerful, powerful experience.

I was worried when I started that I was going to be too directive. I just kept slowing down, and listening, and trusting. And the places it went were just amazing.

I was very aware, too, that without my eyes closed when I was working on the clay, I would have never come up with what I made.

Regarding this last comment, Violet responds that several people have made similar comments to her over the years. She goes on to say that, although time has run out for today, tomorrow morning she will be showing a video-tape of her working with a thirteen-year-old boy using clay as an example of doing this kind of work with children and adolescents.

Reflective notes for day three

In this chapter's reflective notes I will identify and describe some of the shapes and forms of Violet's work that I have discovered over time. I have already discussed some of the parallels between Violet's approach to training adults and her approach to doing therapy with children: both build on relationship, both are experiential, both are playful, both involve a conversation piece, and both involve the same exercises involving drawing, clay, etc.

In the paragraphs that follow, I will use a visual metaphor — the shape of a bowl — to describe another parallel that exists between Violet's approach to the therapeutic process and the training process. I will also describe a consistent form that Violet's work takes with both adults and children. In outlining these ideas, I will use specific examples from Violet's demonstrations involving the Safe Place drawing and the "Clay Experience" on the second and third days of the training.

The shape of training and therapy

Over the ten years that I have been observing Violet at work with both children in therapy and adults in the training, I have come to recognize a consistent shape that her work takes in both these settings. One way to visualize the shape of her work is to imagine a deep bowl with a wide and tapering edge. In the first few days of the training, when Violet is working to establish a trusting and "I/Thou" kind of relationship with the participants, the kinds of experiences that Violet asks the adults to engage in tend to be fairly non-threatening and require less personal disclosure or risk-taking. Put another way, the first day or so of the training stays on the edge of the bowl, metaphorically speaking.

The drawing experiences on the first day of the training are an example of this. The first drawing experience involved Violet's request that workshop participants "draw themselves as a child" and share the drawing in small groups of five. The second drawing experience was the House, Tree, Person drawing during which Violet took guesses about what the drawing might mean about the person who created it and during which she also let that person accept or refute those statements. Both of these drawings served the purpose of "warming up" the adult participants in the training in much the same way that they could be used to help a child warm up to the therapeutic relationship being established with the adult therapist.

As the training moves into the second and third day, however, the experiences that Violet asks the adults to participate in become a bit more challenging. On day two, participants are asked to create a drawing of a safe place and share it briefly with others. Violet later works with an individual and her Safe Place drawing in front of the group. This Safe Place drawing experience, while anchored in reflection on issues of comfort and safety, asks more of the participants in that they reveal some things about themselves and their own experience to others in the group. This openness is exemplified by Lydia's work with Violet in front of the group using her Safe Place drawing.

In the same way that Violet would only ask a child to work on more challenging material in therapy once a strong foundational relationship had been established, so too does Violet wait until the third day before introducing the participants to the "deeper" experiences possible in working with clay. Although Violet does state that clay can be used at any point in the therapeutic process, the level of work that she does with Sabina in front of the group reveals the potential depth of this mode of working.

In these ways, both the therapeutic process and the unfolding of the two-week training take on the shape of a bowl: the deepest and most challenging aspects of the work take place in the middle of the experience while the "edges" — or the beginning and the end — tend to be less deep and less challenging.

There is another way that this metaphorical image of the shape of a bowl works to describe the way Violet structures both her trainings with adults and her therapeutic work with children. The shape of a bowl, with the deepest part being in the middle, is what allows it to be an effective "container" that can hold important things. I see Violet's work in a similar way: she works to build a strong relationship first in order for it to "contain" the more challenging work in the middle of her trainings and therapy.

When Violet sits down to work with Sabina on her clay sculpture, the work begins gently, playfully, with only minor personal risks being taken by Sabina. For example, Violet asks Sabina to pretend "as if" she is the clay piece and to give it a voice. Together, they explore all the possible metaphors that Sabina thinks of in this process: a baseball mitt, a waterfall, a crevice, etc. In this process of starting a discussion based on the clay "conversation piece," the words tend to flow easily from Sabina. They are not yet talking about the serious issues to come regarding the difficulty of struggling with weight issues and the emotional struggle Sabina faces in that area of her life.

But these moments of deeper work do come. Sabina does take greater personal risks and goes deeper into the work, and it is the safe "container" that Violet provides which in large part allows Sabina to go there. Toward the end of their work together, Violet checks in with Sabina to see how she is doing, as she often does throughout a session — taking a moment to reestablish contact and to check in on the relationship — and together they both end the work with the clay on a hopeful and constructive note. In this light, it is not surprising that the first comment made by a participant about Violet's demonstration with Sabina is in reference to the creation of a safe place in which that kind of work could happen with the entire group present.

Throughout the training, Violet emphasizes the importance of bringing clients out of deeper emotional experiences by the time they complete their work, both at the end of each session and at the end of the therapeutic relationship. This doesn't mean that each session is tied up neatly with no loose ends, but it does mean that Violet works to help her clients bring their attention to lighter and easier topics as their work together draws to a close. Violet does this in simple ways, asking what will happen next in the individual's day, what might be for dinner, or just through relaxed chit-chat. She might also ask her clients to look around and describe what they notice in the room or environment in order to help them bring their awareness back into the "here and now."

Thus, each time Violet works with a child or an adult, there is a particular form of that work that is similar to the containing shape of a bowl. Whether that work is a single session with a child or the form of the entire two-week training with adults, Violet eases people into the work before she encourages them to move into deeper and more challenging experiences. She also helps the individuals with whom she works to come up and out of that deep part of bowl at the end of their work, arriving, so to speak, on the opposite edge.

There is another recognizable shape to Violet's approach that I have identified after years of watching her work. Even though Violet uses a variety of expressive materials with both children and adults, ranging from pastels to puppets, each time Violet uses one of these expressive media, the form of the work is similar. In other words, Violet has developed a set of what I call "Therapeutic Experiences" that share a similar form whether she is using clay, sand tray figures, or any other expressive medium.

In the section that follows, I first list the Therapeutic Experiences that Violet leads both adults and children through in their work together. I then describe the consistent form that these varied Therapeutic Experiences take.

Naming the Oaklander Therapeutic Experiences

An interesting discussion usually comes up among the participants in the summer training regarding whether Violet can be described as a "directive" or "non-directive" therapist. There are many ways in which Violet's work with adults in the training and children in therapy can be described as being non-directive, unstructured, and open-ended. Sabina, for example, comes up with the image of a baseball mitt on her own. And the image in Lydia's drawing, a "yellow bed with cookies on it" was entirely her own creation. In each of these cases, Violet goes along with the images and metaphors that are presented to her and helps the person she is working with explore them in a seemingly non-directive and open-ended way.

After watching Violet at work for years, however, I have identified a consistent pattern in her approach that is clearly more directive than one might notice on first glance and which underlies the seemingly non-directive therapeutic work taking place. In identifying an underlying structure in Violet's work, my intent is not to dismiss or argue against the non-directive qualities of Violet's work but rather to paint a more complete and complex portrait of her approach in order to help better understand it. My hope is that a clear description of the structural qualities of Violet's work will allow others to better understand her approach and integrate it into their own ways of working.

Violet herself uses the metaphor of a "dance" to describe how there are times when she leads and times when she allows the person she is working with to lead. Through this dance, Violet creates a loose structure within which there is lots of room to move. The best way to see this dance of structure and openness, of directed and non-directed action, is to focus on what I call the Therapeutic Experiences that Violet uses with children and adolescents in therapy and with adult participants in the summer training.

So far, in the first three days of the training, Violet has introduced the adults to three such Therapeutic Experiences that she also uses with children and adolescents: the House, Tree, Person drawing, the Safe Place drawing, and the Clay work experience. She also opened the training on the first day by having the participants draw themselves as a child, but this is not something she regularly uses with children and adolescents so I do not include it here. Over the course of the training, she will introduce seven other Therapeutic Experiences that will utilize various expressive media. Table 1 contains a list of all such Therapeutic Experiences that she will introduce in the training. Table 1 also names the expressive medium which is used in each Therapeutic Experience, the day on which the Therapeutic Experience is presented in the training, and the therapeutic function that it serves.

Table 1: Therapeutic Experiences
Introduced in the Training

Day	Therapeutic Experience	Expressive Medium	Therapeutic Function
1 M	House, Tree, Person drawing	drawing	building relationship, strengthening contact
2 T	Safe Place drawing	drawing	building relationship, strengthening contact
3 W	Clay work	clay	self-work, emotional expression
4 Th	Anger drawing	drawing	emotional expression
5 F	Music process	musical instruments	strengthening contact, self-work, emotional expression
6 M	Sand Tray experience	sand and toys	self-work, emotional expression
7 T	Demon drawing	drawing	self-nurturing work
8 W	Working with Puppets	puppets	self-work, emotional expression
9 Th	Medicine cards	picture cards	self-work, emotional expression
10 F	Final drawing	drawing	gaining closure

Violet has described to me that she has different purposes and goals in mind when she uses the various Therapeutic Experiences at different times in the therapeutic process with children and adolescents. For example, she uses the House, Tree,

Person drawing to build the relationship and strengthen contact with the child early on in their work together. In a parallel way, she also uses the House, Tree, Person drawing early on in the training as the workshop participants are getting to know her and each other. Violet has also described that the purpose of the clay exercises is related to the objectives of self-work that she described on Wednesday, the third day of the training. The Therapeutic Experience of working with clay also has the function of encouraging deeper emotional expression once some degree of relationship and contact has been established.

As the training progresses, the methods and purposes of each of the ten Therapeutic Experiences listed in Table 1 will be spelled out and become clearer. In the next section, I will describe how these Therapeutic Experiences all share a consistent and identifiable form although the expressive media and therapeutic functions may vary.

The Form of the Oaklander Therapeutic Experiences

My first hint that Violet's approach to both therapy and training had a structural quality was when I identified that she has a set of recognizable Therapeutic Experiences that she uses with both children and adults. When I looked closely at each of these various Therapeutic Experiences as a next step, the structural element of her work became even clearer. That is, my analysis of the Therapeutic Experiences revealed that they all shared a consistent form even though they each had unique names and utilized various expressive media. The Therapeutic Experiences share a consistent form in that they each contain four distinct parts, segments or steps that Violet generally introduces through verbal prompts. This four-step form of the Therapeutic Experiences is consistent whether Violet is using them with adults in training or with children in therapy. In Table 2 below, I describe what is contained in each of the four steps of the Therapeutic Experiences and I give an example, based on the Safe Place drawing, of the kind of prompt that Violet generally uses to introduce each of the four steps.

Table 2: Four-Step Form of the Therapeutic Experiences

1.	An experience using imagination or fantasy Prompt: "I want you to imagine a safe place..."
2.	A sensory expression of that experience Prompt: "I want you to draw that safe place..."
3.	A metaphoric and/or narrative description of that expression Prompt: "I want you to be that safe place..."
4.	A kind of "sense-making" articulation of the three prior steps Prompt: "Does any of this make sense for you in your own life?"

In each of the Therapeutic Experiences, it is through distinct and directive prompts that Violet helps the person with whom she is working to move through four identifiable steps of their work together. Within each step, the client can lead the experience in directions of their own choosing, but as I will show, they are making choices within a clear but open framework of experience through which Violet directs them. In the sections that follow, I describe these four steps of Violet's Therapeutic Experiences in more detail. Although each of the Therapeutic Experiences share a similar structure whether Violet is using them with children in therapy or with adults in training, I will be using only examples of Violet working with adults in the training in order to simplify the descriptions in the following sections. In later chapters, I will provide examples of Violet working with children and adolescents using Therapeutic Experiences that follow the same form.

Step 1. Imaginary Experience: "Imagine it"

The first identifiable part of each of Violet's Therapeutic Experiences involves her facilitating an experience using imagination or fantasy. In the training, this first step most often involves the adult participants closing their eyes and using their imagination to conjure up an image. This image will soon be manifested in some way in the expressive medium at hand, but first it is held only in the mind's eye.

In Table 3 below, I show two complete examples of Violet's prompts for the adult participants to use their imagination in both the Safe Place drawing on Tuesday and during the Clay work experience on Wednesday.

There are two important ideas to reflect on regarding how Violet starts her Therapeutic Experiences with a prompt to use imagination and fantasy. First, paralleling the discussion of "the shape of the bowl," Violet starts these Therapeutic Experiences with a relatively easy task for the participants. In this way, the participants are able to retreat for a moment into the comfort of, as Violet states, "their own space," by closing their eyes and by getting comfortable. Secondly, even though Violet is directing the participants to come up with some imaginary image or form, there is some comfort in the fact that there is no "right answer" that she is after. In this way, the freedom to choose an image is really a seductive invitation from Violet to enter into the Therapeutic Experience from a position of comfort, choice and personal power.

Table 3: Violet's Prompts for "Imaginary Experience"

Safe Place drawing	"I want you to imagine that you can go to a safe place. Whatever safe means for you...Now this place could be some place you remember from your childhood that comes to you, or a place in your life now, or a place you make up. You could make up this safe place. It could even be on the moon"
Clay work	"And what I'd like you to do is close your eyes...And feel the temperature of [the clay] with the palm of your hands...take a deep breath...and when you exhale, imagine the air going down your arms,.down through your fingers, into the clay... I'd like you to begin to form something."

Perhaps most importantly, Violet's initial prompt for the use of imagination reflects a deep respect for children and the developmental strengths of childhood. That is, by starting the Therapeutic Experiences with a prompt to use the imagination, Violet allows children to begin the therapeutic work with one of their most highly developed facilities, the ability to think imaginatively. Significantly, Violet does not start with a prompt that requires children in the therapeutic context to write words down on a piece of paper or to describe in words some experience they may have had in their lives. Instead, Violet builds on what developmental theorists (Piaget, 1962; Vygotsky, 1934) have described as the child's intrinsic ability to imagine, enter, and inhabit "as if" realms of experience in rich, complex and meaningful ways.

Step 2. Sensory Expression: "Make it"

The second identifiable and consistent part of Violet's Therapeutic Experiences also builds on a developmental strength of childhood: the importance of "hands on," sensori-motor experiences in a child's efforts to understand and make sense of the world. After Violet has given the initial prompt to use imagination or fantasy in each of the Therapeutic Experiences, she consistently follows with a second prompt that involves some kind of creative and sensory-based expression of those images springing from the imagination. Whether this creative expression involves the use of drawing materials, clay, or numerous other media that will be utilized as the workshop progresses, both children and adults are next asked to physically and sensorially create an image of what they have already seen in their mind's eye.

Examples of Violet's prompts for sensory expression from the training are shown in Table 4 below, once again for both the Safe Place drawing and the Clay work experience.

Table 4: Violet's Prompts for "Sensory Expression"

Safe Place drawing	"And what I'm going to ask you to do soon is to draw this place, and I want to remind you that I don't have to understand your drawing, no one has to. It's your drawing. It can be any way you want it to be. If you need to draw something you don't know how to draw, it could be a shape, and you'll know what it is. It could be abstract, or it could be as concrete as you want it to be. It could be any way. It could be a mixture. You might have the feeling of the place around the colors, lines, and shapes. Any way that you want to do it. So when you're ready, get your leaning board, a piece of paper, and a handful of pastels..."
Clay work	"With your eyes closed, now that your clay has a lot of your energy in it, I'd like you to begin to form something. Now just let the clay go where it wants to go, and then sometimes let your fingers tell the clay. This might be just an abstract shape, or it might be that you want to make some kind of an object, or an animal, or figure of some kind. So just try, with your eyes closed, just try to make something, but don't look at it yet. Don't worry about what you are making. Just continue working..."

It is interesting to note how the balance of "directiveness" and "non-directiveness" can be seen in these prompts. Although she is clearly directive in her requests for sensory expression, she is also non-directive in the way in which she expects this request to be carried out. Thus, she leaves open for the participants many options in the way they can choose to fulfill her request to draw or make something.

With this prompt to create something from imagination out of the materials available, Violet is asking the adults in the workshop and children in therapy to create the "conversation piece" that will become the focus of their work together. This tactile and visual representation of ideas, images and projections serves as a rich, visual "text" that will in some way be "read" and made sense of by Violet and the person with whom she is working. It is important to note, however, that this physical representation of the client's imagination will not be "read" or interpreted by Violet. Instead, as the next step will demonstrate, it will be up to the creator of this image to speak for it, explore it, give it a voice, and dialogue with it. Violet will be the guide in adding words and meaning to the projective exercise, but she will not step out of this role as guide to become the all-knowing, "interpreter of images" so common in the professional world of psychology since the early days of psychoanalysis.

As in the first part of the Therapeutic Experiences where Violet built upon the childhood strength of imagination, Violet builds upon another universal childhood strength in the second part of the Therapeutic Experiences: sensory-based, artistic expression. Significantly, in both the examples provided above, the sensory experience and expression through drawing and clay are accomplished mostly in silence. Again, it is the non-verbal but very expressive strengths of childhood that Violet emphasizes in this second step of her work. Words will come later, but for now, there is a kind of silent reverie in the tactile and imaginative pleasures of the medium.

Step 3. Metaphoric & Narrative Description: "Be it"

Piaget (1962) believed that in our work with young children in educational environments, we should build up to abstract concepts (such as addition and subtraction, for example) by first using tactile manipulatives that children can sort, divide and add with their own fingers and see with their own eyes. Violet builds on the same principle in her work with children and adolescents in the therapeutic setting. First, she gets children to create a tactile expression of art and imagination, and only then does she work with the children to help them put words and concepts to their creation.

It is also important, however, to notice the type of words and concepts that she uses and also does not use in this phase of her work with both children and adolescents. That is, she doesn't immediately direct the adult or child toward using words and concepts that are abstract and conceptual. Instead, Violet first helps the children and adults with whom she is working to build a story or a metaphor that describes and details the piece they have created and that now sits in front of them. This use of richly detailed, figurative language is accomplished by means of a consistent prompt to speak "as if" the adult or child were the piece they had created. Violet often uses numerous prompts to help children and adults to take on multiple "voices" and fully explore the different aspects of the imaginative piece that has been created. Examples of this type of prompting for metaphoric and narrative articulation from both the Safe Place drawing with Lydia and the Clay work experience with Sabina are shown in the Table 5 below:

Table 5: Violet's Prompts for Metaphoric or Narrative Description

Safe Place drawing with Lydia	"Okay, what I'd like you to do is imagine that you are on the bed, and just say 'I'm on this bed...' and just see what comes from that..."	"So why don't you talk to her. Tell her what you'd like to say to her about this, being on this bed..."	"Well, what I'd like you to do is be the bed. Say 'I'm this bed...'"	"Talk to the bed and say 'I really didn't expect you to...'"
Clay work with Sabina	"What I'd like you to do is, be this piece of clay, say, 'I'm this clay'...and describe yourself to us..."	"Okay, what I'd like you to do is be this part that's not very perfect. And just be that part."	"How does the rest of this piece feel about that. If this could talk, what would it say to that?"	"Well, be the baseball mitt then. Come back to that... 'I'm a baseball mitt...'"

In the training, Violet often describes the differences between working with adults and with children. One main difference is that children will commonly give very brief answers when she asks them to describe what they have drawn or created. In part, this brevity is related to the fact that a child's skill with words does not yet match adult verbal facility with language.

So how does Violet help children move towards using words in her work with them? She does so in a number of ways. First she helps children to create a "conversation piece" that helps get the dialogue going in the first place. She then playfully uses numerous prompts to build the metaphor and the story from that "conversation piece." From those prompts, children, adolescents and adults are gently directed toward the use of words and verbal images to detail, describe and explore what they have created.

It is Violet's theoretical stance that every "conversation piece" that is created, whether it be a Safe Place drawing or a clay sculpture, will by necessity reflect something of the person who made it. It is also Violet's belief that whenever she can get clients to start talking about what they have created, they can't help but describe it in terms that reflect their own ideas, feelings, thoughts, and experiences. This is the concept of "projection" (Freud, 1957, 1959) at work. What Violet has done with these types of Therapeutic Experiences is to create containers wherein participants can project parts of their own experience into a visual format and then add words to it. In the next section regarding the fourth part of the Therapeutic Experiences, I will make visible how Violet helps the person with whom she is working "re-own" and "make sense" of these projections and, in so doing, help them to have a more fully developed and integrated sense of themselves.

Step 4. Sense-making Articulation: "Does it fit?"

In the description of the third step of the Therapeutic Experiences, I outlined how Violet helps the clients with whom she is working to build a metaphor or a story about the image that they first visualized and manifested in the first two parts of the experience. I also discussed how both imagination and sensory-based experience are fundamental aspects of child development that Violet builds upon in her work. Significantly, it is also true that developmental theorists (Bruner, 1990; Bruner and Lucariello 1989; MacCormac, 1990) have identified both narrative and metaphor as cognitive tools that children begin to use at very early ages to make sense of their experience. Very young children can metaphorically use a wooden block to represent a bunny hopping across a field in their imaginative play. Young children also start to understand abstract concepts such as "danger" and "being good" when listening to the narrative account of, for example, Peter Rabbit's adventures in Mr. McGregor's garden (Potter, 1902). In both cases, young children are using a metaphor or a story about some experience in the world to make sense of or think about their own experience. Violet builds on this fundamental human need and skill to "make sense" in the final part of her Therapeutic Experiences.

Once Violet has led the person she is working with through the imaginative, sensory, and metaphoric/narrative steps of the Therapeutic Experience, she will then usually prompt the person to "make sense" of and connect with this experience in a more personal way. The prompt that Violet most often uses is: "Does anything about what you have said make sense for you in your own life?" A variation of this prompt that she has used is: "Does any of this fit for you in your own life?" (A nice example of this prompt shows up in the video that will be used in day four of the training showing Violet's work with an adolescent boy working with clay).

What sometimes happens, however, is that Violet's clients spontaneously make a connection between what they have been saying about their "conversation piece" and their own experience in life. In both of the examples that we have been following — Lydia's Safe Place drawing and Sabina's Clay work experience — these participants from the training spontaneously came to their own personal "sense making" about the metaphors they had been building and the stories they had been describing. In Violet's language, both participants spontaneously "re-owned" the projections they had objectified in their work. In Lydia's case she connects the metaphor of a yellow bed to the experience of being supported by her stepmother. In Sabina's case, she makes the connection between the clay sculpture of a baseball mitt that is "big" and the struggles she has with weight in her own life. Lydia's and Sabina's "sense making" words are shown in Table 6 below.

Interestingly, both Lydia and Sabina not only make a

conceptual connection with their "conversation piece," but they also add what that connection means to them in emotional terms. Gestalt theorists (Perls, et al., 1951) argue that human beings are constantly in the process of finding patterns and making meaning in their lives. In the same way that the ancients looked up at groups of random stars, named them after mythological figures, and called them "constellations," each of us in our own life is constantly working to make sense, create order, and gain closure on what we see, feel, think, and experience. Thus, if an issue arises in our life that troubles us and doesn't easily fit into the known fabric of our life (a divorce, an accident, an incidence of abuse, etc.), we will try to gain closure on this experience by working to make meaning of it in some way.

Lydia: Safe Place drawing	"Maybe it's Sonia and that she's always there for me... It means the world to me, that you're always there for me, and always have been. And it's very unconditional"
Sabina: Clay work	"I'm a baseball mitt. I catch things and I'm big...Which fits for me right now [patting her own hips], I'm big and I hate it..."

Table 6: Examples of Sense-Making Articulation

In this way, Violet can be seen as facilitating the process of gestalt formation and closure with her Therapeutic Experiences in that adults and children alike can project unfinished business from their imagination into the conversation pieces they create.

She then helps her clients to gain closure or work to make meaning of these issues in the last part of the Therapeutic Experiences by asking them if any of what they have said "fits" in their lives.

In the chapters that follow, I will explore each of these four important steps of the Therapeutic Experiences in more detail. To summarize this chapter's reflective notes, I first described a set of Therapeutic Experiences that Violet uses with both children in therapy and adults in the training. I then showed how Violet's Therapeutic Experiences all share the same four-step structure. That is, each Therapeutic Experience contains prompts for imaginative experience ("imagine it"), for sensory expression ("make it"), for metaphoric and narrative description ("be it") and usually for sense-making articulation ("does it fit?").

Another way to look at these Therapeutic Experiences, however, is that Violet simply supports and nurtures the "organismic self-regulation" (Perls, 1947; Piaget, 1971, 1977) of the individuals with whom she works within the safe container she creates with them. That is, she is helping them do the work they are already striving to do themselves. In the supportive environment she helps to create, her clients gain the environmental and self support necessary to be able to work toward "sense making" of the complex experience that make up their lives. Thus, we arrive back at the opening question in this section: is Violet really leading or is she allowing? Is she being assertively directive or supportively non-directive? This will be a theme explored in the examples to come when Violet will work with both children and adults using these structured but open-ended Therapeutic Experiences in the context of the training.

4

Day Four: Thursday
Working with Aggressive
Energy and Anger

Child demonstration: Clay work with Ben

By Thursday morning, most of the participants have made
the choice to sit on the floor, relaxing against the leaning chairs
and chatting with their neighbors. This sense of comfortable
casualness has been increasing in the room since the first day of
the workshop when most participants sat upright in chairs
against the wall politely maintaining their distance. There is
more laughter and a general sense of people checking in with
each other. The tea and coffee service in the hospitality room is
being well-used, as is the library of books that Violet has been
adding to each day. These books, perhaps fifty or more, are all in
some way related to the practice of counseling children. There
are books on using art in therapy, books on therapeutic
techniques with children, and books on different counseling
theories. Participants can check these books out overnight and
many have already done so.

When Violet starts the day with a greeting, she also asks

participants if there are topics they have been thinking about that they would like her to cover. A list of topics is soon accumulated, including: working with parents, working with adolescents, working with groups, sex education in the schools, and what to do with aggression in the counseling session. Violet mentions that she will try to find time to address these topics in the days to come and that aggressive energy in particular will be the topic of this afternoon's session.

Violet refers to the video monitor set up in the corner of the room and says that after yesterday's "adult" experience in working with clay, she would now like to show a thirty-minute, videotaped example of her using clay while working with a thirteen-year-old, African-American boy named Ben. The video, she explains, is part of a series of published videotapes called "Child Therapy with the Experts" (Carlson, et al., 2002). Before she turns on the VCR, Violet tells the participants two things about the context of its production. First, she warns, the video was shot in Chicago just days after she had completed an intensive (and ultimately successful) round of treatments for breast cancer. Second, she and Ben had not met before the cameras began rolling and all she knew about him was that he lived with his mother. In spite of these difficult conditions under which she was asked to demonstrate her approach to therapy, Violet assures the participants that the essence of her approach is visible in her work with Ben. Violet then dims the lights and starts the videotape. The video begins with the image of Ben and Violet sitting at a forty-five degree angle to each other. There are chunks of clay on the table in front of them and on the shelves behind Violet there are markers, crayons, paper, and games.

Violet smiles warmly at Ben in greeting and almost immediately invites him to touch the clay on the table. He reaches forward and picks up a hunk of clay, as does Violet. She tells him she would like him to do some things with the clay but that first she would like to know what kinds of experiences he has had with clay before. Ben smiles shyly and tells her that as a child he used to make people and animals out clay. Violet says, "Well this will be fun. First, I'd like you to see all the different things you can do with clay." Violet then leads Ben through the same activities that she led the participants through yesterday — pinching the clay, poking it, tearing it apart, putting it back together, etc. In addition, she also shows him how to make both snakes and balls with the clay using different rolling motions with the palms of her hands. Ben's genial affect during this part of their work together seems to reflect his playful willingness to go along with this surprisingly different but nice lady.

When they have completed the "getting to know the clay" exercise, Violet prompts Ben to make the kind of "self statements" that she described yesterday in the training. First she asks Ben, "Which of those things did you like the best?" Ben replies, "I liked making the snake, like I used to do in elementary school." Violet also asks Ben if there was "something we did that you didn't like too much." At first Ben says no, but after Violet chuckles and says that she sometimes doesn't like to poke the clay because it gets under her nails, Ben offers that he didn't like "driving a hole through" and that he must have weak fingers.

As with much of Violet's work with both children and adults, there is an easy-going, give-and-take feeling to both the time and the conversation they are sharing, lots of smiles and a few bits of laughter mixed in with the dialogue. When Ben accidentally drops the ball of clay he is forming, for example, Violet dryly adds, "You can also drop the clay and see if it bounces," and Ben chuckles in response. The bright lights of the studio and the intrusive cameras seem to be no longer a part of their awareness at this point as they immerse themselves in playing with the clay and making contact with each other.

About eight minutes into their work together, Violet prompts Ben to begin a second clay exercise in the following way:

Violet: I want you to just take your clay — Let me see how it feels — Oh, that's good, it's not too hard. And I just want you to put both hands on it. I want you to close your eyes. And then take a deep breath, and when you let the air out imagine its going right down your arms into the clay. Try that again [Ben takes a second deep breath and smiles with his eyes closed]. Now this clay has a lot of your energy in it because you've been fooling with it...

Ben: Hm,mm [Ben peeks at Violet, who has her eyes closed, and then closes his eyes again]

Violet: So what I want you to do, with your eyes closed at first, is start making something with the clay. It could be just a shape or you could imagine you're making an animal or a person or, you know, you might think you're making something and it

might not turn out to be that because your eyes
are closed...

Ben: Hm,mm...

Violet: ...and it might just be a shape or it might be a
thing, whatever. Just let your fingers move the
clay. And sometimes the clay tells you where it
wants to go and sometimes you just have to push
so it will know where it wants to go. So just let
yourself, with your eyes closed, make something.
And you'll be surprised because your eyes are
closed...

Ben: Hm, mm

Violet: Yeah...

As Violet has been giving these verbal directions, Ben has
been silently working the clay between his hands on the table.
His formless hunk of clay begins to take on the shape of what
looks like a fish or a whale, with a long, tapering body and two
flukes as a tail. After about thirty seconds pass quietly, Violet
says:

...and after awhile, when you want to, you can open your
eyes and finish it off...and turn it around and look at the
back and finish it, but don't change it, just kind of finish
it when you want to...

Ben opens his eyes, looking first at his clay creation. He
smiles, chuckles, and then looks up at Violet. In the following
dialogue, Violet encourages Ben to speak "as if" he were the clay,

working to help him build and deepen the story or metaphor it
may contain:

> Violet: Okay, Ben. Now since a lot of your energy is in
> this clay, it really is a part of you. So, what I'd like
> you to do is to be this piece of clay and tell me
> about yourself: "I'm this piece of clay." And you
> can just describe how you look or whatever. Just
> tell me about yourself as this piece of clay...
>
> Ben: Um. I don't know how to really describe myself.
> Well, um, this is supposed to be a whale...
>
> Violet: All right. "I'm a whale"...
>
> Ben: ...and whales, um, swim...
>
> Violet: ...Oh, Okay, now here's how I want you to do this.
> You're the clay. So you have to say, "I'm a whale,
> and I swim...," you know...
>
> Ben: Yeah, I, I'm a whale and I like to swim.
>
> Violet: Hm, mm
>
> Ben: I like to go under water [Hm, mm] and go really
> deep [Hm, mm]. Um. I like to eat fish [Hm, mm].
> And that's about it.
>
> Violet: Yeah. [smiles] So, do you get a lot of fish to eat,
> Whale?
>
> Ben: Yeah.
>
> Violet: And are you a young whale or are you an older
> whale?
>
> Ben: Um, an older whale
>
> Violet: How do you know that? Is that because you have
> a lot of cracks and things that you're older?

You've been around a long time?

Ben: Yeah, because it's pretty disabled, you know...

Violet: Pretty what?

Ben: Disabled.

Violet: Ah, it's disabled. And are there some things that you can't do anymore, Whale?

Ben: Probably can't swim that fast.

Violet: Mmm. Has that become a problem for you?

Ben: No.

Violet: No. Do you have anybody after you, anytime?

Ben: No.

Violet: Are you pretty safe in the water?

Ben: Yes. I feel comfortable.

Violet: You feel comfortable. Hm, mm. Well, Whale, are you by yourself or do you have a family?

Ben: Um, I have a family.

Violet: Yeah? Who's in your family?

Ben: My mother, my play-grandmother, and my sister.

Violet: Hm, mm. That's a lot of family...whale family [she smiles].

Ben: Yeah.

Violet: They swim with you or are you pretty independent? Or maybe you'd like to be more independent. I don't know.

Ben: They sort of swim with me.

Violet: They sort of swim with you.

Ben: Yeah.

Violet: Do they bother you?

Ben: No.

Violet: No. They let you kind of go off by yourself sometimes?

Ben: Yes.

Violet: They do? That's good. That's good, Whale. [she laughs]. All right. You're a pretty neat whale.

Ben: Thank you.

At this point in their work together, Violet makes a shift. During this pretend dialogue when she has been encouraging Ben to speak "as if" he were the whale, Violet has been addressing him as "Whale" instead of "Ben." In this next piece, Violet gently, and somewhat falteringly, transitions into the "sense making" phase of the work and uses Ben's real name in the process:

Violet: All right. Yeah. Um, I'm just wondering if there's anything about your whale that fits for you, Ben. That you could say, "Yeah, I'm like that too?" Or, "that's like my life too"? Or...

Ben: [brief pause] Well, during the summer I basically live in the water.

Violet: Really?

Ben: Yes.

Violet: I guess that's one of your favorite things to do, huh? Swim?

Ben: Yeah.

Violet: Hm, mm.

Ben: Swim and, uh, I'm very active. Whales are active...

Violet: Uh, huh.

Ben: Yeah, that's about it.

Violet: That's about it. Well, that's a lot, too, yeah. Do you feel safe in your life? I mean the whale feels safe in the water. Do you feel safe?

Ben: Yeah, very safe.

Violet: Hm, mm. Very safe. And it sounds like the whale family is a little bit like your family. I have a feeling...I don't know. You have a sister?

Ben: Yeah.

Violet: And a mother, and a play-grandmother. What is that, a play-grandmother?

Ben: She's not my real grandmother, but she acts like it.

Violet: I see, I see. I bet that's nice, too.

Ben: Yeah.

Violet: And what about your father?

Ben: Um, he lives in Indiana and I don't see him much.

Violet: Ah. Your parents are divorced?

Ben: Yeah.

Violet: Yeah. Do you wish you could see him more?

Ben: Sometimes, yes, in different situations.

Violet: What do you mean?

Ben: I like to play basketball a lot, and I wish I could see him more to play basketball.

Violet: Hm, mm. Hm, mm. [seriously] Yeah. That's hard when your dad lives far away like that...

Before this videotaped session began, the only piece of information Violet knew about Ben was that he lived with his mother. In speaking "as if" he was the whale, Ben has slowly built a relationship with Violet and revealed quite a bit about both himself and his family, all in less than fifteen minutes. In their next ten minutes of work together, Violet asks Ben to once again go into the imaginary and sensory realm of Clay work and to create a little clay figure to represent each member of his family, including his father. Violet helps him do this, and before long, she has him speaking to each of the clay figures (his mother, his sister, his play-grandmother, and his father) "as if" they are there in the flesh. Violet prompts Ben toward making "self statements" by stating: "Imagine you could talk to them and you could tell them one thing you like and one thing you don't like about them."

When Ben gets to the clay figure that represents his father, he says that what he likes is, "When you have time to spend with me, you use it wisely." He adds that what he doesn't like is that the amount of time his father spends with him is so little. Violet then learns that when Ben is feeling frustrated after a visit with his dad, he often takes out his frustration on his mother:

> Ben: I take things out on my mother sometimes, I
> believe.
>
> Violet: Take it out on her, like when it belongs to
> something else?
>
> Ben: Yes. Like when I come home from my father's house
> and something didn't go right. I don't take it out
> on my father; he doesn't spend a lot of time with
> me anyway. So I can't make it worse. And I know
> my mother will always be there for me so I just go

after her.

For the final fifteen minutes of their time together, Violet helps Ben brainstorm some strategies of how he could express his "mad feelings" without taking them out on his mother. Together, they come up with a list that Violet writes up on a piece of paper. The list includes playing basketball aggressively while being in touch with his feelings, tearing up old magazines, or just simply writing down his feelings on paper. Ben sheepishly admits that he sometimes "beats up on his teddy bear." Violet adds that to the list saying, "That won't hurt anybody and it will make you feel better." To close their session together, Violet hands Ben the list and says, "When you are mad you can do any one of these things, so you won't have to take it out on your mother." Ben smiles and thanks her. Violet asks him to remind her where he has to go tonight, and Ben tells her that he has basketball practice. She then thanks Ben for coming and says, "We have to stop because I want to make sure you get to practice."

After they shake hands, the videotape ends, the lights in the conference room go up, and the participants in the summer training spend the next few minutes, at Violet's prompting, discussing her approach to working with Ben. One participant notes that it was helpful to see the way Violet worked to help Ben build the story and the metaphor of the whale: "He started with so few statements and you helped him come out with so much more." Violet responds that this is what she meant when she said that working with children is different than working with adults: "You have to be willing to be a little foolish, to step in there and play and encourage them a bit." After this discussion, Violet announces it is time for lunch, and she states that the participants will have more practice in playing and being a bit foolish after the break when she presents her approach to working with aggressive energy.

Working with aggressive energy

At one-thirty, when the twenty-four participants have re-gathered in the conference room, Violet asks them where they went for lunch and gets a few varied responses. She then uses a food metaphor to introduce the afternoon's topic of aggressive energy. She pretends to hold a piece of fruit in her hand and to take a big bite out of it, and then she states, "We are always using aggressive energy, like when I'm biting an apple. Otherwise, we would never get our needs met." She humorously imitates trying to bite into the apple with a slack jaw and her lips only mouthing the skin. She goes on to define aggressive energy in a positive light as a naturally occurring form of energy that is used by all organisms to help get their needs met in the environments in which they live. She says that children run into trouble with aggressive energy in one of two ways: "by either withdrawing their natural aggressive energy too much or by externalizing it too much by acting out of bounds." In either case, she states, the natural process of taking care of one's needs in a healthy and productive way is interrupted.

To provide a therapeutic "container" for practicing the healthy expression of aggressive energy, Violet states that four requirements must be in place: 1) aggressive energy work has to be done in close contact with the therapist; 2) the work must be done in a safe "container" or boundary where the child knows the therapist won't let him/her get out of control; 3) the expression of aggressive energy has to be exaggerated; and 4) the work with aggressive energy has to be fun and non-threatening. Violet says that all of these requirements help address the child's concerns and fears about being either overwhelmed by aggressive impulses or shamed for expressing them.

"Later this afternoon," Violet explains, "we will be doing the Anger drawing, but there is a difference between anger work and aggressive energy work." The difference, Violet describes, is that aggressive energy work is a body experience that is not necessarily related to the specific content of anger. She says that she might suggest to a child, for example, that together they punch some clay as hard as they can. This action is a way for that child to feel and express aggressive energy. It allows that child to feel more of herself, to have a better sense of herself and her own power. This improved sense of self provides the child with the "self-support" necessary to address and express other difficult feelings such as grief and anger. In this way, aggressive energy work lays the foundation for deeper emotional exploration but is, in itself, not related to specific issues or content. Violet states that "feelings of grief and anger are at the root of many problems in therapy," and, therefore, a combination of aggressive energy work and anger work may be helpful in addressing these basic issues, one building on the other.

After this theoretical overview of the topic, Violet says, "Just to give you the experience, I need a volunteer." One of the workshop participants, Carrie, raises her hand and steps up to the front of the room where Violet now stands. Violet is holding two red foam bats with black handles; she smiles as she hands Carrie one of the bats. The bats, called Battacas™, are approximately two feet long and eight inches thick. Violet explains to the group that with these Battacas, she and Carrie are going to demonstrate a fun, but contained way to express aggressive energy by having a "Battaca fight." After the nervous giggles of participants subside, Violet says, "But, there are rules: There is no hitting the head or the front of the body, and we start and stop at the sound of the bell. Okay?" Once Carrie has agreed to these rules, the Battaca fight commences with Violet making the sound of a bell and initiating the attack by scurrying behind the surprised Carrie to land a solid, first strike on Carrie's backside. Soon, Carrie picks up the spirit of the exercise and is herself landing cushy blows on Violet's back, backside, and legs. Most of the participants get into the act as well by clapping, shouting, and encouraging both Violet and Carrie to "Go get her! Give it to her again!"

Twenty minutes later, all but two physically-challenged participants have taken part in a brief "Battaca fight" with a partner with the same general results: hilarity, high energy release, red faces, and an increasing sense of merriment at being able to safely "whack" another person without creating harm. Violet asks the participants for their responses to this activity, and a number of them make comments: "It was fun," "It was a great outlet," and "It got my energy going." A few minutes later, after Violet has demonstrated a number of games and toys that are good for the release of aggressive energy (e.g. Whack Attack!™, Splat!™, The Hawaiian Punch Game™, real stone diodes to be broken with a hammer, etc.), my training notes reflect my own surprise at Violet's actions:

> Violet is sitting on the floor shooting foam darts at participants, a very funny image. This mature woman surrounded by brightly colored plastic dart guns, foam Nerf™ guns, alligator squirt guns, a gun that springs a foam fist out at the end of an accordion-stretched arm, a hollow plastic squeeze tube that shoots a soft plastic fist across the room...She says she will not buy play guns that look real and that "these brightly colored ones are hard to find" (workshop notes, 7/17/97 2:47 p.m.).

At the end of this amusing presentation of various approaches to expressing aggressive energy, Violet restates her opening metaphor to describe the satisfaction one gains from "chomping into an apple." She says that is the same kind of experience she is trying to facilitate when she works with children using all the toys and games scattered around her on the floor. She emphasizes that the purpose of this type of work is not to teach children how to be aggressive but to help them find ways to safely express their naturally occurring aggressive energy. She states that this mobilizing of a child's energy enables the child to further gain the self-support and strength needed to address and express other difficult feelings such as anger or loss. Thus, getting in touch with one's aggressive energy is a way of getting in touch with one's personal power and sense of self. She states:

> Especially with kids who get into power struggles all the time, we need to give them a safe place to experience their own power. We should give them that, and encourage them. In fact, I end up a cheerleader. I'm cheering them on. I'm often the model in a session and I will hit the clay first. If I start smashing it, they do too. I pretend I'm smacking the woman who rear-ended my car last year. Of course, I tell kids, "We would never do this in the real world, would we? But in my office it's okay. It's okay to pretend."

Working with anger

After a fifteen-minute afternoon break, Violet explains that she will be transitioning from the aggressive energy work into what she calls "working with anger." Violet introduces the subject of anger work with children by describing how the expression of anger generally frightens children, so they tend to "push it down." But at its root, anger is simply an expression of the self, Violet states, and "when you help them express anger you help them express the self." Anger, she adds, is the way that the self makes clear when a boundary has been crossed. She goes on to describe anger work in the following way:

> Anger is the least tolerated emotion. We expect kids to be afraid and to cry. We tend to think that kids are happy-go-lucky. But when they get angry, forget it. This is confusing to kids because they are expressing the self,

trying desperately to get their needs met. They may use gross terminology and a lot of power because they feel powerless. But adults then equate anger with a bad attitude rather than the message underneath it. Kids don't learn how to deal with these feelings. So that's our job, to teach them to express these difficult feelings in appropriate and safe ways. There is also a difference between "everyday" anger and anger that is about unfinished business. So I help them learn to deal with both kinds.

In order to help children express their anger, Violet states, first we as therapists must help them get more comfortable expressing aggressive energy in the ways she outlined. She then articulates the distinction between what she calls "everyday anger" and "unfinished anger." Everyday anger, she says, is related to the irritation and upset that happens in the ordinary, day-to-day process of living: "If we could always find ways to express our anger and irritation when it comes up, it wouldn't build up into uncontrolled rage." Differing from everyday anger, she describes, unfinished anger, is anger that is related to some unresolved past event such as abuse or neglect. "We need to address these two kinds of anger," Violet says, "in different ways."

She goes on to suggest that we help children deal with "everyday anger" in simple ways, such as teaching them to talk about it and showing children how words can be used to express anger. She suggests making lists with children, as she did with Ben on the Video, about what angers them. She also recommends that we help children learn to identify when they are feeling angry, how they feel in their bodies when they are feeling anger, and to understand that it's okay to express such feelings in healthy and constructive ways. Lastly, she recommends that therapists help children think up their own methods of expressing anger in safe ways, like hitting the bed with a tennis racket or tearing up old newspapers.

Underlying this thinking on anger, she says, is the Gestalt principle of helping a child "restore equilibrium" by helping the child address what has angered him or her and moving on from there. This is highlighted when a participant raises the concern of many parents that teaching a child to punch clay, for example, is "teaching the child to be aggressive." In response to this, Violet states:

> If this work is done correctly, it has the opposite effect. Instead of making them more angry and more aggressive, it makes them calm. It's that equilibrium, that homeostasis. All this work does is give the child an appropriate place to express feelings.

As an example of books that can be used when addressing issues related to everyday anger, Violet reads aloud to the participants "Elbert's Bad Word" (Wood, 1988) in which a little boy gets in trouble at a party for using bad words. In the story, Elbert is taught by the gardener on his grandparent's estate (who, luckily, is also a magician) new powerful words that won't be offensive to use in public (for example, "Zounds and Gadzooks!"). In her reading, Violet uses the accent of upper class folk who are offended by Elbert's bad words. She reads dramatically and playfully, and the participants laugh along with her: "'Snickering wickedly,'" she reads, "I like that!" and repeats the line.

Violet also mentions "The Temper Tantrum Book" (Preston, 1969) and "Alexander's Terrible, Horrible, Bad Day" (Viorst, 1972) as other examples of books that address anger. One of the participants says to Violet, "You read such a good story!" Violet thanks her and laughs. She describes how later in the week, she will be "entering deeper into the storytelling place. You see, everything is connected in this workshop."

Violet then states that she would like to talk about how to work with children who have "unfinished anger" regarding abuse or neglect. Like both "aggressive energy" work and "everyday anger" work, unfinished anger can only safely be addressed when the therapeutic relationship is strong and when the child is feeling a lot of self-support and a lot of support provided by the therapist. As an example of the kind of work she might do with a child related to "unfinished anger," Violet says she would like the participants to do an exercise called the "Anger drawing." The following transcript reflects Violet's verbal prompting for this fourth Therapeutic Experience of the training:

> I'd like you to just get as relaxed as you can. And just go inside yourself and see how you're feeling in there...see how your head feels, and your shoulders feel and your arms, your stomach, chest, back...[5 second pause] ...wiggle your toes, sometimes we forget that we go all the way down to our toes...[5 second pause]. Notice your

breath. Take a deep breath [She inhales], hold it...and then let it out...[She exhales]. Let's do that a couple more times...[20 second pause]. I'm going to make a sound and just listen to the sound as long as you can [she rings a chime three times]...

I'd like you to go back into your childhood and find a time when something happened that made you feel angry. Or maybe you don't remember feeling angry, but you felt frightened, or upset, or hurt, or ashamed, or like you were a bad child. Something that happened when you felt angry or one of those other things. It might not be a big thing! It might just be some small thing, but that's okay. It doesn't have to be a major thing. Maybe something that popped into your mind that surprises you. Rather than find something better or something different, you might want to trust what came to you [5 second pause].

See how far you can go in your childhood. If you don't have any memory of something in your childhood way back, then you can try out different ages. But see how far back you can go with this. Or what pops into your head. If something pops into your head, then just go with that. So notice what it is, what's happening around you, how you look. You might not have a clear memory but that's okay. What's around you? Who's with you? [7 second pause]...

And what I'm going to ask you to do is to draw the scene. And maybe you will draw the feelings of what you're feeling around this memory with colors, lines, shapes, or even words if you'd prefer...[4 second pause]...Again, it doesn't have to be something beautiful that anyone can understand, just something that will express for you, this time. When you are ready, just get what you need and draw your picture...

From the time Violet starts the verbal prompt for the drawing to the time the participants finish their drawings, twenty-four minutes elapse. On the audio tape I left recording during this time, participants can be heard putting their anger experiences on paper with louder scratching sounds and more aggressive, striking sounds than during any of the other three previous drawing exercises.

Adult demonstration:
Anger drawing with Candice

At 3:30 p.m., Violet states that she will work with a volunteer as she has done before. Candice, a hospice coordinator who works at a psychiatric out-patient clinic in Canada, comes up to work after Violet chooses her as the first person of three other volunteers to raise their hands. When Violet asks Candice to tell her about the drawing she has made, the gravity of what the picture represents soon becomes clear. Candice states:

> This is me and this is my older brother and sister. And I'm about 8. And they're 11 and 14, actually I forget exactly what age. But they have teamed up together, stripped me, put me on the bed, took a picture, and

showed me this photograph that they said was magic and they would hang on to it, and every time they put it in the water it would come up, the picture of me naked. And they wouldn't give me the picture...there were a lot of issues...

For the next thirty-five minutes, Violet works with Candice exploring the story around this incident and having her speak "as if" she were different characters in the drawing. She particularly tries to encourage Candice to say things like "I'm so angry" when she is in the character of herself as a little girl in the drawing. Candice has a difficult time with this, and even though the topic of discussion is emotionally loaded, Candice remains quite subdued while talking with Violet: "I feel really blocked," she states.

After a long conversation between Violet and Candice that is so quiet it is inaudible even on the tape machine, Candice finally reveals an even more difficult aspect of the story to Violet. She describes how all three of the children in this drawing were victims of various kinds of abuse by their alcoholic uncle who served as a stern "capitalist patriarch" of the well-to-do family. At this point, Violet says, "Well, maybe you could talk to him. What would you say to him?" The volume and intensity of Candice's voice rises slightly when she states: "You son-of-a-bitch!"

Violet asks Candice, "Would you be willing to try something?" She hands Candice a Battaca, asks her to stand up, and pats the now empty chair that Candice stands over saying, "Here he is. I'll hold the chair so it doesn't fall. What could you say to him?"

At this moment, the focus of Candice's attention shifts from the drawing. She literally turns her back on her drawing and explodes in a verbal and physical rage at the imagined "uncle-in-the-chair." The transcript excerpt below includes a "THUMP!" for each time Candice, now in tears, powerfully strikes the empty chair with the Battaca. Hyphened phrases in the transcript indicate rushed speech, while capital letters reflect words loudly spoken or yelled:

> Candice: Okay, you son of a BITCH! [THUMP!] You ruined a family full of [THUMP!], full of [THUMP!], brightness and JOY [THUMP!] and humor! But you ruined [THUMP!] us all, and we all came to be [THUMP!] drunks and abusers. [THUMP! pause] You son of a bitch! [THUMP! sobs, sniffles] And you tied us in with your money [THUMP!]; so we all [THUMP!] depended on you for money [THUMP!]; so we all lived beautifully and sickly [THUMP!], and you were so awful to us all [voice cracks THUMP! deep inhale] You hated us girls! [THUMP!] I remember that [THUMP!] you hated us and you made [THUMP! falters]...
>
> Violet: [softly] Yeah! Just TELL him...
>
> Candice: God! You were sooo... DESTRUCTIVE! [very loudly, wailing]
>
> Violet: Yeah!
>
> Candice: GOD! You were so awful [THUMP!], and

nobody could say NO [THUMP!] to you. [THUMP!] You'd sit there and... Look at you [THUMP!] with your goddam [THUMP! THUMP!]...

Violet: Hm, mm!

Candice: [THUMP!] FUCKING silver [THUMP!] cocktail shaker, and you'd SIT there [THUMP!] while you'd be by the fire... [THUMP!] OH! we'd be [choking] quiet [THUMP!] quiet [THUMP!]... good little girls while you'd stand [THUMP!] there and PONTIFICATE! [THUMP! sniffles]

Violet: Yeah!

Candice: And your kids were a mess [THUMP!], and you were a mess... You bastard! [THUMP!... pause... inhales]

Violet: Hm, mm...

Candice: [THUMP!] We were all quiet and DRUNK! [THUMP!] GOD! [THUMP! sobbing THUMP!]

Violet: [murmuring] Ohhh... hmm

Candice: [pauses. takes a deep breath, and releases it]

Violet: He certainly deserves a lot more of that, doesn't he?

Candice: He ruined so many lives! [choking up, sniffling]

Violet: yeah...

Candice: [quieter crying sounds... then deep breaths]

Violet: [10 second pause]... boy...

At this point, Violet and Candice talk quietly together about the expressive work just done and share a private joke, inaudible on the audio tape. The tone between them has returned to the quiet level of earlier in the session. There are long pauses, further conversation, and a few more tears from Candice, as well as deep breaths. Eventually, there is some hearty laughter regarding Violet's suggestion that Candice could work on this further by actually buying a silver martini shaker and beating it like she did the chair today. Candice replies, "What a great idea! Beat the shit out of a martini shaker!" At this point, relative equilibrium has returned to the room. The strained calm of Candice's voice when she first started working with Violet and the violent outrage she expressed later are now resolved, for the moment, with a few small jokes shared between the two.

Violet first checks in with Candice a final time, then opens for comments and questions from other participants, many of whom first move to reassure Candice. One participant from Sweden quotes a poem from her native country. She translates, "No child has done such a hard job as to grow up while all the adults are chattering." Another participant comments that the demonstration "made me sympathize with what I am asking my clients to do." To this, Candice replies, "If I had felt afraid to do this with you, I couldn't ask a child to do this." She also adds, "I would have loved to have done this work as a child."

When another participant asks Candice how she is doing after such a powerful piece of work, Candice states:

We've been talking about the container, and it really did feel that way to me. It did take me a few minutes to come

back after the session and be able to make eye contact
with the rest of the folks here. But then the anger was
over. That's different than my being bitchy all day long at
everyone I see. I think that's because it was directed, it
was contained, it was expressed.

Soon after this discussion, Violet has the participants pair up
and briefly share their drawings — "not doing this level of deep
work" — with each other. When everyone has regrouped, Violet
says that before the day is over, she would like to give an
example of doing this kind of "unfinished anger work" with
children. She proceeds to tell the story of Gina, a twelve-year-old
girl who had been repeatedly sexually abused by her stepfather.
In the therapy sessions with Violet, Gina would act unfailingly
polite, obliging, and very shy. This was Gina's manner at home
and at school as well, and Violet notes that she was generally
having problems assertively standing up for herself and getting
her own needs met at school and with her siblings. Gina was also
very reluctant to talk about or address any of the feelings she had
about her step-father and about being abused by him. In one
particular session, Violet had Gina make a head out of clay to
represent her stepfather. Violet goes on to describe:

She proceeded to make the head of her stepfather out of
the clay, and she worked very hard on it. She was making
eyelashes and eyebrows and generally avoiding doing
anything else with it. I finally had to say to her "I would
like you to finish it." Usually I won't interrupt a child
when they are working on something. In this case, I was

pacing the session and I had in my mind that we needed a little time to work with her clay piece.

So she finished it and I said, "Here is your stepfather. Here he is. Now you can say anything you want to him. He's not really here, it's just clay. He won't know it. But here he is. What do you want to say to him?" And she said, "I can't talk to him. I can't talk to him." I saw that she was really agitated, so I said, "Okay, do you mind if I talk to him?," and she said, "Sure, you can talk to him." So I started yelling at him: "I don't like you! I don't like what you did to my friend, you really make me mad!"

Gina started laughing at this and she thought that it was the funniest thing. Then I picked up the mallet. I said to her, "I think we need to give him a whack. And she said, "You do it, you do it." I said, "Nope, you have to do this." So Gina takes the mallet and goes like this [Violet pantomimes Gina stalling by adjusting her chair, then adjusting her grip on the mallet, then adjusting her chair again]. Then she suddenly put the mallet down and stood up and said, "I didn't know you had one of these!" as she took a sand tray toy off the shelves and sat down again. Finally, she was able to pick up the mallet and quickly gave the clay piece a couple of small whacks. Then she said to it, "You'll get more later."

After finishing this story, Violet describes again how the work is done in small segments with children. She mentions that clients are most often not done with all their unfinished anger at the end of one particular session. Sometimes, she says, they need help getting refocused or grounded, doing a bit of breathing or looking ahead to positive things so they can leave the session in a relatively calm way. She says she often sees children leave off on a piece of difficult anger work in one session (regarding an abusive parent, for example) and then come back to the issue in later sessions.

In support of Violet's experience and story, a participant named Andrea recounts a story of how she used an inflated "punching clown" with a child whose father had been murdered. The boy, with his mother's help, drew a picture of the murderer's face on a piece of paper and taped it on the punching clown. Andrea states that this provided both the child and the mother with a safe way to deal with their anger. Violet builds on this theme of a "safe way" to deal with anger by stating:

> It's taking it into a playful realm, it's the contact, the safety, the container. They know that I'm there and that I will continue to be there for them. We've already established that I have limits about what they can and can't do in my office and that I'm very clear and not wishy-washy.

At 4:50 p.m., Violet lets the tired-looking participants know that tomorrow, Friday, will have a less intense quality to it. In the same way that Violet helped Candice transition back to a less emotionally labile state by sharing small talk and humor at the end of their work together, the week itself will end on a less intense note. Violet ends the day by stating reassuringly, "We'll have a nice half day tomorrow...with music."

Reflective notes for day four

In the reflective notes at the end of Chapter Three, I outlined the consistent, four-step process that Violet uses in her various Therapeutic Experiences. I described in those notes how Violet guides both adults and children through experiences that engage and utilize 1) the imagination, 2) the senses, 3) the figurative language of stories and metaphors, and, 4) the sense-making step of asking "Does any of this fit for you?"

In this chapter's reflective notes I will add to this discussion of the structural dimensions of Violet's work by showing how her work is not always simply a linear movement through these four steps, but that it is often circular and recursive. That is, she frequently "loops back through" the same four steps of the Therapeutic Experiences after having gone through them once in a session with a child or an adult. Functionally, Violet tends to use this "looping back" to address new or deeper issues that emerge in her work with her client. Thus, this looping can be seen as a deepening spiral in which she engages individuals in layers of the work as the child or adult is ready to take them on (Figure 6).

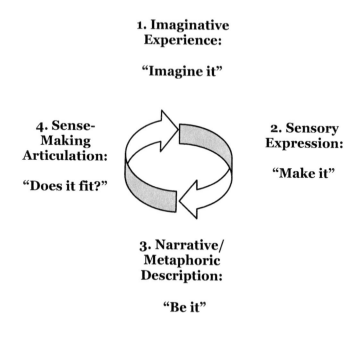

1. Imaginative
Experience:

"Imagine it"

4. Sense-
Making
Articulation:

"Does it fit?"

2. Sensory
Expression:

"Make it"

3. Narrative/
Metaphoric
Description:

"Be it"

**Figure 6: Recursive Aspect of the Therapeutic
Experiences**

Before describing and detailing this recursive aspect of
Violet's work, I will first highlight how the basic, four-step
process of Violet's Therapeutic Experiences is reflected in her
demonstration sessions with both Ben and Candice.

The four-step process with Ben and Candice

The four-step process described in the Reflective Notes of
Chapter Three is easily identified in Violet's work with Ben using
clay in the videotape that she showed to the participants on

Thursday morning. The table below excerpts each of the prompts that Violet gave to Ben at the beginning of each of the four steps that comprised the Clay work experience.

Table 7: Violet and Ben During Clay Work
The Four Steps

Steps	Violet's Prompts to Ben
(1) Imaginary Experience: "Imagine it"	"I just want you to put both hands on it. I want you to close your eyes. And then take a deep breath. And when you let the air out imagine its going right down your arms into the clay. Try that again."
(2) Sensory Expression: "Make it"	"So what I want you to do, with your eyes closed at first, is start making something with the clay. It could be just a shape, or you could imagine you're making an animal or a person."
(3) Narrative/ Metaphoric Description: "Be it"	"So, what I'd like you to do is to *be* this piece of clay and tell me about yourself: "I'm this piece of clay." And you can just describe how you look or whatever."
(4) Sense- Making Articulation: "Does it fit?"	"I'm just wondering if there's anything about your whale that fits for you, Ben? That you could say, 'Yeah, I'm like th too?' Or, 'that's like my life too'?"

Later in the day when Violet worked with Candice on her Anger drawing, the four-step process was also easily discernible. First, Violet had guided all the participants in a brief relaxation exercise that began with her saying, "I'd like you to just get as relaxed as you can. And just go inside yourself and see how you're feeling in there...." Next, Violet asked all the participants to:

> ...go back into your childhood and find a time when something happened that made you feel angry. Or maybe you don't remember feeling angry, but you felt frightened, or upset, or hurt, ashamed, or like you were a bad child.

This prompt for an Imaginary Experience was quickly followed by a prompt for Sensory Expression of those images when Violet asked the participants to draw what they had remembered:

> Again, it doesn't have to be something beautiful that anyone can understand, just something that will express for you, this time. When you are ready, just get what you need and draw your picture...

When Violet began working with Candice in front of the group, the first thing she asked Candice to do was to "tell me about your drawing," thus prompting her for Narrative/ Metaphoric Description. The story that unfolded in the first part of this intense piece of emotional work (being tied down by her siblings) obviously related to Candice's personal experience. In this way, Violet did not have to prompt Candice to "see if any of this fit for her own life" as part of the Sense-Making Articulation component of the work.

What did happen next, however, was that Candice's story of being tied down by her siblings immediately led to a deeper and more troubling aspect of her young life. What had been a description of Candice's abuse at the hands of her siblings became a story about all the siblings' abuse at the hands of their uncle. In this way, this second piece of work (Candice expressing outrage at her uncle by pounding the chair with the Battaca) can be seen as a kind of sense-making of her original story. In other words, understanding and addressing the broader context of Candice's original picture and story lead her to a deeper emotional expression and resolution of the underlying issue.

As Candice was describing the details of the story behind her drawing, her affect was flat and she spoke in a hushed tone. At one point during the first few moments of their work together, Candice confided to Violet that she felt "really blocked." What was it that enabled Candice to move again emotionally? What was it that enabled her to express some of the understandable rage she must have felt and still feels toward her abusive uncle?

What helped Candice move emotionally was Violet's move to lead through the same four-part structure of the Therapeutic Experiences for a second time. This is a key point in understanding Violet's approach: The four-part structure of the Therapeutic Experiences is often repeated within a particular piece of work. This "recursive" element to Violet's work allows further exploration of new or similar themes at a deeper level. In this way, the deepening spiral graphic shown in Figure 6 more accurately represents Violet's approach in the Therapeutic Experiences than does the linear description of the four-step process first introduced in the reflective notes of Chapter Three.

The recursive aspect of the Oaklander Therapeutic Experiences

When Violet discovers through Candice's unfolding story that all the children in the picture had been abused by Candice's uncle, she asks Candice "Would you be willing to try something?" After Candice agrees, Violet leads Candice through another round of the four-part sequence. This time around, Violet prompts Candice to have a second Imaginary Experience by pretending her uncle is in the empty chair. Violet then prompts Candice towards another experience of Sensory Expression by handing her the Battaca (clearly not the same as pastels or clay but certainly based in sensory expression). Violet then quickly prompts Candice toward both Narrative and Metaphoric Description by asking her, "What would you say to him?" At this point, Candice does not need much more prompting and explosively engages all her imaginative, sensory, narrative and metaphoric capabilities in recounting and expressing deep feelings about her horrific experience.

This recursive, "second time through" aspect of Violet's approach is also clearly represented in the videotaped example of her work with thirteen-year- old Ben that the participants saw earlier in the morning. In his first fifteen minutes of work with Violet, Ben had gone through the initial round of the four-part Therapeutic Experience with the clay that culminated in him speaking "as if" he were the clay whale and in talking about how the "whale family" was similar to his own.

Just after this piece of their work together, Violet once again led Ben back through the four-part sequence, still using clay but in a different way. She asked Ben to use his imagination and fingers to "represent each member of your family in clay." She then had him speak to the clay pieces "as if" they were real, saying one thing that he liked about each one and one thing that he did not like about each one. It was this second round through the four-part sequence that led Ben to more fully explore and "make sense" of his relationship with both his mother and father and how he might manage his feelings of frustration and anger in those relationships.

These examples involving Candice and Ben demonstrate that the four-part sequence of the Therapeutic Experiences is consistent whether Violet is working with an adult or a child. These examples also show that she follows this sequence whether she is using clay or pastels (or, as I will show in later chapters, music instruments, sand-tray toys, or puppets). Violet's work with Ben and Candice reveals that she often uses the "first-round" of the four-part sequence in the Therapeutic Experiences to explore what issues may be relevant for the individual — in Gestalt language, to see what issues emerge and come into figure — before using repeated iterations of the four-part sequence to further explore or address these issues.

As Violet helps individuals move recursively through this four-step process, the fourth step — involving Sense-Making Articulation — appears to be the least consistent or explicit. In interviews, Violet has said that she does not always ask children or adults if the work they have done in the first three parts of the Therapeutic Experiences "fits" for them in their own lives. Sometimes, she says, she assumes a kind of integration has taken place, a kind of internal "ah ha" moment, and that it does not need to be spoken. This stance is aligned with Violet's Gestalt therapy theory orientation in that the experience of "closure" is not always a verbal one but one that can instead happen at a deeper, non-verbal level of experience for the individual.

It is also true that after the first round of the Therapeutic Experiences, a connection has usually been made to the individual's life and therefore it is not necessary to keep asking about that connection in additional "go rounds." Think, for example, of Lydia exploring her safe place drawing of the big, yellow bed with cookies on it. After Lydia had recognized in the first round that the bed represented her relationship with her stepmother, Violet encouraged her to explore her feelings about her stepmother in a second go round (through imagining her step mother was on the bed and then talking "as if" she were there with her). In the second go round, Violet didn't need to ask again if what Lydia was talking about fit for her in her own life. The same is true of her work with Ben. Once he began talking about his family and his relationship with his father after he made the connection between the "whale family" and his own, Violet didn't need to ask him if any of the following fit in his own life. It was his own life that he was talking about.

In Gestalt language, Violet uses the first round through the Therapeutic Experiences to help individuals find a "figure" that has relevance to their own lives, and she uses subsequent "rounds through" to work on sharpening that figure so the individual can fully address it and make sense of it.

In the Reflective Notes at the end of Chapter Three, I introduced the idea that Violet's work in the various Therapeutic Experiences can be seen as composed of four progressive steps (i.e. Imaginative Experience, Sensory Expression, Narrative/Metaphoric Description, and Sense-Making Articulation). In this chapter's Reflective Notes, I have introduced two additional ideas that help to more completely describe the complexity of Violet's work using these Therapeutic Experiences: 1) Violet's work in the Therapeutic Experiences is often recursive, and, 2) These "go rounds" are not always symmetrical. In summary, there is usually more than one round to Violet's Therapeutic Experiences and the fourth step is usually less explicit after the first round.

Over the next few days' worth of Reflective Notes, I will be "sharpening the focus" on each of these important four steps of the sequence of Violet's work in these Therapeutic Experiences to show how they are both consistent and occasionally different, given the medium and the context. My intention is to differentiate these four steps in order to highlight their individual value and function as well as to make clear how they work in concert as a powerful, integrated, and developmentally appro-priate therapeutic approach. Put another way, I will be highlight-ing how these Therapeutic Experiences are at the heart of Violet's unique contribution to both child therapy and adult training.

5

Day Five: Friday
The Music Experience

At the end of Thursday afternoon, Violet had told the group that today would be an emotionally "less intense" day. She has planned for this in a couple of ways. For one thing, today is only half a day, running from nine a.m. to twelve noon. This gives participants an early start on the weekend in and around Santa Barbara, which is a beautiful coastal town, especially during the month of July. Also, the centerpiece for Friday is the "Music Experience" which tends to help individuals focus more on positive group membership than on personally difficult issues.

As the participants wander in this morning to the conference room, the first thing they see is a large pile of musical instruments strewn all over the floor: mini-xylophones, tambourines, rain-sticks, wooden cláves, bells and whistles, wood-frame drums, gourd shakers, etc. Participants are "jumping the gun" a little bit — in their own words — by playing with the xylophone, the shakers, and the other assorted musical instruments they find at their feet. Quiet music is also playing on a tape-deck in the background. As more participants arrive, there is a growing volume of lively chatter and one participant remarks loudly: "This is like the 'Mickey Mouse club' for adults! Every day

137

we have a new theme! First it was drawing, then clay, and now music!"

At 9:02 a.m., Violet warmly states, "We're going to start now, friends." First, there are some business items that need to be addressed. For one, a friend of Violet's will be coming at the beginning of the lunch break with oversized, stuffed bears that some participants have ordered after seeing the one that Violet uses in the training. Violet's big bear has been making the rounds each day, with different individuals hugging it close for long periods of time while the training goes on. There is also some talk and planning about Monday, "Sand Tray Day," which will take place at Violet's office in her nearby house.

After this preliminary discussion, Violet says the she wants to say a few things about the Music Experience before demonstrating it. She first describes how this experience was adapted from workshops that she attended with musician Paul Winter at his "Music Village" on a farm in Connecticut. Winter plays the alto-saxophone and has had a successful recording career pioneering a blend of Jazz and Brazilian music. Winter (1978) is perhaps best known for combining his music with the songs of animals recorded in the wild, such as whales and wolves, to startling effect.

Violet goes on to describe her experience with Paul Winter and his music workshops. She says that even though the workshops were mostly filled with professional musicians, Winter's approach was to emphasize that "there's no such thing as a wrong note." Like the sounds of nature that Winter includes in his recordings, the workshop was meant to be an appreciation for, as Violet says, the "sounds we can make together in community." Violet remarks that she left the richly creative and expressive atmosphere of the Winter workshops with a question: "If I feel so much of a sense of myself doing this here, how can I incorporate this into my work with children?" She says that she adapted the process that she learned from Winter to better fit her needs, and it is that revised process that she wants to now demonstrate with a volunteer.

Adult demonstration: Music with Isabel

From the six hands that are raised, Violet chooses a volunteer, Isabel, and they sit on the floor amidst all the instruments. Violet tells Isabel that when she is working with children she will slowly—and noisily— empty the large box of instruments on the floor for maximum dramatic effect. She then tells Isabel that the first thing she wants her to do is to look through all the instruments and experiment with them to hear the sounds that they can make. Isabel responds by playing with the spoons first, then an African, beaded shaker, then a small tambourine. After Isabel has played with a number of the instruments, Violet explains the structure of the first activity they will do together:

> Okay, this is how the structure goes. You pick an instrument and play it alone for a few seconds. Then I'll pick one and we'll play together. Then you stop, and I'll play alone for a while, then you pick a new instrument and join me. So you play alone first, then we play together, then I play alone, then we play together again,

and we keep on going...

What follows is a fascinating "dialogue without words." Violet appears to choose instruments that match Isabel's sound closely so that when they play together there is a blending. There are also moments when one of them is playing alone and only that "voice" is heard. When they are finished a few rounds of this activity the other participants spontaneously applaud. Both Violet and Isabel smile broadly and Isabel states, "That was fun! I couldn't keep my eyes off all the instruments, it was like a cornucopia. I felt like laughing." Other participants remark that it was nice to see so much communication with no words: "I could clearly see both the leading and following," states one participant. Another states, "It was just like watching the good social skills of conversation. There was turn taking and active listening being acted out through the instruments you were both playing."

Violet explains that another exercise that she does with children is ask them to play different moods with the instruments. Not only does this exercise help children learn to better differentiate their feeling states, she says, but it also gives them a chance to broaden their expressive repertoire. Violet then asks Isabel if she would be willing to do this next exercise with her. When Isabel eagerly agrees, Violet asks her to pick an instrument with which she could "play joyful." Isabel picks a xylophone and Violet picks a shaker. When Violet gives the signal, they both happily go at it. For "playing angry," Isabel bangs away at a heavy wooden drum and a Violet torments a wooden "scratcher" instrument. To "play sad," Isabel picks up and plays a mournful whistle and Violet taps away quietly and half-heartedly at the xylophone's upper register. Both Violet and Isabel then use loud shakers and big arm movements when Isabel suggests that they "play crazy" [Figure 7].

Figure 7: Violet and Isabel "Playing Crazy"

As a last calming exercise, Violet leads Isabel through a guided imagery exercise. She asks her to close her eyes and imagine a kite flying gently in the breeze, then to pick an instrument to accompany this image. Violet eventually talks the kite down to the ground and Isabel's gentle rustling of a shaker is stilled. At the end of all this activity, Violet asks Isabel how she feels. Isabel responds, "Calm and good. I thought I might be frenzied with all this noise, but I'm not frenzied at all. I feel good."

Still sitting on the floor but talking to the whole group, Violet describes how this structured activity is very "freeing" for a restricted child and at same time "containing" for a child who is too often out of control or "out of bounds." The concept of contact is reintroduced by Violet as she states:

> I make contact with the child by joining in her rhythm and she too has to listen, wait, and join when it is her turn. It becomes on exercise in both making contact and in withdrawing from contact appropriately.

Whole group exercises

Violet then goes on to describe how the whole group of participants will have a different kind of musical experience in smaller groups of six to end the day and the first week of the training. She lays out the following guidelines for this small-group experience:

- six people at a time will sit in a circle on the floor around the pile of instruments
- each person will pick two instruments after trying them all out
- the lights will be turned down and everyone will close their eyes and be quiet for a few moments
- when so moved, someone in the group will begin making sounds, and others in the small group will join when they are ready
- all kinds of sounds can be made with the instruments but participants may not play a sustained rhythm or melody
- it's okay to be quiet and just listen to other's sounds
- it's okay to respond musically to the sounds others are

making
- usually the small group doesn't need to be told when to stop and will spontaneously do so at some point
- those in the room who are not in the small group will keep their eyes closed too, listening to the sounds, and seeing what imagery or metaphor arises while listening to the group

Being a musician myself, I did not like "no sustained rhythm or melody" rule when I first participated in this music experience a number of years ago. What I have come to realize, however, is that this rule in the small group exercise allows for a much more spontaneous and negotiated experience. One ends up listening and responding quite a bit more to what others are doing instead of falling into a steady and predictable rhythm or melody — or feeling lame that one cannot sustain the rhythm or complement the melody that someone else is playing!

After Violet's introduction of this large group music experience, each of the small groups takes a turn in the center of the room. Surprisingly, each small group sounds completely different from the others. Most of the small groups start out somewhat quietly, building to some kind of crescendo (or cacophony?) before settling down to some kind of mellow or quirky ending. One group in particular has a particularly mournful sound defined particularly by a wistful whistling on a ceramic flute. At the end of each group's turn, Violet asks the individuals in the group to make a comment about their experience — a kind of individual Sense-Making Articulation of the group metaphor created by using imagination and sensory expression. These individual comments tend to project something about the speaker's experience as a group member: "I now realize that I must have been playing louder than others in the group," "I felt right at home contributing my part and hearing others in return," "I felt like I was very aware of everybody in the group," and, "I had my eyes closed and it felt more like two, not six people playing".

Violet also asks the participants in the larger group to describe the images they imagined while the smaller groups were playing. Some comments include: "To me it sounded like a village waking up in the morning," "I distinctly heard the sound of carpenters at work," "That last one made me think of a forest with all the animals rustling around at dusk."

After a short break in which many participants continue to play around with the musical instruments on the floor, Violet says that she would like to describe an example of the music process in her work with one boy in particular. She states that this kind of work, along with many of the other sensorial experiences she has been sharing, "support the child's world and way of being, because children are stronger in physical expression than in words."

She then details the case of a boy whose parents were both alcoholic. The boy's life tended to be quite chaotic as a result and his response to the music exercise was to relish the role he could play in controlling the experience to the maximum extent. Violet describes how the boy worked out an elaborate system of signaling with his fingers when it was time for her to join in, or to stop playing. Violet makes many of the participants laugh out loud with her pantomimes that accompany this story (e.g. pointing, gesturing dramatically, repeatedly slicing her finger across her throat as a "cut" signal, etc), but she states with some seriousness that it was therapeutically important for this child to experience the sense of control that he did in this activity. By allowing this boy to experience a "sense of control" through the use of musical instruments, Violet underlines the idea of "self work" that she outlined on Wednesday where "power" was one of the items she discussed. Regarding this boy's experience with the music activity, she states: "There is something about the structure that helps the children engage. It is amazing what kids can come up with when they feel free to engage."

Before the participants leave for the weekend break, Violet again encourages them, as she did on the opening morning of the training, to connect with each other, have dinner together, and invite others along to whatever activities are planned. In fact, many of the participants have already made plans together to have dinner downtown, go on shopping expeditions, and to take day trips to local areas of interest. By encouraging the continued development of such contacts between and among the participants of the training in their free time, Violet is building on a theme — the centrality of relationship to both the therapeutic and the learning process. It is quite amazing, in fact, that such a strong sense of community and authentic relationship has been established within this group of strangers who, five days ago, arrived unknown to each other from all points of the globe.

Reflective Notes on Chapter Five

In this chapter's reflective notes, I will first offer some ways of looking the first week of the training as a whole, as it unfolded and as it came to a close. I will then focus on the first part of Violet's Therapeutic Experiences to take a closer look at the role that Imaginary Experience plays in them.

The flow of the first week:
Crescendo and diminuendo

As I have discussed in the reflective notes of previous chapters, Violet works to build a sense of community in the training before she addresses the more difficult topics concerning therapeutic work with children. This makes sense in light of the fact that she asks the participants of the training to experience for themselves most of the techniques that she uses with children and adolescents — for example, the House, Tree, Person drawing on Monday, the Safe Place drawing on Tuesday, the Clay work experience on Wednesday, the Anger drawing on Thursday, and the Music experience on Friday. In this way, the training is structured so that participants engage themselves at a deeper level of commitment and personal investment as the days go by. As noted earlier, this is parallel to the way that Violet works with children in therapy: she first focuses on "making contact" and building a relationship with the child before addressing areas of distress in the child's life. The self support a child gains from making good contact with both themselves and the therapist, she asserts, can then be built upon to tackle more difficult personal issues.

I foreground this information because it helps explain how, by yesterday afternoon, the intensity of the material covered in the training was reaching a kind of crescendo. Participants had already observed Violet work with Lydia on her Safe Place drawing Tuesday afternoon which turned out to be a very emotional, if still positive, experience. They had also seen Violet work with Sabina on the more difficult issues that she brought up with the Clay work on Wednesday afternoon. On Thursday, participants intently watched Violet work with teen-aged Ben for thirty-eight minutes on the video and discussed with her what they saw afterward. Then, after lunch on Thursday, they experienced a few moments of humor and playful energy release with the "aggressive energy" experiences before observing perhaps the most powerful and challenging example of Violet's approach when she worked with Candice on her Anger drawing.

With such a rich and intense set of experiences in the first part of the week, participants tend to come into the training on Friday morning looking a bit wrung out. They are usually relieved that the activities for the day are more connective and light and less challenging. It is important to note that Violet's attention to the overall structure of both the therapeutic process with children and the training process with adults is another way that she can be seen as being "directive" in her work. By making Friday a lighter day, and by using the Music Experience with children for similar purposes, she reflects an understanding of not only how to encourage individuals to move into challenging areas of experience, but also how to balance that challenge with moments of lighter contact and enjoyment.

It is also significant to note that Violet works with this balance in micro as well as macro ways in her work with both children in therapy and adults in training. By this I mean that, even within sessions with individual adults and children, Violet repeatedly "checks in" with her client to make sure the relationship is strong enough and that the client has enough self support to move forward into deeper and more challenging work. For example, when Violet worked with Isabel during the demonstration of the Music Experience, she repeatedly asked her, "How was that for you?" when they had finished a piece of the experience. Violet also made sure that she asked Isabel if she would be willing to try another piece of the experience before they moved ahead. In this way, Violet facilitates movement into deeper and more challenging work by making sure that she has good contact and a strong relationship in place with both individuals in therapy and with the group as a whole in the training.

Thus, although there are many ways in which Violet helps to create an environment free of expectations and demands with both children and adults, there are also ways in which she offers opportunities for such individuals to both turn up or turn down the intensity of their experience at appropriate moments.

Focus on imaginary experience:
Facilitating involvement

In a discussion regarding the role of imagery and detail in conversation, Deborah Tannen (1989) quotes a line that was spoken to her by a friend during a long distance phone call: "I wish you were here," stated the friend, "to see the sweet peas coming up." In reference to this conversational fragment, Tannen asks:

> Why is this more moving than the simple, "I wish you were here?"...it is because of the sweet peas — small and ordinary and particular. The sweet peas coming up provide a detail of everyday life that brings everyday life to life. The sweet peas create an image — a picture of something, whereas "Wish you were here" suggests only an abstract idea of absence. (p. 134)

Tannen goes on to state that we use details in conversation to create images and that these images then act to facilitate "involvement" and intimacy for those in conversation. Both the speaker and the listener are involved in the process of imagining and trying to make sense of a scene through the details provided. Tannen states:

> details create images, images create scenes, and scenes spark emotions, making possible both understanding and involvement...it is in large part through the creation of a shared world of images that ideas are communicated and understanding is achieved (p. 135).

Tannen's ideas about the way in which concrete details and images from ordinary life help to foster involvement and intimacy in conversation highlight the importance of imagery and imagination in Violet's work with both children and adults.

Such powerful images, laden with both emotion and potential meaning, form the centerpiece of Violet's Therapeutic Experiences such as the Safe Place drawing or the Clay work. It is in the first two parts of those Experiences when Violet prompts for both the envisioning of an image (e.g. "close your eyes and imagine a safe place...") and a physical expression of that image ("now I'd like you to draw it..."). These imagined and expressed images create the "conversation piece" that was discussed in Chapter Two and that serve as the opening focus of the therapeutic work that Violet engages in with both her clients.

Let's review what "small and ordinary and particular" images emerged in this first week of Violet's training and all that sprang from those images. On Monday, participants shared images from their own childhood as a way of getting back in touch with the experience of their lives as children. Later on that day, each participant had their image of the House, Tree, Person drawing held up by Violet in the group and discussed. On Tuesday during the Safe Place drawing, there was the image of Lydia's yellow bed with the cookies on it that led Lydia to reflect on the depth of support she receives from her stepmother and the depth of feeling she shares with her. On Wednesday, there was the simple but powerful image of a "baseball mitt" created out of clay that lead Sabina to delve into some difficult issues related to both weight and self worth. On Thursday, the day began with participants watching Violet working with Ben as he created the image of a whale in clay that served as a springboard for further work about his family and his father in particular. Later on Thursday, the dam holding back Candice's emotions broke when she remembered the mundane but emotionally charged image of a "silver martini shaker" that her uncle had owned. And today, on Friday, the imagined scenes inspired by the sensory expression of sound —animals in a forest or carpenters at work— served to create a more calming and soothing experience to bring to a close the intense first week of the training.

That each of these detailed images held strong emotions for the creator of that image is clear. Just as important, however, is the role these images played in creating the "understanding and involvement" of both self and others that Tannen discusses. It was the image of the yellow bed, simple and uncomplicated at first, which allowed Lydia to understand and become involved in her own emotional experience of the rich and complex feelings she felt towards her stepmother. It was also this image of the yellow bed as a "conversation piece" which allowed there to be a starting point in Violet's quickly deepening relationship with Lydia in the time that they worked together. It may also be true that the simple image of the yellow bed, seen by the whole group at an early moment in the training, was part of what enabled a sense of understanding and involvement to begin developing in the group of participants regarding not only what Violet had to teach, but about what the participants might learn from each other and from children through the sharing of personal images.

These simple images start from imagination and are expressed through sensory engagement into some medium— paper, clay, or musical instruments, for example. They form the base of Violet's Therapeutic Experiences and often lead to rich stories and metaphors that help children and adults understand themselves and their world better.

Three of the most important lessons that Violet has been imparting during this first week all involve these imagined and expressed images: first, such images are inherently powerful when they are allowed to come from the individual. Second, these images need to be handled with care and should not to be interpreted or evaluated by someone other than the image's creator. Third, and perhaps most importantly, adults who work with children need to have the messy and sometimes awkward experience for themselves of creating such images in multiple media in order to truly understand their power and relevance and how effectively they can be used to connect to issues of personal importance.

When the group reconvenes on Monday morning for the second week of the training, they will have appropriately longer periods of time during Sand Tray Day to delve into the process of imagining, expressing, and working with such powerful and evocative images.

154

6

Day Six: Monday
Sand Tray Day

Description, experience, and comments

The second Monday of this two-week training is a uniquely different experience for the twenty-four participants from any other day in the training. Instead of meeting in the hotel conference room as usual, they have car-pooled up the hill to Violet's house to meet at the office where she sees clients. Her office is in a private studio in her backyard, attached to, but separate from, the rest of her house. This office is usually a revelation for participants: Violet has consciously filled it up with just about every "play therapy" object imaginable to serve as a kind of ideal model of what such an office might look like. The participants make lots of exclamatory comments as they enter through the waiting room doors and begin to look around such as "Wow, this is impressive!" and, "I love all the stuffed animals!".

Inside the office, there is a sitting area toward the back wall arranged with two arm chairs and a small table a couch. Various stuffed animals are slung atop the back of the couch: a black and white cow, a couple of bears, and a fat kangaroo with babies. In

the closet next to this seating area are shelves of boxed games —
The Storytelling Card Game™, Trouble™, Blockhead™, Chutes
and Ladders™, Knock-out™ — and other shelves containing a
play telephone, a cash register, some Lincoln Logs™, a pig
puppet, a toy clown, a Mickey Mouse™ doll, and a little girl doll.

There is also a large basket on the floor near the closet that
contains about sixty puppets of all kinds: a stern looking teacher
puppet, a fairy princess puppet, a bumble-bee, a ghoul, a seal,
and many others. Next to the puppet basket are two miniature
garbage cans with tight lids that contain both gray and red
pottery clay.

A bookshelf against the opposite wall holds many volumes
with titles like "Put Your Mother on the Ceiling: Children's
Imagination Games" (De Mille, 1955) and "The Gestalt Art
Experience" (Rhyne, 1973). There is a puppet stage that is
propped behind the door, and a doll house that Violet says
children like to use a lot. Standing near the center of the room is
Boppo the Clown™ an inflatable punching toy that looks like a
sports referee.

In the corner of the room opposite the seating area, there are
six vertical rows of small shelves that are built into the walls and
that hold hundreds of sand tray objects. These objects and
figurines are very colorful and range in size, shape, and
appearance though they tend to be about two inches high or less.
Amazingly, they are all organized by type: there are shelves with
scary stuff (witches, tombstones, skeletons, etc.), shelves with
ocean-related objects (shells, rocks, fish, and octopus), and
shelves with fantasy figures (knights, dragons, princesses, etc.).

Additionally, there are snakes, lions, birds, animals, toy children of all sizes, and families of all colors and shapes. There are also houses, bridges, fences, army-men, nuns, ghosts, horses, gorillas, a Batman™ figure, dinosaurs, trees, miniature coffins, glass stones, boats — you name it, she's got it.

Before the participants arrived, Violet set up eight "sand tray stations" around the room and out on the shaded patio. These stations are composed of 3 chairs positioned around one sand tray. The sand trays are either made of wood or plastic and are approximately two feet wide by three feet long and about six inches deep. These trays are filled with about two inches of white sand and each of them has a blue bottom that, with a little imagination, can become a lake, river, or ocean. The three chairs will be used by small groups of participants as they take on the roles of "therapist," "client," and "observer" throughout the day while working with the sand-trays. Because participants will spend most of the day in these roles and less time listening to presentations or watching demonstrations by Violet, this day will become the most deeply experiential one for the participants thus far in the training — a day to put into practice all that they have been taking in over the past week.

When the participants have settled onto the couch, into seats or upon pillows on the floor and the buzz of excitement has died down, Violet says she would like to tell them about her approach to working with the sand tray. She describes to the participants that sand tray work follows many of the same principles that frame her other projective and expressive experiences involving drawing, clay, or musical instruments. That is, the work begins with a child creating an imagined scene in the sand which then becomes the centerpiece and starting point for discussion in the session. In a handout entitled "Notes on sand tray work" that is provided to the participants, Violet writes about the process in this way:

> I usually say to the child, "I would like you to make a scene in the sand. You can use any of the objects you see here, and if there is something you don't see, ask me — maybe I have it. Your scene doesn't have to make sense, or it can. You can choose things because you like them and want to use them. Or you might want to make something special. It can be real or imaginary or like a dream. Anything." I usually show the child some photographs of sand trays to give them the idea of what I mean. Sometimes I will ask the child to do a special theme. For example, "Do a scene representing the divorce in your family," or "Make a scene that shows how you feel these days"...

Violet also describes in the handout that there are multiple "levels of the work" that can take place with a child and the sand tray. Some of these levels include paying attention to the child's process in making the sand scene (e.g. "Is the child slow and methodical or fast and frenzied?"), the general look of the sand tray that the child has created (e.g. "Is it organized? Chaotic?"), and what Violet calls the "making sense level" which she describes in this way:

Children always attempt to make sense out of the scene, just as they try to make sense of their lives. I will say, "Tell me about your scene." They'll look at it and then say, "Well, this is a..."

As with the clay and drawing techniques presented in the first week of the training, another level of the work is reflected in helping the child to "own" any of their projections that they may have put into the sand tray scene. Violet writes in her handout that she may ask, "Does anything here remind you of you or anything in your life?" or, "Do you ever feel like you need a place to hide like the rabbit in your story?"

Violet goes on to explain that today the participants will have a lot of time and many opportunities to practice working at these various levels of the sand tray experience. When they are in the role of therapists, she explains, they will try to help their "client" make sense out of the scene that they have created by starting a dialogue or having the client tell a story about what they see before them. As clients, they will have the opportunity to experience what this kind of therapeutic work is like first-hand. As an observer, their job will be to watch the unfolding dynamics of the work between the client and therapist and foster a discussion after the session as a kind of processing of the work done. The therapist may also stop the session to consult with the observer if the therapist is feeling stuck or in need of advise. The focus, asserts Violet, is on the role of the therapist and on the practice of this approach.

After this overview of her approach to working with sand

trays, Violet says that she would like to do a short demonstration session with one participant in front of the group. Nicolas, a child and family psychotherapist from Montana, raises his hand first and Violet then hands him a small, red, plastic bucket. Violet asks Nicolas to take a few moments collecting sand tray toys and objects that he would like to use in creating his sand tray scene. After a few minutes in which Nicolas silently looks over the many figurines, picking some, leaving others, he rejoins Violet in the center of the room and the two of them sit on the floor on either side of a blue plastic container partly filled with sand. Violet then asks Nicolas to "create a scene in the sand" and without more prompting, he begins to do so.

Nicolas almost immediately asks Violet if he can "take a little of the sand out. It's too much sand." Violet gives Nicolas a container with which he scoops out some of the sand and pours it into a nearby sand tray. In this process of removing some of the sand from his tray, Nicolas uncovers more of the blue bottom the tray and then begins to create his scene. Quietly, Nicolas moves the sand around with his hands, smoothing it out in some places. He then begins adding the figures and objects that he has chosen for his scene. Eventually, a scene emerges in which a house sits near the edge of a large body of water. The house is protected by a large tree, and a male and female figure stand outside the house. An angel figure occupies one corner of the sand tray, with bright bits of glass and a few beads scattered around its feet. In another part of the sand tray are a number of animal figurines, some cows and dogs and a horse. At the edge of the water is a small, white boat with a sail that looks damaged and which lies flat across the hull of the boat.

When Nicolas has finished his scene and sits back, seemingly pleased with his efforts, Violet says: "Okay. Would you tell me a little bit about this, as much as you can right now?" Nicolas tells Violet that, "As I started laying it out it became clear to me what it was". He goes on to say that the scene is composed of the comforting things in his life now, an angel to represent his spiritual side, a cow to represent his grandmother's farm where he spent a lot of time as a child, and a female figure to represent his supportive wife.

Violet then asks Nicolas to "be" a number of the figures in the scene. For example, at one point Violet refers to the angel figure and says to Nicolas, "What I would like you to do then is be her and speak as her." After a few more moments, Violet then asks Nicolas to "be one of these cows." In the process of exploring a number of the sand tray figures together with Nicolas, Violet points to the boat down near the water's edge and the following dialogue ensues:

> Violet: Be the boat.
>
> Nicolas: I am the boat [Laughs]. I was the boat the other day with the clay. Somehow the clay became a boat, and it was in need of repair, and I notice this boat is in need of repair too. I am the boat, and I have a sail here in need of repair. But I enjoy being on the water. It's very calm. It's very soothing. It's rocking. It's just very peaceful on the water. I like being on the water, and riding around in the harbor, and going out to sea,

       actually. I like going out to sea too. And I like taking people places. I need to get repaired.

Violet: You need to get repaired.

Nicolas: I need to get repaired. Yes.

Violet: What are you thinking about as you say that? Now, what are you thinking about now?

Nicolas: Its kind of the same thing that came up with the Clay work. That I need to take better care of myself, take more time for myself. Get to the gym [Laughs]. Get repaired so I can continue on the journey.

After Violet has asked Nicolas to speak as most of the figures in the sand tray, she returns to something that Nicolas said earlier in their discussion. Nicolas had said that halfway through making his scene, he decided that he would not be able to fit all the objects and figures into the sand tray without it looking too crowded. He decided instead to leave some of the figurines out, including ones that represented all four of his now almost fully-grown children and two of their spouses. Returning to this theme, Violet asks Nicolas to speak to these figures that he has left out of the sand tray scene. Violet later asks Nicolas to incorporate back into the sand tray one figure that was initially left out. Nicolas identifies this figure as "the working Nicolas," and begins to have a dialogue with it.

In his fifteen-minute, demonstration session with Violet, Nicolas ends up exploring aspects of his life that give him support as well as aspects of his life that worry and challenge him. In his sand tray scene, most of the objects that he included represented supportive and peaceful aspects of his life (e.g. his spirituality, his house, his wife) while the objects that were not included in the scene represented some of the more worrisome aspects of his life (e.g. his working self and one of his daughters who has recently left the family home).

In the group processing of Violet's demonstration session with Nicolas that follows, one participant says, "I was real curious to hear from those parts that weren't in the tray. So I was really glad that came up in the process." Another participants asks Nicolas, "As you were going through picking the figures, did you start out with an image in your mind of what you were going to create, and if not, when did that begin to take shape for you?" Nicolas responds that as he put the scene together he started to be conscious of how he was including "peaceful" objects and excluding the objects that represented more difficulty for him. As the brief processing time comes to a close, Violet states that the process of putting together the sand tray scene is just as important as the product itself. She adds that when she is working with children in particular, she will watch the way they pick objects, work with the sand, and place objects in the different parts of the tray, sometimes asking the child about this aspect of the work later in the session.

At 10:15 a.m., after the demonstration with Nicolas, Violet asks the participants to count off into eight groups of three. She then has each member of the eight groups decide if they will be the client first, second, or third. She then points out the schedule on the wall which outlines the flow of the day (Figure 8).

9:00-9:30	Overview of the day
9:30-10:15	Demonstration
10:15-11:30	First person as therapist
11:30-12:00	Check in with large group
12:00-1:00	Lunch
1:00-2:15	Second person as therapist
2:15-2:45	Check in with large group
2:45-4:00	Third person as therapist
4:00-4:30	Check in and closing

Figure 8: Sand Tray Day Schedule

Before sending the small groups of participants off to work with the sand trays at their stations, Violet describes the steps of the process that each session should take. She describes that the client should first take approximately twenty minutes to choose the objects and compose a sand tray scene. The client and the therapist will then work together on the sand tray scene for approximately thirty minutes. This work will be followed by a fifteen-minute period of time when the observer shares feedback and the client and therapist can process how the experience went for them. Lastly, before the client cleans up the sand tray, Violet will walk around and take a Polaroid shot of each scene for the client to keep. After each round, the whole group will regather for a check in and report back about what was learned, particularly by the person in the role of therapist.

The rest of the morning and early afternoon are a quieter time for Violet as she sits in close proximity to most of the small groups and makes herself available for questions and concerns. The participants in the small groups spend concentrated moments picking out figures and objects from the many shelves around the room, placing them in a small blue, red, or yellow bucket provided for them to use, and then going back to their station and creating wildly imaginative and colorful scenes in the sand. In one participant's case, the scene involves a farm with rows of crops and a farmer looking out over open, blue water where a mermaid and octopus swim. In another part of the room, a client can be overheard describing her scene in which trees and feathers stuck in the sand create a peaceful alcove for a wooden, Aphrodite-type figure. The day proceeds with hushed discussions as well as exclamations of surprise and laughter.

At the end of each practice session, when the large group has been reformed for a check-in, Violet asks the participants how things are going and what is being learned. Throughout the day, many participants share comments related to the "powerful" aspects of this mode of therapeutic work. In a quick survey of hands, Violet discovers that while 10 of the participants had never worked with a sand tray before, everybody found it "meaningful in some way." She then half-jokingly asks, "Okay, how many cried?" and 8 participants raise their hands. One participant described her experience in this way:

> I have never done sand tray work myself, I have only seen children do it. And whoa, It's so powerful! I don't know why I picked what I picked. Just because it popped out at me. And when it unfolded, it was like a revelation to me. My own work was a revelation to me. It never ceases to amaze me what comes out of that work. When you really become the bicycle. You may think, "That's

stupid, why become a bicycle?" [laughter]. But I just felt like I wanted to keep exploring the scene in the sand tray.

During one of these check-in periods, another participant brings up the question of how directive to be in this kind of work, which stimulates the following conversation regarding what's it like to "be" different parts of the sand tray:

Lindsey: We talked about being directive. For example I asked the client, "Would you like to..." But it may have been more powerful or better to just say, "Do it."

Violet: Well, I usually say, you know, "I'd like you to be the dog," or "Have the dog talk to..." Yes, I'm pretty directive. It's like if you say "Would you like to be this..." then the person doesn't know really what to answer [laughs], it puts them on the spot...

Liz: Being more directive also gives more permission. Asking her "Would you like to do this?" doesn't really communicate that it's okay to do this.

Lindsey: And often a client will say, [cringing in feigned embarrassment] "Oh, I can't be a bicycle." But if you say, "Be a bicycle" you give the support: "Even if its a little funny, be the bicycle, and don't doubt it." I think it's better!

Violet: That's it. With kids I'll say, "I want you to be the bicycle," and they look at me funny [laughs]. I tell them, "Just say, 'I'm a bicycle!'" And then we'll

start: "Well tell me, Bicycle, tell me what you
do?" It begins a kind of dialogue...

Later in this group discussion, this same issue of "being"
different parts of the sand tray scene comes up again, this time
revealing a bit more of the participants' own experience. The
following exchange between Liz and Sheri reflects the
participants' deep, personal involvement in today's work:

Liz: I found that when I was the person doing the sand
tray, I was so surprised by what came out of my
mouth when I became the turtle. I said stuff like,
"I'm really moving slow." It really got to the
underlying issues of what was going on for me.
What came out was my level of frustration with
things going so slowly, with progress in my
career. And I think I really needed to become the
turtle to say that, because as I said it, it was
almost like it felt real true and genuine. But it
came as a real surprise. It was like, "Where did
that come from?" So I don't think I would have
had that insight if I had not become the pieces in
the sand tray.

Sheri: You know, I can echo that by saying that when I
did my sand tray, I got into my feelings when I
became things. There was a lot of expression
when I was talking about it. But when I spoke
from the turtle — I had a turtle in my tray also,

and the dog — that's when the tears came...

Liz: Yeah. It brings up a lot. It's a whole different level. And the respect that the therapist had to let me be with that for a minute and not do the interpreting, I found very valuable.

The discussion after the sand tray day is so lively that Violet does not stop it even though it's after 4:30 p.m. Helen, a participant who has come to the workshop from Sweden, raises the question as to the difference in doing this kind of sand tray work with children as opposed to adults. Helen states that she found it difficult to stay in the "play mode" while working with an adult client and ended up talking more about the client's real life outside the sand tray. She asks Violet, "Is it different for you when you work with children?" Violet provides the following response:

Well, children are not very serious about it. We just play with it and talk about it in a very playful way. And so it's quite different. For instance, when I work with an adult, tears might come and I might say, "What's that about?" We might leave the sand tray, and then maybe go back to it, and all that. Children don't do that. They don't usually start crying about the sand tray [laughs]. Sometimes they do, but not usually. But kids are very playful with it. They enjoy working with it. Even if they're doing a scene on divorce, they really enjoy it. You don't go as deep with kids. You stay at a much more surface level. They don't have that capacity usually.

Helen adds that in her approach to working with children, she usually become a part of the sand tray scene as a lion or tiger, for example, and then she has a dialogue with the child:

> Helen: I have the idea that both the child and I know what we are talking about, but we do it through the symbolic way, because it's not allowed to talk about it directly just yet.
>
> Violet: Very good, yes! You don't even have to talk about it in that way!
>
> Helen: No, you don't have to talk about it. You know that it's reality in a way but it's not ready to put into formal terms, but you can still do it symbolically.
>
> Violet: I agree with that and have had that same experience a lot when working with children.

Child example: Tommy's sand tray

Violet says that before the day ends, she would like to give one example of doing sand tray work with a child by telling the following story:

> I was working with a fourteen-year-old boy named Tommy whose parents were going through a bitter divorce, and he was an only child. The parents were having terrible arguments. They really disliked the way the other one was parenting and they were fighting for this child. The courts insisted that the parents take

Tommy to therapy and that they go too. I could not see both parents in the same room because they were so difficult. I don't mind couples fighting and arguing, but this was extremely bad.

So Tommy comes in alone the first time I saw him and his attitude was, "I don't care about the divorce, it doesn't bother me." Pretty typical of his age. But his grades were falling and he was showing other symptoms that something wasn't right. He was also pretty resistant. He didn't say anything, but his manner was like, "What am I going to do here with this lady? I'm not going to talk, I have nothing to say."

Anyway, this is not necessarily what I always do the first time that I see a child. I can't remember why I said this, maybe because he walked over to the sand tray and was fooling around with the sand. I said, "I'd like you to make a sand scene, anything you want." And he says "Okay." He finds a basket of cake-decoration figures and takes these three little surfers and he puts them in the sand. Then he moves the sand around a little bit to represent the waves, and says, "That's it."

So I said, "Tell me about your scene." All he says is, "There are three surfers," which is typical of the way children will respond. They just don't know what else to say. So I said, "Well I'll tell you what, you be one of the surfers. Which one are you?" So he says, "All right, this one." And I began to dialogue with him. I said, "Okay, well what are the waves like? How's the water? Is the water cold?" He is reluctantly answering these questions, and as he's talking one of the other surfers falls over. So I said, "What happened to him?" And he said, "He fell." And I said, "Well what's going to happen?" And he kind of got into the spirit of it and says, "His surfboard is going to hit him in the head and he's going to drown."

It's interesting because at that point he sort of began to pull in again emotionally. He had been kind of playing with me, but now he began to pull away again. But I kept going on because he hadn't quite closed down yet. I said, "Well what about you, could you help him?" He said, "No, and then it'll probably be my fault that he drowns."

I could see at this point that he wasn't going to go any further with this. So I said, "Is there anything about this story that reminds you of your life?" And he said "No." But I said, "You know, you kind of said it was your fault that the surfer drowned. I'm just wondering if, in your own life, there's anything you think is your fault?" At this point Tommy bursts into tears and said, "Everything that is happening with the divorce is my fault."

It occurred to me then that children don't get rid of that egocentric stance they have as young children when it's an emotional issue. I think it's important to remember that kids blame themselves and it's not true when they say, "I don't care, it doesn't bother me." The more they deny it the more that you can assume they probably blame themselves. So that is one example of working with a child with the sand tray.

At this point, Violet looks at her watch and notes out loud that it's almost five o'clock. At the end of this long Sand Tray day, Violet reminds everyone that tomorrow we will all be meeting back in the conference room. There are many thanks given to Violet at this point from the participants who are grateful for having had the opportunity to see Violet's own working space. Not too many participants are in a hurry to leave this unique room, and many linger before departing, checking out all the many child and adult friendly things the room has to offer.

Reflective notes for day six

In the reflective notes at the end of Chapter Five, I focused on Imaginary Experience, the first step of Violet's Therapeutic Experiences. In this chapter's reflective notes, I focus on the second step — Sensory Expression — and part of the third step — Metaphoric Sense Making — of Violet's Therapeutic Experiences. I am only focusing on part of the third step of Violet's Therapeutic Experiences, Narrative/Metaphoric Sense-Making, because this step is really composed of two aspects that are sometimes combined and sometimes separate. By this I mean that Violet encourages both the children and the adults with whom she works to build a story or a metaphor, and sometimes both, from the imaginary piece they have created. In the second part of this chapter's reflective notes, I will take a closer look at the role of metaphor in this sense-making process. In the next chapter's reflective notes, I will focus on the role of narrative sense-making in the Therapeutic Experiences.

Focus on sensory expression:
Encouraging activity

Sand, miniature toys, clay, drawings, musical instruments, and later this week, both puppets and storytelling — by the time the participants have completed this training, they will have been introduced to a slew of expressive media with which to work with children and adolescents. At some moment during the third or fourth time that I went through Violet's intensive summer training it struck me: in using these media so centrally in her work, Violet is dipping from a deep and very old well of human expressiveness. In fact, each one of these media have been around as an expressive tool for thousands of years in every known culture around the globe. Just because they have been around for a long time, however, does not mean they are necessarily valued in the therapeutic context. By embracing and incorporating these media so completely in her work, Violet is bucking a dismissive attitude about the role of such expressive media in the world of applied psychology. In this technologically-obsessed time, psychological interventions are more likely to be based on pharmaceutical medications than they are on puppets or clay. The only place you're likely to find puppets or clay taken seriously in our culture in general is in the production of Saturday morning cartoons or in "family oriented" animated films.

 Yet these ancient media still have power. In some ways, Violet's training is akin to being gathered around a campfire under a shroud of stars and being told deeply moving stories through these almost forgotten media that remind us of what is important in our lives. Time and again, I have heard participants describe their experience in the training as a "refresher course" or as a "shot in the arm" when they had begun feeling burned-out in their work. Violet's relational way of being with people is certainly key to why these folks leave feeling so refreshed and invigorated about the potential of doing healing work. I am also convinced that it is the participants hands-on experiences with these creative, expressive media within Violet's approach that helps to revive in them something deep and vital. Violet approach leads the participants to the water and they do drink.

Participants who struggle in their daily professional lives with deadening amounts of paperwork and professional demands for "effective, short-term interventions" often come away from Violet's training with a new-found faith in the power of these expressive media to help an individual or a group feel more whole, more integrated, and more alive. In short, healthier. They have experienced it themselves and they have seen adults and children experience it when they have worked with Violet. Significantly, participants who come to the training with deeply held beliefs that they are not artistic or creative come away from the training having experienced something akin to the way they felt as kids when they made up rich and detailed scenarios in a sand box or drew wild scenes on a piece of paper with colorful crayons.

Often, some participants groan on the first day when they hear that Violet expects them to draw something. Yet Violet strips away all the expectations about being artistic and about drawing like an artist and instead tells them to "just make line or shapes" on the paper. Last Friday, she also told them intentionally that they could not make "real" music with rhythm and melody and instead they just had to wing it and make sounds. In this way, Violet reintroduces them to the child-like sense of spontaneous invention that both adulthood and bureaucracies seem to thwart. Deeper still, she is helping them remember how to engage in these powerfully expressive media so that they can support the children and adolescents with whom they work to do so as well. If an adult participant isn't willing to go out on a limb and talk to a clay whale as if it's real, then a reluctant adolescent most likely won't either.

During her description of her approach to working with aggressive energy, Violet called herself a "cheerleader," and she does cheer on both adults and children in a number of ways. First, she encourages them to say things they would not normally feel comfortable saying (e.g. "Yeah! Just TELL him..." she said when Candice was screaming at her imagined uncle). Second, she encourages them to jump in and get their hands dirty using materials that might otherwise be left to "real artists" (e.g. "So just let yourself, with your eyes closed, make something" she tells Ben as he works the clay). Thirdly, and perhaps most importantly, she encourages adults, adolescents and children to take these media and what they have to offer seriously. By the very fact that she owns and knows how to use more than fifty puppets (as the participants will soon see on Thursday of this second week of the training), this author of one of the most popular books in the world on doing therapy with children lends her credibility to this approach to working with young people. The adult participants feel encouraged by seeing Violet in action: "If Violet can put on a puppet show, then maybe I can too," one of the participants will say later this week.

In an age where behavioral plans are certainly given more credibility than puppets as "interventions" for our children's well-being, Violet seems to take on the role of the playful-yet-wise sage who reminds us of what powerful things we have forgotten in our rush to be both modern and adult. One of those powerful things that we might have lost is the idea that children need a strong sense of self to deal with the difficult world they face. Violet's inclusion of sensory-based activities in therapy help children to recover a strong sense of themselves by actually allowing them to have an experience of themselves.

Last Friday, after the music experience was over and the participants were just about to launch off into their weekend adventures, one of the participants taught the group to sing a verse from a Paul Winter song that he knew called "Common Ground." One of the verses of this song states: "In a circle of friends, in a circle of sound, all our voices will blend, when we touch common ground." I believe that Violet helps the participants touch such common ground in part by encouraging and engaging them in the simple human act of making things out of basic substances like clay, color, and sand. It isn't so much the art that is emphasized in this process, however. It is both the experience itself as well as the personal meaning that might be derived from that creative process. In short, Violet takes these expressive media and the messages they may contain very seriously, but with a light touch that feels like an exciting but unthreatening invitation to simply begin to "play with" and "make something".

Having encouraged adults and children to step into the sensorial, creative process with these expressive media, Violet next helps the individuals with whom she works to "build a metaphor" from the piece they have created. This process is explored in the next section.

Focus on metaphoric sense-making:
Borrowing meaning

At the end of Sand Tray Day, Violet told the story of using the sand tray with a young client named Tommy. In that story, Tommy "borrows" meaning from a metaphor he created about surfing and, in a manner of speaking, "ferries" it over to his own life. That is, first it is the pretend surfer in his sand tray scene that feels responsible, then it is Tommy himself who realizes he feels responsible in his own life. The word ferry comes from the Greek "Pherein," which means to transfer, or carry across. That same Greek root is at work in the word "metaphor" and the same function is implied — to "carry over." When Lydia used the image of a yellow bed to describe the feelings she had toward her stepmother, she was carrying that meaning across from the image of the drawing into her personal life. The same was true of Sabina when she created the clay image of the "baseball mitt." Sabina carried the idea of the mitt being big and awkward over and applied it to her own body — and her own hips in particular

— as a way to describe how she felt about herself. This is the essence of metaphor: we find meaning in something we already understand and then try to apply it to something we are still trying to figure out. Like a ferry then, metaphor helps us make connections between things, and bring important and relevant ideas from one place to another.

This ability to put together familiar things with unfamiliar things in what is often, as noted by MacCormac (1990), an "unusual juxtaposition", starts at a very young age in human beings. Even before the vocabulary of infants grows beyond a few words, they have the ability to, for example, run a stick along the ground and claim that it is a snake. Metaphor, in fact, is an important early-developing and universally-used cognitive tool that humans employ to make sense of the world around them. We build on what we already know to make sense of what is new. In this light, it is easy to see how metaphors serve such a central role in Violet's approach to working with both adults and children.

In her story about her work with Tommy and his sand tray, Violet recounts how he took some pretend responsibility for one of the surfers drowning and then how it wasn't long before he was able to carry some of that same meaning over and into his own life. Soon, he was able to make an emotional connection about how much responsibility he felt regarding in his parents' divorce. Tommy may have been able to make that personal connection with that pretend metaphor simply because metaphors, by their nature, tend to force us to feel things. They do this in a couple of ways. First, metaphors make us feel things because they tend to be built upon something we are familiar with and already have feelings about — a comfortable yellow bed or the act of surfing and struggling in the water, for example. In this way, they tend to be "emotion laden" from the outset. But metaphors also force us to feel things by the very fact that they are composed of a strange coupling of images and ideas and don't immediately make sense to us. For example, when Lydia first claimed that the yellow bed she had drawn might be like her stepmother, she was forced to make sense of this awkward statement. Internally, she had to ask herself, "What do I mean by that?" and come up with some satisfactory answer in the process.

This sometimes emotionally uncomfortable process of making sense of metaphors also seems to play a role in the way that Violet works. For example, Violet had Ben make something out of clay and he came up with a whale. Then she had Ben speak "as if" he was that whale. She then asked him if that whale had anything to do with his own life. That question is, by its very nature, an emotionally perplexing one: "How can I possibly be like a whale?" By asking such questions in the way she does, Violet seems to gently force the adult or child she is working with to enter the emotional world of metaphoric sense-making. In doing this, Violet helps make the experience of the children or the adults with whom she is working an emotional one. Or, in other words, she encourages them to have an emotional experience and then work to address those emotions and to integrate them with their other thoughts, feelings, and experiences. In this way, the use of metaphor in Violet's work supports one of the main goals of her approach to therapy: to help children "become more whole" by becoming more aware of their emotions and by helping them integrate those emotions with the rest of their larger self.

Stirring up the client's emotional world through the engagement of their imagination and senses to create images and emotion-laden metaphors also has another function in Violet's work. That is, this stirring up of the emotions allows "unfinished gestalts" to come up to the surface and to the foreground of the individual's awareness. From a gestalt therapy perspective, such unfinished pieces of emotional and cognitive business — how Sabina feels about her weight or how Ben feels about his father, for example — are always ready to emerge and be addressed if we are allowed the time and space to become aware of their existence. Violet's work in this way promotes the process of gestalt formation and closure in that such unfinished gestalts can rise to the surface through imagination, image, and metaphor and then be addressed in more conscious, "sense making" ways in the Therapeutic Experiences.

One last idea before I close this section on the role of Metaphoric Sense-Making in Violet's work. In their book, Metaphors We Live By, Lakoff and Johnson (1980) say that the essence of metaphor is "understanding and experiencing one kind of thing in terms of another" (p. 5). This concurs with what we have already discussed. However, they also propose a new idea: that metaphor is as much a part of human functioning as any one of our five senses. They go on to conclude:

> It is as though the ability to comprehend experience
> through metaphor were a sense, like seeing or touching

or hearing, with metaphors providing the only ways to perceive and experience much of the world. (p. 239)

I think this idea is particularly relevant to looking at Violet's approach to both training adults and doing therapy with children. For one thing, the adults in her training have been learning about Violet's approach to therapy through creating and making sense of their own rich metaphors in the Therapeutic Experiences. Thus metaphor plays a key and perhaps irreplaceable role in the way they are able to "perceive and experience" the content of Violet's training. That is, they learn about the power of "building the metaphor" through working with metaphors themselves.

There are even deeper implications regarding Violet's work with both adults and children regarding Lakoff and Johnson's idea of metaphor serving as a "sixth sense" by which we learn about ourselves and the world around us. Throughout these chapters I have identified the ways in which Violet's approach to both therapy and training involves the five senses in a rich and significant way. If, as Lakoff and Johnson suggest, metaphor is equally as important to us as our other five senses (and may even be a kind of sense in itself) then Violet's consistent use of metaphor in her work with both adults and children truly does reflect a commitment to a great degree of multi-sensory involvement and integration in both training and therapy.

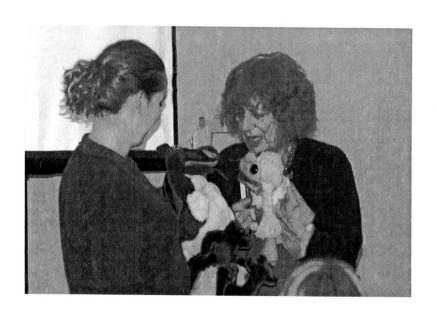

7

Day Seven: Tuesday
Stories, Metaphors and
Puppets

Child demonstration: Elisa's work with Violet

On Tuesday morning, participants are still abuzz about their experiences with Sand Tray Day. More discussion and follow-up questions of sand tray technique take up the first half-hour of the morning. At about 9:30 a.m., Violet mentions that she wants to share the case history of Elisa, the fourteen-year-old guest who is coming in for a demonstration session at 10:00 a.m.

As with many of the stories of child clients that Violet has told throughout the training as case examples, this one is not easy to listen to: Elisa, now almost fifteen, was abandoned by her mother and found in a completely neglected state along with her two brothers. After she was discovered by social workers, Elisa and her two brothers spent time with a foster mother with whom she grew very close. Elisa had a very difficult time leaving this foster mother when she was adopted at six years old, in large part because Elisa was adopted but her brothers were not. The couple that adopted Elisa thought at first that she was developmentally delayed because she would not speak or show that she understood statements made to her. All in all, there has been a history of difficulty with bonding between Elisa and her adoptive parents.

Violet describes to the participants that she has been seeing Elisa for a year and was able to establish a good relationship with her in a short period of time. Violet holds up Elisa's House, Tree, Person drawing which was completed in their work together. Violet also shows a drawing of a broken heart that Elisa drew after the divorce of her adoptive parents, stating that Elisa "loves to draw and is very artistic." Violet also explains that one of Elisa's biggest therapeutic concerns is the grief she has experienced at being separated from her brothers, both of whom now are in juvenile institutions. She explains that Elisa expressed excitement about coming to the training today and is aware that there will be twenty-four participants observing her work with Violet.

After this twenty-minute case presentation and a short, morning break for the participants, Elisa arrives with her mom and is greeted by Violet outside the conference room. Elisa is asked if she would like to have her mom stay with her, to which she answers yes. Inside the conference room, Elisa sits down on the floor with Violet, surrounded by puppets, drawing materials, and a board with clay tools and a hunk of gray clay on it. Violet asks each of the participants to say their name and where they have come from. Elisa expresses surprise that so many people are "from so far away." After these introductions, Violet tells Elisa "all these people are here to learn about how I work with young people. We can just forget about them for now, okay?" Turning toward Elisa on the carpet, Violet asks her what she would like to work with this morning and points out the puppets, clay, and drawing materials.

Elisa starts to check-out the pile of puppets and soon goes along with Violet's request that she "pick one that appeals to you." Elisa picks a puppet with a star for a face and Violet picks a puppet of a Bald Eagle. A conversation follows in which the Bald Eagle puppet asks the star-face puppet many questions (e.g. "Do you know Elisa?" "Do stars have feelings?") Elisa responds to these questions in a playful but brief manner.

As with her work with Ben on the videotape, Violet next asks Elisa to pick a puppet to represent each member of her family and then asks her to "say anything" she wants to each puppet. During this exercise, Elisa mentions her two brothers and how much she misses them. After Elisa makes this statement, Violet asks her to do a drawing of how she feels about missing her brothers and the following dialogue ensues:

Violet: Because you've mentioned your brothers, Matthew and Jason, I'd like you to maybe draw a picture of that feeling you have missing them. You know, like colors, lines, and shapes...

Elisa: Okay—With Jason...

Violet: You know, how you feel about not having your brothers around anymore...

Elisa: With Jason, I lived with him longer and so—it feels like sometimes, when you're just sitting there [Hm, mm] there's just like this really big, dark tunnel (Elisa draws a dark circle). I never really told anybody before, but there's a big chunk missing. Because Jason had, he was a lot of me. People don't really understand sometimes why I miss him that much. But in life he was—he was a *really* big part of me. It was like, he was part of me and, when he'd leave, I kinda fall down. Like if I was like a table? He'd be one of the legs (Elisa draws a three-legged table)...

Violet: Wow...

Elisa: ...and he'd go and I'd be *sitting* there going all crooked...

Violet: Wow...Yeah...

Elisa: ...and it'd be really hard to live my *life* without him because he was always something that when I made decisions—it was his part too. And so, ummm— (Elisa begins to cry quietly, wiping her nose) it was just like all my life depended on him too, even though he had his own feelings too. But, I never really told him *that* either, that he was a lot of me...but...

Violet: Hm, mm...

Elisa: So when I think of him, it's like...

Violet: Now, how old is he now?

Elisa: He's going to be sixteen in September. So, he's going up (Elisa draws a line going up) and I'm staying down (Elisa draws a descending line). So he's kinda like living his life—he just keeps going, but I'm still down here trying to figure out what to do, so (pause)...

Violet: Hm, mm—If he were here, how would it be different for you?

Elisa: Actually, it'd probably still be the same. I'd have to get adjusted to having him back. And it'd be awhile before he started being part of me again? See, because I've lived—now I've lived like—a year I think, or *two* years—without him, and so, I've gotten used to sort of being on my own. I've gotten used to making decisions, without me asking "Jason, what do you think?" A lot of the reasons I got my answers was from him 'cause he helped me. So if he *did* come back, I'd get used to—*having* him there. But I don't think I'd be so much with him anymore.

Violet: And maybe you've learned—you've *had to* learn a lot of how to do that yourself?

Elisa: Yeah... That's happening a lot where—I live my life on my own, without having Jason there...

In the reflective notes that follow this chapter, I will spend more time on this first piece of work that Elisa completes with Violet regarding her brother Jason. To me, it is a distinct piece of work in itself with a sense of closure just as it concludes. It begins with Elisa feeling bereft at loss of her brothers, but finishes with her realizing how far she's come since their departure. In the reflective notes, I will take a closer look at the role that narrative plays in Elisa's sense-making of this loss. For now, I will move on and describe the rest of the work that Elisa and Violet do together. In a different manner than in other chapters, however, I will also be interspersing "reflective comments" throughout the remainder of this rich depiction of Violet working with a child "live" in the training setting.

Just after Elisa finishes this first piece of work, she spontaneously begins a new drawing about her feelings regarding her other brother Matthew, whom she didn't live with as long as she did with Jason:

Figure 9: Elisa's Drawing of a Tree

Elisa: ...If you think of a tree with all its branches and stuff (she draws image in Figure 9). When you think of Matthew, he's just kind of like a part that, just a *little* part that has been cut out (she draws an indentation in the tree). Because if I'd have lived with him for a longer time, he probably would have been like the whole tree. Since I haven't, it's only like a little part that's gone. Mostly when I cry it's always for Jason...

Interestingly, after drawing and talking about this image of the tree, Elisa expresses concern that she is not crying about the loss of her brothers as much as she used to. She worries that this might mean that she doesn't care about them anymore: "I always think...that I'm a bad person that I don't cry like I used to." This new problem that arises for Elisa is a good example of Gestalt theory in practice. That is, just as Elisa gains a bit of closure on her first unfinished piece of business (missing her brother Jason), a new unfinished piece of business arises for her (missing the feeling of missing both her brothers). In the next segment of their work together, Violet offers Elisa a reframe of this concern, suggesting instead that she is growing into more of a "whole person." Elisa picks up on this idea, agrees with Violet and then extends the metaphor of "wholeness:"

> Violet: I think that the reason you don't cry so much is not only because you understand more, and it's not as painful, but because you're more of a whole person...
>
> Elisa: Yeah, that's true...
>
> Violet: See when they left it's like part of you...
>
> Elisa: [interrupting] Yeah, but now I've grown back, and it's true. It's like a sore, you cut yourself...
>
> Violet: That's it!
>
> Elisa: ...and you're missing part of your skin. And then

you grow a scab, so you'll heal! So when Jason left it was like a big sore, but now it's growing back...

Violet: It's like *you* have grown more whole yourself...

In her work with Violet, it's important to note how Elisa's metaphors shift to reflect the emotional change in the way that she is viewing herself. She began the session by using images that included a "big dark tunnel," a table that was "going all crooked," and a tree with "a little part missing." As her work with Violet progresses, the metaphors she uses carry a different emotional tone. In this last passage, Elisa uses the image of a scab that grows over a "big sore." Next, when Violet asks her to think of an image that somehow represents how she has "become more whole within yourself," Elisa comes up with a new metaphor:

Elisa: Well I guess you could use like an apple (Elisa draws first of four apples in Figure 10). When Jason left, there was always this center part that like... would never fill up! But then it gradually got to (Elisa draws second apple)...lesser...

Figure 10: Elisa's Drawing of Four Apples

Violet: lesser...

Elisa: And finally, I get to the part where it's not so much that I miss him anymore (Elisa draws third apple). But then it will get to the part where (Elisa draws fourth apple) it's a whole apple! Yayyyy!

After Elisa has drawn and described all four apples, Violet chuckles in response to Elisa's enthusiasm but then reminds Elisa that she will probably still have times when she does not feel so "whole," adding that she thinks this will be "pretty normal." As earlier with the "scab" metaphor, Elisa picks up on Violet's ideas and adds a new metaphor of her own:

Elisa: Yeah. It's like if you're married to somebody and the person dies...

Violet: Hm, mm

Elisa: And you feel like you've lost somebody that's always been there, but then after a while you get used to them not being there...

Violet: Hm, mm

Elisa: It's a lot like that...And losing your pet is a lot like that! Because I felt the same way when I lost my dog...

Violet: I remember, yeah...

Elisa: ...and then he left, and I'd always walk outside and he wouldn't come up and lick me...and so I was sad...

In a little over a half an hour, and in front of a large group of people, Violet and Elisa have covered a lot of ground together. Although their work centered around Elisa's issues regarding the loss of her brothers, it did address distinct aspects within that larger theme. In her first two drawings of a "dark tunnel" and of two lines going up and down, Elisa addressed her feelings of loss about her brother Jason. With her third drawing of the tree with a "little part cut out," Elisa began to explore how she felt about missing her brother Michael. Interestingly, what emerged next was how she felt about not missing her brothers as much as she used to. With her fourth drawing of the apples, Elisa represented her emerging sense of wholeness and recovery after her traumatic loss.

There are two aspects of Elisa's work with Violet that I'd like to highlight. First, I think the work is a good example of the fluid movement through emergent topics, or pieces of "unfinished business" that is central to Violet's Gestalt-centered approach to therapy. Second, I think the work clearly shows how Violet works through the four steps of her Therapeutic Experiences in recursive ways. This recursive movement, discussed in reflective notes of Chapter Five, allows Elisa to stay on topic, but to explore issues at a deeper level. Violet leads Elisa through multiple imaginary and sensory experiences with both puppets and drawings in their brief but productive time together. These experiences help Elisa create powerful metaphors and stories that she uses to help "make sense" of both her past experiences and her present-day situation.

To wrap up their time together in the training, Violet asks

Elisa if there is anything else she would like to do with the puppets or "anything you can think of." Elisa says, "No, not really," so Violet begins to close the session by changing to a lighter topic. She asks Elisa how her summer vacation has been going, and where she went on vacation. Then, after just a few more moments, Violet tells Elisa that it's time to end and thanks her for coming in this morning. Elisa gets up with her mom to leave, smiles and waves good-bye to all the participants, many of whom thank her for coming, and then steps outside with Violet.

When Violet returns to the room, she opens up the floor to questions or comments by saying, "Let's talk about what you saw." There are a few complimentary comments about how helpful it was to watch Violet at work with a child client (e.g. "It was helpful to see you work with two different expressive media — the drawing materials and the puppets — in the same session"). There are also some comments expressing concern about whether Elisa might have felt too vulnerable in front of such a large group of observers. Violet restates that Elisa very much wanted to come and understood the context. She adds that in her experience of bringing children into the group over the past ten years, she has never had one child come back to her with a negative reaction: "I think that, having done this work in front of the group, Elisa left here with a very strong sense of herself," she says.

Near the end of this discussion, and just before lunch break, a participant states: "It was a real learning for me to see that you didn't try to 'fix' her bad feelings in the session." To this, Violet responds, "The goal is to express what they're feeling, exaggerating it. Our goal is to get those feelings out. That's what's healing."

Story-telling, puppet shows, and therapeutic metaphors

After the regular hour-and-a-half lunch break, the participants return to the room to find that the floor has been cleared of all puppets, clay and drawing materials and instead they find Violet sitting amidst a scattering of books. When everyone is settled, Violet begins to describe the way that she combines storytelling, metaphor, and the use of puppet shows in the therapeutic process.

She begins by holding up a particular book called "Dinosaur Divorce" (Brown Brown, 1988) and says, "It's a funny book! But it addresses this a very serious matter." This same theme of playfully addressing serious matters is represented in "A Very Touching Book...For Little People And For Big People" (Hindman, 1983) which is about helping children distinguish between being touched in healthy or abusive ways. Essentially, Violet says, stories that serve as metaphors for children's own experience help them feel that their experience is understood and affirmed. She goes on to say that she often will read a book to a child when she is aware that a certain book reflects an issue that children are having in their own life.

A related way that stories and metaphors can be used in therapy, Violet suggests, is to perform puppet shows that dramatize stories or scenes that have important meaning for the child. After setting up a modest puppet-show stage by crouching behind a chair, Violet demonstrates an example of a puppet show that she put together for a little girl who was painfully shy and struggling with the ability to be assertive in her life. Violet says that this puppet show, called "I'm going to the park," is about the adventures and misadventures of a little girl puppet who begs her mom to let her go to the park alone because she thinks she is now old enough to do so.

Hidden behind the chair, Violet begins the show with a little-girl puppet merrily skipping along and singing aloud, "My mother said I that I'm old enough to go to the park all by myself! I'm going to the park! I'm going to the park!" Suddenly, the little girl encounters a crocodile puppet that tells her he is lost and, "looking for the swamp." After the girl states vehemently that she does not know where the swamp is, the crocodile says that he is also quite hungry and he makes a move towards the girl. The little-girl puppet shrieks, runs off and hides until the crocodile is gone. When the little girl reappears, she vacillates between going home or proving to her mom that she can make it to the park all by herself. With newfound courage, she starts out once again singing, "I'm going to the park," but with a less enthusiasm in her voice than the first time and with a few suspicious glances to left and the right.

Once again, the puppet's progress to the park is blocked by a shark puppet that pops up and says that he too is lost and is looking for the ocean. "Have you seen the ocean?" he asks disingenuously. When the little girl replies that she has not seen the ocean, the shark puppet also makes a move to eat her like the crocodile puppet did. Once again the little girl puppet shrieks, runs off and hides. This time when she reappears, after the shark has gone, the little girl is crying and telling herself that she should go home, "But then my mom won't ever let me go to the park by myself," she moans. So once again she musters enough courage to go on. She looks around cautiously and begins her sing-song chant of, "I'm going to the park," but this time she sings with no enthusiasm at all and she hardly makes any progress forward (To this, the participants murmur empathetic "Ohhs"and "aahs" regarding the little girl's situation).

When the last villain puppet arrives on the scene — this time a scary-looking wolf — and starts to make a move in her direction, the little-girl puppet angrily and assertively bonks him on the nose and says, "Get out of my way and leave me alone! I'm going to the park!" The wolf howls in hurt and says as he sulks off, "You didn't have to hit me!" In the final moment of the puppet show, the little-girl puppet turns to the audience and says proudly and confidently, "Well, I'm going to the park!" and marches off.

The participants in the training break out into applause as Violet emerges from behind her chair. After some discussion, and as a kind of encore performance, Violet demonstrates another puppet show that she says she has used with a client who is a young boy. The opening scene of this second puppet show involves a "mom" puppet who is busily cooking dinner and an impatient "dad" puppet who eventually hits the mom puppet when he finds out dinner is not yet ready. At this point, Violet peaks out from behind her chair for a moment to tell the participants that the first time her young client saw this scene, he said, "That's just like my life!"

In the remaining scenes of this second puppet show, Violet introduces a little-boy puppet that is actually a puppy (Violet later describes that she tends to use animal or caricature puppets instead of real-looking human puppets, preferring not to be too literal). This puppet representing a little boy discusses what he witnessed between the mom and the dad with his sibling (a little monkey puppet): "I don't like it that Daddy hurts Mommy! It scares me and I don't like it!" The sibling puppet urges his brother to confront the dad and tell him how he is feeling. In the last scene of the show, the dad puppet at first denies it when the little-boy puppet says, "I don't like it when you hit Mommy. It scares me!" But then the dad puppet finally concedes that the son is right and that he will stop being mean to the mother.

Violet pops out her head from behind the chair to explain that the purpose of this puppet show was to give voice through the puppets to the feelings she assumed the boy was having but could not identify or express. She then goes on to demonstrate another puppet show that she created for this young client in which the puppy puppet says to the "mom" puppet, "Mommy I want to tell you something, but I'm afraid you will get mad at me." The Mom puppet responds by saying, "Oh, go ahead son, I won't get mad at you." The puppy puppet explains to his mom that, "even though I know you don't want to see Daddy again now that he's moved out, I still do." Although the mom puppet is flustered at this news, she tries to take it well and eventually ends up hugging the son and thanking him for telling her what he feels. The mom puppet tells him she'll have to think about his request that he be able to see his father.

As Violet emerges from behind the chair, she explains that the little boy who was her client actually performed a version of that last puppet show for his mother and that it helped them discuss the situation afterwards.

During all three of Violet's puppet shows, the participants were held rapt attention and many of them later described how surprisingly engaging and powerful the shows were. One participant commented that she learned something important from watching Violet perform the puppet shows:

> I used to think that in order to do puppet shows, you had to do all those strange and funny sounding voices for each character. That's why I never wanted to do them. It felt dumb. What I saw you doing was speaking in a voice that sounded more natural for all the characters. Your voice carried real emotion instead of getting all wrapped up in silly voices. I liked that a lot and found it more effective.

Adult demonstration:
Lark and the Medicine cards

After a short afternoon break, Violet demonstrates other metaphoric and story-telling techniques that she has used with children. One such technique involves the use of a commercially-available pack of tarot-like cards called "Medicine Cards: The Discovery Of Power Through The Ways Of Animals" (Sams Carson, 1988). These cards each contain a detailed drawing of a variety of animals, insects, and birds that are significant in the spiritual tradition of North American native tribes. In a book that accompanies the cards, a description of each animal's habits and habitat and what they represent in Native American folklore is described. Regarding the mouse card, for example, the text of the accompanying book states: "It is good medicine to pay attention to detail, but it is bad medicine to chew every little thing to pieces".

As a demonstration of how she would use the Medicine Cards with a child, Violet chooses a volunteer from the group and, sitting with her on the floor, asks her to pick three cards: "One that represents who you are now, one that represents who you used to be, and one that represents who you would like to be in the future."

Lark, a child and family therapist from New Zealand, picks a butterfly to represent who she is now. About this card, Lark states, "I feel like I've developed wings and I can fly. I can appreciate my color and my difference." Lark next picks a mouse for who she used to be, "sort of scurrying around. You know, hiding." Lastly, Lark picks an owl for who she is becoming. Describing how this animal metaphor fits for her, she says, "What I like about the owl is the ability to step back and to observe, and also that ability to come forward when it needs to."

These three cards serving as rich metaphors for Lark's experience become a starting place for a broader discussion between Lark and Violet. At one point in this discussion, Violet asks Lark, "What do you need to do before you can become more like the owl?" Lark's response to this question reveals her own surprise at the emotional identification she feels with the butterfly card:

> Lark: Well I guess I'm a bit...Oh! Hmm...(she chokes up and her voice becomes shaky) I'm a bit like the butterfly...
>
> Violet: What just happened?
>
> Lark: Well, I just recognized what the butterfly does. It sort of lives its life really quickly and then it sort of...[pause]...
>
> Violet: Ooh...Huh. And that makes you feel sad when you think about it...
>
> Lark: Yeah...

Because of time constraints making this is a brief demonstration (about ten minutes long), Violet does not pursue Lark's identification with the butterfly metaphor further. Instead, Violet describes both to Lark and the other participants what she might do next if she were working with a child:

> Violet: I'm not going to do this, but the next step would be to have you draw a picture using these three figures. Not copying them, but using those three figures in one scene, in some way. And, well, would you like to do that?
>
> Lark: I could do that myself at home, actually...
>
> Violet: Okay. And then, what's interesting is to look at the picture and have the animals talk to each other, and you would be each one, and see where

you position them, in terms of how close and how far away, or what. It's always so interesting to see that...

Violet checks in once more with Lark and then thanks her for working with her in front of the group, and, for the last few moments of the day, she highlights one more method of the "many ways of using metaphors and stories." She describes the "mutual story-telling technique" which she adapted from Richard Gardener's (1971) work. As an example of the "mutual story-telling technique," Violet describes herself holding a microphone for six-year old Adam to speak into as he becomes a "guest" on a pretend story-telling hour on a radio station. She tells Adam that story-telling has some rules and the rules are "the story has to have a beginning, a middle and an end." Violet then describes how she started the story with Adam ("Once upon a time, a long time ago, there was a..."). She then describes how she looked at Adam expectantly and paused. Adam then caught on and contributes to the construction of the story by responding, "...a shark who ate some people." Violet asks Adam to tell her more about the shark and then builds on Adam's responses by weaving a tale that metaphorically references Adam's real-life experience.

Adam had come to therapy because he fought with other children so often that he was having a difficult time keeping friends (he had, in fact, thrown a dozen eggs at children who had come to his door to play with him). In Violet's metaphorical story, the shark can't find anyone to play with because all the fishermen are afraid of being eaten by him. By the end of the story though, the shark has found a child who wanted to play with him, "because the shark was nice to him." Violet tells Jimmy, "I guess what that story tells me is that the shark needed to be friendly if he wanted to have friends." This story became a centerpiece for Adam's work with Violet, she says, and was often referenced and told repeatedly at Adam's request.

With the end of this example, Violet notes that it is past 4:30 and therefore time to go. Tomorrow, she says, will be the day-long Practicum experience where "all the media we have been talking about will be available for you to use and practice with. See you then."

Reflective notes for day seven

In the reflective notes at the end of previous chapters, I have focused on three aspects of Violet's Therapeutic Experiences: imaginary experience, sensory expression, and metaphoric sense-making. In this chapter's reflective notes, I will focus on narrative and it's role in sense-making. I begin with a piece entitled "Stories are more than just stories" and then I move into a section that focuses on Violet's work with Elisa earlier today as a particular example of the role that "narrative sense-making" plays in Violet's approach.

Stories are more than just stories

When I first started conducting research on Violet's trainings, I was most interested in discovering the answer to one basic question: what does Violet do in these trainings that attracts people from around the world every year to come and study with her? My method in working to answer this question was basically anthropological: I would sit in on Violet's trainings as if I were visiting a foreign culture and see what I could learn. I recorded each day's events on audio- and video- tape, conducted interviews, and took detailed notes. I paid close attention to the moment-to-moment interactions and transitions in the training to uncover the themes, practices and patterns of this mini-culture. By doing this, I was able to step back and view what Violet actually did in these trainings at any particular moment as well as over time. In other words, I was able to understand the structures and processes that made up the content of Violet's trainings and that provided participants with such a valuable and meaningful experience.

Many of the themes and patterns that I have written about in these reflective notes stem from discoveries I made in this process of trying to understand the shape, form and content of Violet's trainings. These themes and patterns include the "parallels between training and practice" that I discussed in chapter one, the "conversation piece" that I discussed in chapter two, the "four-step structure of Violet's Therapeutic Exercises" discussed in chapter three and four, as well as the focus that I put on images, sensory expression and metaphors in chapters five and six.

Some themes in Violet's training popped out at me almost immediately (the parallels between training and therapy, for example), but other themes and patterns were not as easy to identify, even when they were staring me in the face. One such theme was the role of stories and narrative in Violet's work. For years, I sat through Violet's trainings with my notebook in hand and would repeatedly scribble in the margins lines like: "Violet tells another case story," or "Jan tells a story during her demonstration session with Violet about her childhood," or, "Violet says she wants to help the child build the metaphor or story."

I didn't pay much attention to these notes because I must not have considered such stories to be all that important. In part, I had been trained, like most of us have, to think of stories as entertainment or maybe as a way to pass the time, but certainly not something worth of study in a dissertation research project. I also now believe that, like most of us, I was so used to being immersed in the stories of everyday life — stories that friends told me, stories I heard on the radio, stories that I read in the newspaper, stories in movies, novels, songs, etc. — that they were invisible to me, like water is invisible to a fish.

One day the cultural anthropologist in me woke up and said, "Hey, stories are obviously a significant part of Violet's training, you had better take a close look at this!" So I did. I started reading about stories and was surprised to learn that narrative is a huge field of study in disciplines as wide-ranging and diverse as cognitive development, religious studies, law and education. I learned that in the last thirty years, narrative studies have become central to the inquiry process of many of these disciplines after being ignored for hundreds of years previously. Donald Polkinghorne (1988) describes that after the scientific revolution, "Figures of speech, including metaphors and narratives, were...understood to contribute nothing to a person's cognitive understanding." In short, figurative language such as stories and metaphors were considered ornamentation while reason, logic and mathematics were considered the real thing.

Recently, narrative studies have become key to the way that many researchers in the human sciences in particular are learning about the ways in which people understand their lives and construct their identities, both as individuals and as social beings. Stories, it turns out, are fundamental to way we "make sense" of ourselves and of the world we live in. Think of all the stories that serve as a backdrop and a foundation for our lives (where our parents came from or what our childhoods were like, for example). Think about the stories that help us define and think about who we are (what career path we decided upon and why, or how we met our significant other, for example). Such stories help us puzzle out significant topics and events and to see ourselves and others in a broader context.

Stories serve both individuals and large groups: there are personal stories of overcoming hardship, there are stories from our religious congregations that help us figure out right from wrong, and there are national stories about what we stand for as a people. We both listen to and tell stories, reinforcing them each time we share them. As Toni Morrison (1993) states: "Narrative is radical, creating us at the very moment it is being created."

Focus on narrative sense-making:
Addressing trouble

In this section, I will be showing a particular example of how narrative can help both children and adults to "make sense" of their own experiences and help construct their identities as they grow and change in a world that is also changing. Specifically, I will first show how Violet, through her use of a Therapeutic Experience involving drawing, encourages Elisa to build on metaphors and to tell a story that describes and puts into vibrant, emotion-laden images the difficulty Elisa has experienced in losing her brothers. Second, I will also show how Violet helps Elisa to "make sense" of that narrative and her experience in a way that enables her to try on a new sense of herself, one that more truly reflects who she is in the present and not who she was in the past. In this way, I want to highlight how the narrative aspect of Violet's Therapeutic Experiences (along with aspects that involve imagination, sensory expression and metaphors that I have highlighted in prior chapters) serves a central function in Violet's work. This central function serves to help both children and adults to make sense of prior or present troubles in their experience and to move to new understandings about themselves and their world. This section then, is a closer look at narrative sense-making.

As Violet has described in earlier parts of the training, she will occasionally prompt a child to focus on a particular theme in their work if she feels it will benefit the child to explore it. When Elisa raises the issue of "missing her two brothers" after Violet has her speak to puppets "as if" they were her family members, Violet prompts Elisa to draw a picture of the feeling she has missing her brothers using "colors, lines, and shapes." In this way, Violet leads Elisa into a Therapeutic Experience that will recursively follow the same four-part sequence we have been exploring in prior chapters. That is, Violet will lead Elisa through multiple passes of the following four steps: 1) imaginative or fantasy experience; 2) sensory expression of that experience; 3) metaphoric and/or narrative description of that expression; 4) sense-making articulation involving all the prior steps.

To summarize her steps thus far, Violet has been playing with Elisa using puppets when she then asks Elisa to imaginatively put her feelings into form using the sensory expression of pastels and paper. Unlike some children, Elisa needs little prompting from Violet to "build the story and metaphor," and, in fact, she begins telling a story and using metaphors while she is still in the process of drawing the "long dark tunnel" to represent her feelings for missing her brothers.

Within moments, Elisa has described a vivid set of images that help to tell the story of how she felt before and after her brother Jason left. She uses repeated phrases throughout this first part of her story to tell Violet how much Jason meant to her:

"he was a lot of me"
"he was a really big part of me"
"he was a part of me"
"my life depended on...him"
"he was a lot of me"

In doing this, Elisa does what most of us do when we tell a story. We first describe and emphasize the way things were before something significant happened. In Elisa's case, these past norms included a close and important relationship with her brother Jason. This equilibrium of Elisa's life was rudely disrupted with Jason's departure. To describe how she felt after this troubling change of events, Elisa uses a set of vivid but bleak metaphors that are spoken and in most cases also sketched out on paper:

> "there's this really big, dark...tunnel"
> "there's a big chunk missing"
> "when he'd leave I'd kinda fall down"
> "if I was a table, He'd be one of the legs and he'd go and I'd be sitting there...going all crooked"

Narrative theorists (Bruner, 1990; Labov, 1977; Propp, 1928) have a name for what Elisa is describing in this part of her story: they call it "trouble" or "disequilibrium" and it appears at the core of most stories we tell. That is, we tend to tell stories about "non-ordinary" things, either positive or negative, that happen to us. This trouble or disequilibrium in our story contrasts strongly to the norms that we usually describe at the outset of our story. In Elisa's case, the way she felt after Jason left is in sharp contrast to how she experienced life when Jason was someone she could count on in her life.

Importantly, narrative theorists also identify a consistent "third part" of our stories that usually follows the first two parts where norms and trouble are described. This third part of a story is where we try to "make sense" of our new situation in light of the trouble that has happened to us. In short, the first part of the story is about how we used to be, the second part of the story is about the trouble or unusual occurrence that has happened, and the third part of the story is an effort to describe who we are now and how we have been changed: "I used to be this, then that happened, and now I..."

In this third part of our stories, we often describe how we see or experience things differently in light of the trouble or challenge that we have faced. The fact that change has happened cannot be ignored by us, so we must "reweave" a narrative that accounts for it, that addresses these changes and somehow integrates them into our present life story.

Interestingly, the simple and common word "so" is often used to begin this third part of a story: "So this is what I learned", or, "So I'm really better off now than I was then." In Elisa's case, she begins this third part of her story with the commonly used "so," but the way she "makes sense" of the trouble she has faced in losing her brother is not particularly positive. Even though it has been nearly two years since Jason left, Elisa still feels as if she has not moved on from this difficult experience:

> "So he's—going up and I'm staying down"
> "So he's kinda like living his life—he keeps going, but I'm
> still down here trying to figure out what to do, so..."

What happens next in the interaction between Violet and Elisa is important. Violet asks Elisa a simple but intriguing question: "If he were here, how would it be different for you?" In answer to this deceptively simple question, Elisa revises and almost completely reverses the "third part" of her narrative that she just told to Violet. She seems to suddenly realize that she is different now, that a lot of water has gone under the bridge, and that she has learned a lot about standing on her own two feet in the time that she has lived since Jason left. She again initiates this revised third part of her story with multiple sentences starting with "so" and again uses repetition of certain phrases to get her point across:

> "So, I've gotten used to—sort of being on my own."
> "I've gotten used to making decisions"
> "So if he did come back, I'd get used to—having him there.   But I don't think I'd be so much with him anymore"
> "So…I live my life on my own, without having —Jason there"

It's impossible to say exactly what inspires Elisa to so fundamentally rethink her experience and her story at this point in her work with Violet. One thing that is certain is that no story is told in isolation and how we tell a story depends on who is listening and what their response is. We don't usually share our personal stories with someone we don't trust because such a person might evaluate or judge us negatively based on what they hear or highlight in our story.   The opposite is true when it comes to people we do trust. When we tell a personal story to someone we trust and have a good relationship with, we are willing to hear and consider what they think about our story. In fact, a trusted listener often helps us see things about our own stories and about ourselves that we may have missed ourselves (Capps Ochs, 1995).   In this way, stories are often the "co-construction" of both the teller and a trusted listener.

In Elisa's case, I suspect that she is suddenly able to see herself in a different light when Violet implies in her question that a lot of time really has gone by since Jason left and that Elisa might in fact be different now than she was just after his departure. All at once, Elisa seems to become aware that she is not who she used to be, and that maybe the way she used to end this particular story no longer fits for her. Violet's simple question seems to invite Elisa back into the "here and now" instead of dwelling in the "there and then." In this way, Violet's question almost forces Elisa to come up with a new version of her story, or at least a new ending for her story which more aptly describes who she is now and what she knows about herself in the present moment. Perhaps this is Violet's greatest contribution to Elisa's story: as "co-editor," she helps Elisa span the distance from "back then" to "now" and, in that process, Elisa sheds an old story and rewrites a new one that suits her present experience better.

Something that I find fascinating in this case is a connection between Gestalt theory, which is fundamental to Violet's working model, and narrative theory, of which Violet was not familiar when she did this piece of work with Elisa. As I noted in the reflective notes for chapter six, in Gestalt theory emotion-laden images that are created in various media allow "unfinished business" to come into the foreground and be addressed by individuals (e.g. the clay image of the "baseball mitt" allowed Sabina's unfinished business regarding her body image to emerge). The interesting thing is, in narrative theory, the evidence points to stories serving the same function. That is, stories also help us enfigure vivid, emotion-laden images that reflect unfinished business. We tell stories about things that we are still grappling with, things we are still trying to "make sense of" (e.g. Elisa's story of losing her brothers). Stories, then, are told in order to gain closure in some way on our past so we can move into the present and the future with some clearer understanding of who we are and what we are about.

On this day with Violet, Elisa certainly leaves the room with a sense of who she is and what she is about that is different from the one with which she walked in. In her work with Violet, Elisa was given the opportunity to create powerful and personal images that brought to the surface some difficulties she was presently facing but that, when addressed and wrestled through with Violet's help, provided her with new ways of looking at herself and her experience.

Later in the day, Violet also provided the training participants with other ways that stories can be used to help a child see and "make sense" of their lives and experiences in new ways. Through the puppet shows that Violet demonstrated, children are able to see their own experience set in the form of a narrative that offers them a new way to make sense of the issues with which they struggle. Through the use of the Medicine Cards, children and adults are able to tell a story, in three parts, composed of who they used to be, who they are now, and who they wish to become. This approach gives the child or adult practice in seeing their lives as an unfolding story in which they are a central narrating and creative force.

To summarize this section, I have given examples of how

narrative and sense-making both form a central core to the Therapeutic Experiences that Violet uses with both children in therapy and with adults in the training. Along with the imaginative, sensorial, and metaphoric realms I have already discussed in these reflective notes, narrative seems to serve as the "deepest place in the bowl" where the most work is done by those who engage in these Therapeutic Experiences. Importantly, Violet leads individuals to use this rich word-play and verbal sense-making only after they have first had the chance to use their imaginations and senses to create images with which to work. Elisa tells her difficult story of loss and regained strength only after she plays a bit with Violet and a few puppets. Elisa also uses pastels and paper to draw images of dark tunnels, of lines moving up and down, and of trees with pieces missing.

To me, this is more evidence that the first two steps of Violet's Therapeutic Experiences involving the imagination and the senses offer a familiar kind of support and grounding from which the more difficult emotional and cognitive work can be done in the subsequent, more verbal parts of the experiences. In this way, Violet builds on children's developmental strengths and on the safety of the relationship she establishes with children before leading them into the challenging realms of deeper therapeutic work. Through this approach to her work, Violet acts as master of attachment theory (Bowlby, 1988) in that she is constantly making sure the necessary supports — or "secure bases" as Bowlby puts it — are in place so that the next level of risk is able to be taken on and successfully addressed.

Tomorrow, during their full-day Practicum experience, the training participants will also be given a rich opportunity to take on new levels of challenge themselves using all they have learned thus far in the training.

8

Day Eight: Wednesday Practicum Day

Overview of the day

As the participants enter the conference room on Wednesday morning, they have to step carefully. Separated piles of various expressive media cover large parts of the floor before them. There are pastels, paper and other drawing materials, clay, clay tools and cutting boards, boxed games, puppets, musical instruments, Medicine and Story-telling cards, Nerf™ guns and battacas. There is also a "portable sand tray" made of lacquered wood that opens up like a suitcase, with sand on one side and tiny figurines in plastic storage boxes on the other side. All of these therapeutic tools will be available for training participants today as they take on the practicum roles of therapist, client, and observer in a structure similar to Monday's "Sand Tray day".

The excitement in the room as the morning begins is reflected in the noise level of the participants and their exclamations over which materials they might choose to work with when it is their turn to be client. As everyone gets settled in their seats, Violet greets the participants and asks if there is any "left over business" from Tuesday. She then begins to organize the whole group for the day ahead. First she has the participants count off, resulting in eight groups of three people who gather around the room in small clusters. She then describes how the members of each group will rotate through the three roles of Therapist, Client, and Observer. Pointing at the schedule of today's activities that is posted on the wall behind her (Figure 11), Violet describes the timing and roles of the three practice sessions in which the participants will take part: in session #1, one member of the group will be therapist; in Session #2, that same person becomes the Client; and, in Session #3, that same person becomes the observer.

9:30 - 10:30	Session #1
10:30 - 10:45	Break (optional)
10:45 - 11:45	Session #2
11:45 - 12:00	Regroup
12:00 - 1:30	Lunch
1:30 - 2:30	Session #3
2:30 - 2:45	Break
2:45 - 4:30	Regroup

Figure 11: Practicum Day Schedule

After she describes the day's schedule, Violet has the small groups of participants decide who will take which role for the first practice session. When this is accomplished, Violet then explains how this day will be different than Monday's Sand Tray experience:

When you take on the client's role, you will be yourself as a child. You can be any age between 6 and 16. I have found that this approach of being yourself as a child is how the most genuine work comes out. It also helps the person in the therapist's role to think about working with children and their issues. During today's practicum, when the client comes into the session, each of you will tell the therapist why you have been sent to therapy and a little bit about the surrounding factors: "My mother is worried because I bit my brother," or "I'm shy," or "I don't know why they sent me." Pretend that it is not the first session that you have had together and that the parents are not there.

Usually the session should only be about a half hour. Even with a real child, it is not much longer than that, so pace yourselves. This is not therapy, so as the therapist you don't have to feel obligated to go on and on. As a client, you may get some therapeutic benefit from the work, but the focus for the day is on the practice of being in the role of the therapist and doing this kind of work with children. As a client you will also learn from being yourself as a child how a child might feel in that situation. It's good for the therapist to know how to make closure at the end of the demonstration session. Try to help ground the client before they leave.

The observer's role is also very valuable. The observer helps facilitate discussion after the demonstration session and gives feedback regarding what they noticed as the session progressed. Also, I'd like the observers to be responsible for contributing something they learned from the small groups to the large group when we re-group at the end of the day.

Throughout the rest of the day, participants leave the conference room with their hands full of various materials and return every so often to pick up something they forgot, or something that they realized they wanted to work with. The portable sand tray is immediately "claimed" by different participants for each of the three sessions. Musical instruments are also very popular, and at one point in the afternoon, the energetic pounding of the drums can be heard out under the trees and near the pool of the hotel and conference center.

In their groups of three, participants have chosen different locations in which to work. Most groups have chosen to work in one of the participant's hotel room, which give them more privacy for this sometimes intense work. Other groups, however, have chosen to work under the umbrellas at poolside or just outside the conference room on tables on the back porch. Violet makes herself available, as she did on Monday, for questions and concerns from the participants.

During this quieter time for Violet, I take the opportunity to ask her some questions about her approach. At one point in the interview, with the sound of participants talking "as if" they were puppets drifts into the room from outside on the patio, we discuss the central role of fantasy in this type of work:

Violet: A lot of what we do involves fantasy. In my workshops I will often lead all kinds of fantasy exercises, open-eye exercises, closed-eye fantasies — "Imagine you could go home right now, what would you see?" — those kinds of things. And the point of these is to help the participants get comfortable with fantasy.

Peter: What is it about fantasy that is important?

Violet: It's interesting about fantasy, because I always say you have to learn to let go to do fantasy, but when you do that, you come back to yourself. It's almost like you eliminate or go through the shield, or the armor. You have to relax it, you have to let go to do fantasy. If I'm like this (she tightens up her face and arms and pinches her eyes closed) I can't imagine anything. But when I let go and I can allow myself to imagine these things, I'm actually coming back to myself because they're always projections. Even in a guided fantasy — if I say, "Okay, you're walking through the woods and you're looking around..." — I don't know what kind of woods you're thinking about. It's your projection. So ironically, fantasy gives us an access to our own real experience.

Violet further describes how the training is structured in such a way as to have the participants "let go" into fantasy more and more as the training progresses. According to Violet, the participants experience the real power of the work the more they let go into these experiential exercises.

Later in the afternoon, during the last of the three practicum sessions, Joan gives me permission to sit in on her session as she role-plays the client while Teri takes on the role of the therapist and Paul takes on the role of the observer. Joan, the only participant this year to have traveled from Germany to come to the training, is both a child therapist and the equivalent of a "special education" teacher in her home country. During her session, she presents herself as a very quiet and withdrawn young girl who has come to therapy because her mother thought it might help her deal with the depression she seems to have been in for the past year or so. As the adult therapist, Teri eventually finds a way to start a flow of conversation with Joan through having the "young princess" puppet that she has chosen talk directly to Joan's "goldfish" puppet.

Participant comments

After this last session of the day, when all the participants have re-gathered in the conference room and Violet has stated, "I'd like to hear what you learned from this exercise and how it was for you," Joan shares the following comments:

> I imagined I was about eight years old when I was the client and found it very difficult to talk. But with the puppet it was a little bit easier to express myself. It was the first time that I had worked with puppets and I found myself able to deeply identify with it. It was so full of life

for me, and I think it helped that it was an extension of my own arm, almost a part of my body.

A different perspective is shared by Teri who was in the role of Joan's therapist and found the work "a struggle." After one participant states, "I learned that you make it look easy!" Teri makes the whole group laugh loudly with her comment, "I just want to add: damn you, Violet!" She follows up this comment with a more serious explanation of her difficult experience as therapist:

It's not as easy as it looks. I think experience is something that teaches you to be with the moment. It is a struggle to not try and fix what is going on. I felt myself consciously saying, "Stay in the moment. Don't try and make this child feel better. Let them feel the sadness that they need to feel."

Another participant shares the difficulties she encountered in taking on the role of the therapist, but also adds that she found the structure of the practicum experience helpful: "The support of the other two I was working with allowed me to make mistakes but felt supported and not defeated by it. The observer especially gave me some ideas for good possibilities." To this, Violet responds, "This is why we do this practicum at the end of the training. People feel safer to make mistakes. It wouldn't work to do it earlier in the training."

Altogether, over an hour and a half are spent processing the practicum experience. At times, there are long pauses before someone contributes another comment. The mood is thoughtful and reflective, with participants speaking about all three of the roles they have taken on as well as the materials and subject matter of the practice sessions. There is more verbal give and take around the circle, with participants sharing equally as much as Violet. Toward the end of this period of time, Violet asks those who have not spoken to contribute something about their experience. One of the last comments is made by Mary, who is one of the quieter participants: "I realized how hard it is to be the client, not just the therapist." Violet responds to this comment by saying that this is why she thinks the capacity to play, fantasize and be expressive as a therapist is so important, especially with issues that are difficult. She says, "That's why we do all this in the training, because that's what we are asking the child to do."

After the training on Wednesday, I had the opportunity to talk with a number of the participants who were sitting around the pool at the conference hotel. We discussed in particular the issue that Violet raised about adult therapists being able to play well with children. Jenna, a clinic director in a city near Sydney, said that the most meaningful aspects of this workshop for her had to do with a strengthening of her convictions about which direction to go in shaping her clinic. She described her learning in this way:

> Before this trip to the workshop, I knew I didn't like that many of my therapists were well-trained academically but didn't know how to "make contact" with children. We would often have kids who wouldn't return to the clinic

saying that they thought it was boring. Now I plan on visiting the director of the University training program — a woman I know — and demanding, really, that the therapists who come out of her program will not just be the types who can work from their head up, but are willing to engage in playful contact with the children.

Jenna also described an important dream that she recently had one night during the training. In this dream, the offices in her clinic were being emptied and she was directing the movers as to which old things would be cleared out and which new things would be brought in. She said this dream was a metaphor for her about her new-found confidence gained from this workshop about a important style of working that had been reinforced and elaborated on by Violet during these two weeks.

Reflective notes for day eight

While the participants were engaged in the different roles and activities of the Practicum Day, I took the opportunity to interview Violet about the roots of her approach to working with children. Primarily, I was interested in learning about what had contributed to the development of her unique approach of combining a Gestalt orientation with the process of working therapeutically with children. What follows is a transcript of the story Violet shared during this interview explaining the evolution of and the influences upon her style of working with children in the therapeutic context. The interview began when I asked her about early influences on her approach:

Interview with Violet: Origins of the work

I'm going to have to go way back. I worked with kids a lot, and adults too, and I've always been interested in the creative process in working with them. I remember when I was about twelve and I lived in Cambridge, Massachusetts, there was a little girl who was a neighbor that was having trouble reading. The mother asked me if I would tutor her. I hadn't the slightest idea what to do so I started telling her stories about every letter. I would tell a whole story about the letter "A" and the sound it would make, and she became really interested. I watched her start learning to read which was fantastic!

I also worked in summer camps starting at age fifteen. I was the art and crafts director even though I had never done that kind of stuff before. I remember I had some pieces of leather that someone had donated and I said to the kids, "I don't want you to make ordinary things. Take these pieces of leather and see what they make you think of. I was doing that kind of thing even then, so I guess it's kind of been evolving.

I also remember I ran a Sunday Play Day at the Jewish Community Center when we lived in Denver, Colorado. They had a Sunday afternoon session for kids and I was in charge of this. I would play the guitar and we would sing and do all these creative things. But I remember the director saying, "The trouble with Violet is that she can do so many things, but she's not really expert in any one thing. She's not focusing on any one thing." It was kind of hurtful to hear that, but I think being able to do all those creative things, and not being a master in any one of them, eventually helped me in developing my approach. I think I knew that someday it would all come together.

One time in Albany, New York, after I was married and had kids of my own, I remember I did a PTA event at my house. I had all these people over and I showed them how to make toys and things out of boxes and just junk and found objects. I had these different stations set up and it was a lot of fun. I've always done this kind of thing, I guess, being creative with things in an unusual way.

The truth is that I learned it from my mother. She was like that. We were kind of poor when I was a kid, certainly not anything I was aware of, but I had very few toys that you bought in a store. I did have all kinds of stuff my mother made for me out of cloth and out of boxes and jars and cans. She would decorate them and make me toys and things to play with. She used to take snippets of plants as we'd walk down the street. She'd see a bush that she liked and she'd take a snippet home and put it in water until it grew roots and then she'd plant it. When I was a kid I was very intrigued by all that, I thought it was wonderful. So I guess I learned a lot about being creative from her.

I think I always did a lot of that kind of stuff with my own kids too. I taught nursery school for a year when my oldest child was three and a half. I would go to work and I'd learn things about the way kids develop that would fascinate me: what they were interested in and how they were intrigued by exploring and touching and singing and moving. I was always so interested in that aspect of development and I was a really good nursery school teacher. But unfortunately, because I'd only had one year of college, the board of directors wouldn't hire me back. That was kind of a sore spot with me: I wanted to go back to school, but it was very difficult financially with three kids and husband who was a social worker.

Then we moved to California and I found out that it was very inexpensive to go back to school, so I did. I was thinking I'd be a nursery school teacher. They had a child development program. It took me three years to do the two-year program and then I transferred to Cal State University at Long Beach and ended up graduating with an elementary school teaching credential. I was hired in the Long Beach School system.

I was about thirty-four by that time and I just hated the job. I didn't like being a teacher because I had to follow a curriculum. I liked doing different things. I'd say that was the beginning of really moving off in my own direction. I was always doing unusual things. You could say I was an alternative teacher before I knew what that meant. I'm really proud of myself now when I remember some of the things I did with the kids. But I was always in trouble because of it. I just couldn't do it any other way. I used to come home and cry and I'd say to my husband, "I'm not cut out to be a teacher." But actually I think I was really a very good teacher. I had that sense of how to connect with kids. But my principal at that time said to me, "Have you ever thought about going into recreation?"

My move towards doing therapeutic work with kids all started because the counselor in the school where I was working said to me, "You ought to teach emotionally disturbed children because you would probably be really good at that." I learned that they were starting a new program at the University and that they were getting funds from the government. So I went to observe a class and I said, "I can do this: teaching twelve kids with an aide and you can create your own curriculum!" So that's when I found my calling, working with those kinds of kids. I mean it was hard. It was really hard. But I struggled. I just followed my instinct a lot being with the kids. During the six years I did that kind of work, I won a fellowship and went on to get my Masters degree in Special Education. But then my son Michael got sick and that totally changed my life.

Michael, my middle child, was thirteen and a half when he got sick. He had never been sick. He was my healthiest kid. They thought he had kidney disease, but the doctors kept giving him these different tests and finally diagnosed it: Systemic Lupus. They took him to a famous doctor who wrote a book about Lupus and he confirmed the diagnosis. He told me that Michael had eighteen months to live. I mean, can you imagine being told that? Still to this day, just remembering that is painful. He was pretty sick. He was going to school and he'd have to stay home sometimes because he'd be tired. He also spent a lot of days in the hospital.

Then six months before he died he became very ill and had to go into the hospital and that is when I realized that he was dying. I got depressed and started going to one therapist that I knew. He cried and couldn't deal with it so he wasn't any help. Then I went to this famous therapist from the University and he was totally inept. Then I went to some other guy who decided that I should have medication and I didn't want medication. None of those therapists' approaches helped.

I didn't know what to do until finally a friend of ours said, "I'm going to Esalen. Fritz Perls is going to do some demos and Jim Simkin is doing a group for a week. Why don't you come?" This friend who asked me was a psychiatrist. He was a really good friend of ours, so I thought, "Okay, I'll go." I was really just exhausted. Michael was in the hospital, but he was pretty stable at that point. So I asked my mother-in-law to take care of Sarah, my 11-year-old daughter — my other son, Arthur, was at U.C. Berkeley — and I went to Esalen for a week.

That was my first exposure to Gestalt theory. It was interesting. I was in a group of eighteen people and Jim Simkin, a close associate of Fritz Perls, worked with me.

I mean he really worked with me. He worked with me on my grief, on my anger, on all that stuff. He really worked with me. He wasn't affected by my story. He didn't start crying. He didn't say, "Oh my God, that's terrible!" He was incredible. He kept himself separate, but he had this whole way of just being there, guiding me through the work. Outside the group he was very compassionate the whole time. I became a different person in that group because of that work I did with him.

After Michael died, I decided to go through the Gestalt training program in L.A. and eventually went back to school to get a Masters in Counseling Psychology at Chapman College. I also got my Marriage and Family Therapy license in California and went into private practice.

After my Gestalt training, I began to wonder how I could use the theory and practice of Gestalt therapy in my work with children. I was still working with children in schools and I had groups of children in private practice and I would try all these things out with them. For example, one boy was referred to me for getting into terrible fights at school. He got disciplined at the school but it didn't stop the problem. So I used the "empty chair" with him. I would have him pretend he was speaking with the other boy he had fought with and have him say everything he needed to say to that other boy. I saw him get in touch with lots of feelings that way, not only his anger but also grief and sadness. He ended up coming into my office on his own later and saying to me, "I need to talk with the chair!"

I also did sensory work with boys who were considered hyperactive. I had these twelve-year-old boys standing around with trays of finger-paints. They thought it was weird at first, but when I would tell them, "You have to do it," they relaxed and loved it. They would start talking to each other in ways you can't imagine they knew how to — it centered them enough to do that. After they would finger-paint all over these trays that I borrowed from the cafeteria, then I would take a blank piece of paper and make a block print of their work. They felt so good that they had created such a beautiful thing. All of these experiments were ways that I was trying to help them get better in contact with themselves and with each other.

Later I started working on my Ph.D. and my book evolved out of the writing I did for that and out of the practice I maintained in Long Beach, California. I was also teaching a class in child counseling at Chapman College during that time. The book was finally published in 1978. Altogether I was in private practice for about 25 years, in L.A. and here in Santa Barbara.

I started the summer trainings when I was working in L.A. in the Eighties. For a while, I had two trainings each summer and now I'm down to one, even though I have a waiting list every year. They are just so exhausting. I have been doing the trainings for more than twenty years now and have traveled all over doing other trainings — Europe, South America, South Africa, Australia, Canada, and lots of other places. Now I'm working on my second book. Anyway, that's the story of how my approach evolved.

9

Day Nine: Thursday
Self Nurturing Work

The Demon drawing and Self-Nurturing work

Back in the conference room on Thursday morning, the last full day of the training, Violet greets participants at 9:03 a.m. by asking them with a laugh, "How did you all survive the practicum day?" She also asks them, "Is there anything you would like to say right now." One participant says, in a playful tone, "I'm exhausted." Many participants laugh along with her, but Violet takes her seriously saying, "Yes, this training is an intense experience."

After a bit more discussion, Violet smiles and announces that she forgot to give them each a gift from the day before. She pulls out two boxes of colorful, foam balls, each about the size of a tennis ball, and starts to pass them around the room, telling participants that they should pick their own color. My notes from Tuesday morning describe the scene:

> Now lots of "oohs!" and "aahs!" as balls are passed around. The label on the boxes reads: "Sports relax balls:

prescription for stress." One participant exclaims, "The colors!" as she chooses one and starts squeezing it. They come in four colors — blue, green, yellow and red — and all are very bright with little flowers painted on them. They are a present from Violet. "Thank you SO much!" says more than one participant.

Violet tells the participants that she had ordered these balls from a toy catalogue that specializes in "bulk" sales. She had ordered what she thought was just two of the colorful balls for her office, but she received two boxes instead, each box containing a dozen balls. Most participants enjoy a good laugh with this story. Continuing in the spirit of fun this morning, Violet then holds up a book with a cartoon-like drawing on the cover. The book is entitled Demons, by Randy La Chapelle (1975), and Violet reads part of the preface that states:

> I believe we are far too serious about our demons. They are serious, but that does not mean we have to be so somber in our approach to them. In fact, such an attitude seems to breed more of them.

Violet leafs through and shows the participants the rest of La Chapelle's book which is composed of hand-drawn caricatures of various "demons," including: "The Demon-Who-Thinks-Too-Much," "The Demon of Time," "The Loneliness Demon," and "The Compulsion Demon" (Figure 12).

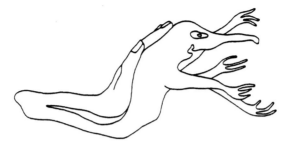

Figure 12: "The Compulsion Demon"

As participants are shown these drawings, there are many remarks and exclamations such as "Oh, I know that one!" and "Yes!" accompanied by knowing laughter and moans. After she finishes the book, Violet announces, "We are going to do a drawing of our own demons!" Without the usual relaxation exercise, Violet gives the following prompt for this drawing:

> So what I'm going to ask you to do, and I know we all have several demons, is think about one of your demons. It could be a part of yourself that you don't like, or that gets in the way sometimes. It doesn't have to be totally horrible and it could be something that's not that bad, but something you still wish you didn't have. It could be one of these or it could be another one you think of. You can use the kind of style from the book, or you could do it any way you want to draw. But you can see that it can be very abstract, just colors and shapes if you want. It doesn't have to be artistic as I keep saying. And it doesn't have to be as clever as his are. Just express your own demon using whatever you want. Then name your

demon, give it a name on your page. So that's what I'd like you to do right now. Get your leaning board, and paper, and crayons and pastels...

After a twelve-minute period in which all the participants focus on the task of bringing their demons to life through color, line, and image, Violet states "What we're going to do is go around the room and share our demons." There is much groaning laughter at this idea and yet one participant raises the ante by suggesting that the demons should be presented in pantomime. Violet says that she thinks this is a "fantastic idea" and adds: "We're going to go around the room. If you're going to work with children, you're going to need to let yourself do this stuff. By now you shouldn't be afraid of pantomiming."

Many participants groan again in a playful way at this news. Before long though, the front of the room becomes a stage for each participant's spoken prologue about their picture accompanied next by pantomimed gestures that enact their "demon" in ways that often bring loud laughter or sympathetic moans from the rest of the participants. Jill, for example, introduces her drawing by saying: "This is the Demon-Who-Gives-Too-Much." She then acts out her Demon drawing by scurrying around the room while frantically reaching into her pockets and pretending to give away everything she owns to the other laughing participants. At one point, she even takes off her shoes and hands them over to another participant as well. After each "performance," everyone spontaneously breaks into applause. After one particularly vigorous round of applause one participant states, "It's strange that we are applauding demons!"

Many people laugh at this comment also, but Violet quickly reframes it by stating, "We are actually applauding the courage to bring our demons up here!"

Adult demonstration:
Beth and the Demon drawing

When all participants have shared their "demons" with the rest of the group, Violet chooses a volunteer with whom to work in front of the room. For the next half hour, Violet works with Beth with her drawing of "the demon-who-can't-let-go-of anything." Beth's drawing has a person in the middle of what look like numerous tethers that extend out octopus-like and cling to lots of different objects all around her. A story emerges out of this work (through Beth talking "as if" she were different aspects of the drawing) of Beth's relationship with her now-deceased mother and how difficult it was for Beth to receive any love from her mother while she was still alive. Beth also describes how hard it has been to let go of any family possessions since her mother died, thus the "demon-who-can't-let-go." Near the end of their work together, at Violet's suggestion, Beth ends up holding one of Violet's large, stuffed Teddy Bears in her lap and talking to it "as if" she were talking to herself as the love-starved child she once was, stroking the bear's fur softly and murmuring to it in low tones.

In the group discussion that follows, Violet describes the kind of work that springs from the Demon drawings as "Self-Nurturing work." An example of this was how Beth talked to the bear "as if" it were herself as a needy child, thereby nurturing the child that "still functions in us, especially under times of stress, usually representing one of our demons." Beth finally leaves the chair next to Violet for her own seat on the floor, but she brings the bear with her that she has been stroking for the duration of the discussion.

Violet goes on to describe that in order to do the Demon drawing and Self-Nurturing work with children, "the relationship has to be strong." A workshop participant asks whether it was intentional that the Demon drawing was used well into the second week, not some time in the first week, for example. Violet agrees that this was an intentional part of the design of the workshop so that participants would be ready for this kind of work.

Violet then tells a case story regarding Justin, a 12-year-old boy with whom she did the Demon drawing and a piece of the Self-Nurturing Work. Violet holds up Justin's Demon drawing, entitled "Mr. Klutz" for the group to see. In Justin's drawing, "Mr. Klutz" is depicted as a grotesque and awkward figure covered with cuts, bruises, blood and bandages from head to toe. Violet says that in a pretend dialogue with Mr. Klutz, Justin stated, "I hate him! I hate how he is always breaking things, crashing into things, dropping things or blowing it at sports!" Justin went on to describe how the cuts and bruises on Mr. Klutz represented all the times he has hurt himself or just plain felt clumsy.

Violet describes how in the session with Justin she picked up a "fairy godmother" puppet and asked the boy, "What might this fairy godmother say that is nice about you?" After some prompting Justin came up with the idea that the fairy godmother could say, "Even if I make a lot of mistakes, at least I try new things a lot."

One of the goals of this type of work, Violet says, is to "help kids understand that it's okay to be nice to themselves." Such demons, she explains, are the result of early negative introjects, or negative messages about the self that were taken in at an early age. Self-Nurturing Work is designed to confront these negative introjects in a very proactive way. This work, she explains, proceeds with a few steps: First, children are helped to "differentiate" the demon by drawing it and speaking "as if" they were the demon. Next, children are asked how long this demon has been around and an effort is made to identify the age of the child when the demon first showed up. Violet then describes how she usually tries to have children "speak to" themselves at that earlier age from the more compassionate voice of a "fairy godmother" type character. In this way, children learn to replace or at least to contradict the negative internal voice with a more supportive and nurturing one.

When Violet has finished describing this process, Beth notes that during her demonstration session with Violet a bit earlier, "the kinesthetic aspect of stroking and talking to the bear was what got the supportive messages across to me even better than someone else's words could have."

Child demonstration: Jessie's work with Violet

After the lunch break, Violet tells the group that she will be giving another demonstration of Self-Nurturing Work when she works with Jessie, a ten-year old, Asian-American girl who is the second child to visit the training (or the third, if you count Ben's "visit" on video tape). Before Jessie arrives, Violet says that she has seen Jessie previously in private therapy sessions and that the circumstances surrounding Jessie coming to therapy are two-fold: 1) her parents are going through a difficult divorce; and, 2) Jessie suffers from an extreme case of eczema, which leaves her skin red, flaky and irritated all over her face, neck and arms. Jessie also suffers from asthma. These physical challenges have limited her ability to connect well with other kids as well as subjected her to harsh treatment from some of them regarding her appearance.

Jessie and her mother arrive at the door of the conference room at 2:00 p.m. and Violet introduces both of them to the group. Jessie's mother joins the group by sitting in an open chair while Violet and Jessie sit on the floor. In front of the two of them are boards loaded with clay and clay working tools. Violet begins her work with Jessie when the two of them pick up their hunks of clay spontaneously and almost simultaneously. Violet first leads Jessie through many of the tactile experiences of working with clay with which workshop participants are now familiar (e.g. squeezing the clay, pinching it, rolling it, etc.).

After about ten minutes of this activity wherein Violet and Jessie play with the clay and talk quietly with each other, Violet gives Jessie a prompt for further Clay work that is related to the Demon-drawing exercise. In doing so, She initiates a piece of Self-Nurturing Work with Jessie by asking her to "make a part of yourself with the clay that you don't like." Jessie looks attentively but somewhat quizzically into Violet's face as Violet makes this request of her. Violet follows her request with, "You know, like the part of you that doesn't like to get out bed in the morning, or something like that."

Jessie quietly says, "Okay," and spends about five minutes calmly patting, smashing, and shaping the clay into a form that she finally presents to Violet. At first it is not clear what Jessie's clay piece represents, and it doesn't help that she and Violet discuss the piece in very hushed tones. At one point though, Jessie states in a louder voice: "This is a bowl of ice-cream that tastes good. I hate it because I'm allergic to so many things and so I can't even eat ice-cream!"

After Jessie says this, Violet takes another piece of clay and says to Jessie, "Pretend that this piece of clay is the you that is allergic to things. What would you like to say to it?" Jessie responds, "Go away!" Violet then asks Jessie if she could hit this piece of clay with the mallet while telling it to "Go away!" Jessie tentatively strikes the clay and Violet asks her, "What is the hardest you can hit it?" Jessie hits the clay somewhat harder while telling Violet how the kids tease her at school and how she has been allergic as long as she can remember.

After a few more minutes in which both Violet and Jessie play with the pieces of clay that are in their hands, Violet tells Jessie that she would like her "do a drawing a picture of how it feels to be allergic to stuff." Jessie proceeds to draw a little red box on her paper that is filled with red and orange dots and says to Violet, "these are my allergies." Jessie then draws a round cage on top of the red box to "trap the allergies." Continuing to draw, she adds a few mice with a blue crayon. Next to this drawing on the same piece of paper, Jessie draws another image similar to the first one but this new image is missing the allergies (Figure 13). The mice, she explains, are fatter in the second drawing because they ate up all the allergies: "These mice can eat anything," says Jessie.

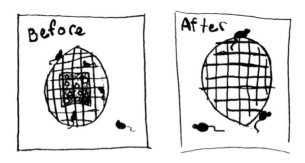

Figure 13: Jessie's Drawings

While Jessie has been drawing, Violet has been asking her questions (e.g. "How many mice are there?"), encouraging her (e.g. "What are the mice going to do?") and laughing with her when Jessie has completed the picture. In this way, the drawing as a finished product is a collaborative effort between the two of them. After Violet asks Jessie if there is anything else she would like to draw or to make out of the clay, Jessie energetically makes a clay pizza. Toward the end of Jessie's time with Violet, I write the following in my notes:

> Even for this very shy and quiet child in a very large adult group, there is little resistance to engaging in these kinds of activities with both clay and drawing. Even in this

crowded setting, Violet elicits "verbal material" about the child's issues from these "non-verbal materials." Now that she is about to leave, Jessie is noticeably more relaxed than when she first came in. Seemingly pleased with herself, she sits back on her knees, rocking and smiling.

After Jessie is thanked by Violet and the participants, she leaves the conference room smiling, with her mother at her side. Violet then asks the participants for comments on "what you observed." One participant mentions that before Jessie did the drawing, she was very hesitant to hit the clay very hard. But just before she left, while she was making a pizza out of clay, "boy was she pounding it, and slapping it, getting out and using all that aggressive energy that you talked about." Another participant notes that although it didn't unfold in exactly the same way as with the Demon drawing examples, Jessie's work in front of the group did start with "something about herself that she didn't like" and ended with the "Self-nurturing actions of those hungry mice who made her allergies go away." Violet affirms that, especially because Jessie was such a quiet child, it seemed important to help her confront her "demon" allergies and to develop a stronger and more affirmative sense of herself in the process.

Toward the end of the day, the conversation turns from Jessie's severe allergies and asthma to other children with more severe disabling conditions. In response to a participant's question regarding if Violet had any specific books that she would read to children with a disability, Violet pulls out a book called Little Tree (Mills, 1992), a metaphorical story about loss and self-acceptance. In the story, which Violet reads aloud to the group, a tree loses half of its limbs in a lightning storm and eventually comes to terms with its loss. After this reading, Violet makes the point that she prefers "metaphorical books" rather than books that deal with specific disabilities.

Show and tell

With just a few minutes remaining before 4:30 p.m., Violet notes that some of the participants asked to share some of the things that they have purchased as therapeutic tools while in Santa Barbara. She smiles and tells the participants that this will therefore be "show and tell" time. For the next few minutes many participants share puppets, sand tray toys, books and musical instruments that they have purchased during their stay in Santa Barbara. Near the end of this sharing, one participant says that sometimes she worries that only people who can afford to have all the "right stuff" can do this kind of therapy. There is a moment of profound silence before Lark tells this story:

> Where I am in practice in New Zealand, I've had the opportunity to work with a number of Maori clients, the native people from my country. In my experience, these native Islanders can't relate to the white-faced puppets at all the other stuff that sometimes fill up our offices. However, I have used Violet's approach in doing some wonderful work with these Maori children using nothing but shells, nuts, and sticks as projective and expressive

tools.

Violet thanks Lark for this story and says she would like to emphasize that "it's the approach, not the stuff" that is important in her work. She goes on to give an example of how she once did sand tray work on a public beach with a colleague, just to try it out. They both used anything from the beach — dried sea weed, feathers, rocks, shells, bits of garbage, etc. — to "create a scene in the sand." Violet says that one interesting result of doing a sand tray scene in that context was how they were able to spread out the placement of the objects that they chose for their "sand tray scene." On the expanse of beach, they placed some objects closer together and some very far apart in order to represent the closeness or distance they felt in some of their most important relationships. After a few more moments of discussion on this creative approach to "minimalist therapy," as one participant describes it, Violet closes the day at 4:45 p.m. She states: "We have had a long and full day. I am sad to say that tomorrow will be our last day, but it will be a good one. Even though it's only a half-day, I have a full agenda so please be on time."

Reflective notes for day nine

This will be my last set of reflective notes for the two-week intensive summer training. At the end of the day on Friday, Violet will ask each of the participants to make their own closing remarks regarding the training and the eloquence of their comments will serve as an appropriate way to reflect on the meaning and value of not only the last day of the training, but of

Violet's training as a whole.

In this set of reflective notes, I present a set of summary tables in which the four-step sequence of each of the Therapeutic Experiences demonstrated in the training is outlined. In the introductory comments for these summary tables, I offer my views on what this type of analysis of Violet's approach can provide us, as well as what it cannot provide us.

Introduction to the summary tables

Violet's work with Jessie on Thursday afternoon represents the last piece of work with either an adult or a child that Violet will demonstrate for the participants. Over the past nine days, Violet has worked with six adult volunteers and two child guests in front of the other participants. All of these demonstration sessions, though differing in form and content, share much in common. Her last demonstration session with Jessie focused on the particulars of doing Self-Nurturing Work with children. Even with this particular focus, Violet's work with Jessie reflected the underlying, four-step structure of her approach that I have described in the reflective notes of previous chapters.

After making contact with Jessie and working for a few minutes to "build the relationship," Violet gave Jessie prompts to conjure images and to use her senses to express those images (e.g. "make a part of yourself with the clay that you don't like" and "move to drawing a picture of how it feels to be allergic to stuff"). Violet also engaged with Jessie in long stretches of dialogue that were dedicated to what Violet has previously described as "building the story or metaphor" and to making sense of Jessie's experience with her allergies: "Pretend that this piece of clay is the you that is allergic to things. What would you like to say to it?" "How many mice are there?" "What are the mice going to do?"

This particular example of Violet's approach to doing Self-Nurturing Work also reflects the basic structure of her work that we have seen in each of the Therapeutic Experiences demonstrated throughout the training. Regardless of the materials Violet uses (e.g. clay, drawings, sand tray scenes, etc.) or the particular topic that she addresses (e.g. a Safe Place, an Anger drawing, or Self-Nurturing work) the same four-step sequence serves as the foundation for her therapeutic approach, whether she is working with a child or an adult.

This four-step sequence is certainly not performed in a "lock step" manner, nor is it something that Violet consciously thinks about using and/or building upon. Before I did this analysis of her work, in fact, Violet never realized there was a consistency to her work across all the media with which she works. Although she agrees with the analysis I have done of her work, she says she does not think consciously about the steps I have described when she is working: "I'm focusing on the relationship, on contact, and on where the work is going," she says.

Of course, Violet is already a master of her own approach, so why should she need to think about it? Instead of being consciously employed, the four-step sequence seems more like a set of already-memorized chords upon which Violet improvises, in much the same way that a jazz musician might work. Like any great jazz artist, Violet has an intuitive understanding of how to work with the form: when to add something, when to be quiet and listen, when to start something new, and when to revisit an important theme. Also like any great jazz musician, the true artistry of Violet's work cannot be captured by a simple analysis of the chords she is playing, or, in her case, of the four-steps she uses in her work.

The four-step structural analysis I have been presenting in these chapters, therefore, is dangerously close to reducing the complexity and subtlety of Violet's work to a few over-simplified chords. My main concern with providing such a "reductionist" analysis is that those interested in learning Violet's approach would simply reproduce this four-step sequence without taking into consideration the broader context and subtlety of her approach. One doesn't become a jazz musician by learning to play a few major-seventh chords, and one doesn't come close to modeling a complex approach to therapy like Violet's without having a deep appreciation for what lies at the heart of her work.

What lies at the heart of Violet's work is complex and manifold: her rootedness in Gestalt therapy theory; her fundamental and moment-to-moment respect for the I/thou relationship; her ability to give her clients the freedom of having "no expectations" for their work with her; her willingness to engage deeply and openly in play; and her basic faith in the processes of contact and organismic self-regulation that allows her to "let the work unfold" instead of anxiously pushing for something to happen.

Violet's work is more art than technique. By this I mean that she has artfully woven rich threads from Gestalt therapy theory, from child development theory, and from the expressive arts themselves to create her own approach to doing therapy with children. In doing so, she has created a vivid tapestry that must be looked at as a whole if is to be understood and appreciated. To pull out and separate any particular threads might ruin the whole piece. Moreover, it is important to note that Violet has been very creative in the way she both developed and is still adapting her approach. In other words, she has brought a lot of her own personality to her work and continues to do so. If anything, then, a central lesson to Violet's approach is that it is important to bring your own personality, style and creativity to this difficult work and not simply follow a cook-book style recipe for doing therapy.

This being said, I also believe that there is value in looking at and trying to understand the parts, the steps, the general sequence, and the basic moves upon which Violet builds her work. Charlie Parker's Jazz solos have been transcribed note-for-note and now provide up-and-coming saxophonists with a "window" on his work. Without the opportunity for such close study of a mentor's work, another musician can never hope gain and equal level of fluency in the rich idiom that is jazz music.

It is in this spirit of offering a "window" into Violet's work that I present the summary analysis provided in the following tables. In these tables, I have included mini-transcripts of each demonstration session that Violet offered during the training. These tables and mini-transcripts are presented as evidence of Violet's moves through the basic four-step sequence across different Therapeutic Experiences (i.e. Clay work, Sand Tray work, etc). These mini-transcripts are not meant to serve as a recipe for how to do the Therapeutic Experiences from which they are taken. Instead, they are meant to provide a window into Violet's work by showing a fundamental structure that underlies her flexible artistry. Because Violet herself cannot be duplicated, it is my hope that this way of looking at her work can serve two purposes: 1) it can be used as a starting point to understand the greater complexity of her approach; and, 2) it might be used as a kind of template from which we might be able to creatively build upon and adapt her approach to our own needs, settings, and styles.

Violet working with children and adolescents in the training

In Table 8 below, I show the four-step sequence of Violet's approach as it unfolded in her demonstration sessions with children and adolescents in the training. I have included Violet's work with Ben from the videotape example she showed as well as her work with Elisa and Jessie during their actual visits to the training. In Column A of Table 8, I show Violet's prompts regarding imagination and fantasy that begin the Therapeutic Experiences. In Columns B, C, and D, I have included the children's verbal and non-verbal responses to the remaining three steps in the sequence.

In all three cases presented in Table 8, Violet's work with the child is certainly fluid and responsive to the relevant themes that emerge in the "here and now." However, Violet can also be seen leading the child down a familiar path that helps the child move through the challenging emotional terrain of the issues that arise. Near the tope of each of the columns that represent the four-step sequence, I have added shorthand references for the type of prompt that Violet might use to help the child engage in each step of the therapeutic process (i.e. "imagine it", "make it", "be it", and "does it fit?").

In these examples, one can see Violet helping the child to engage the imaginal and sensory realms of experience to facilitate a process of creating rich, metaphoric and projective images that the children then relate to their own experience. A whale, a tree, and a bowl of ice cream come to represent significant aspects of the children's lives. These images help Violet to build a relationship with and to learn about the children with whom she is working. The images also lead to the creation of a "conversation piece" that facilitates a way of talking about the childrens' experience in both concrete and metaphoric ways.

Table 8: Therapeutic Experiences with Children and Adolescents

Types of Therapeutic Experiences ←	Parts of the Therapeutic Experience ↓			
	a. Imaginary Experience "imagine it"	b. Sensory Experience "make it"	c. Metaphoric/ Narrative Articulation "be it"	d. Sense-making Application "does it fit?"
1 Ben and Clay work	Violet: "with your eyes closed, make something."	Ben forms a whale out of the clay.	Ben: "I'm a hale...I like to swim...I like to go underwater."	Ben: "during the summer I basically live in the water."
2 Elisa and drawings	Violet: "draw a picture of that feeling you have missing them."	Elisa draws a tree with a "part cut out," with pastels.	Elisa: "If you think of a tree with its branches and stuff."	Elisa: "If I'd lived with him longer, he would have been like the whole tree."
3 Jessie and Self-nurturing work	Violet: "make a part of yourself with the clay that you don't like."	Jessie uses clay to make a bowl of ice cream.	Jessie: "This is a bowl of ice-cream that tastes good."	Jessie: "I hate it because I'm allergic to so many things and so I can't even eat ice-cream!'"

Violet working with adults in the training

In Table 9 below, I show mini-transcripts from each of the Therapeutic Experiences that Violet demonstrated with a volunteer in front of the rest of the participants during the first week of the training. As in Table 8 above, Violet's prompt for some type of fantasy or imaginary experience in Column A begins a movement into and through the other steps of the Therapeutic Experience that follow. In Column B, the varied sensory expressions explored during the first week of the training are identified, including pastels, clay, and musical instruments. The seemingly random set of metaphors listed in Column C (a window, a bed, a baseball mitt, etc...) resolve in each case into some kind of personal sense-making in Column D where the statements uttered by the volunteers are listed.

In the Table 10 below, I include an analysis of the three examples of Therapeutic Experiences from the second week of the training. Like the examples from the first week, each of these three examples provides clear evidence of the four-step sequence of Violet's approach, though the expressive media vary widely.

In all three of the tables presented above, I think it is important to note the deep and personal explorations represented in these demonstration sessions that took place in front of 23 other participants. There are a number of possible explanations for how such personal openness occurs in such a public setting. First, many participants had the training recommended to them by a friend or acquaintance and they were therefore ready and perhaps even hungry for this type of rich, experiential learning environment. Second, as I noted early in the reflective notes of Chapters 2 and 3, Violet sets a safe tone early on in the training and only gradually raises the level of personal risk that the participants are asked to take. In this way, the sense of both safety and "groupness" that develops in the training corresponds with the amount of risk and challenge presented to individuals within the group as the days pass.

A third reason for this level of openness seems to have something to do with something I've thought of as the "summer camp" phenomena. That is, the participants are able to share more openly with each other precisely because they know their time together is limited. Since participants come from around the world, there is little chance that they will bump into each other again unless they make an effort to do so (and many do keep in touch after the training ends). This combined sense of both intimacy and anonymity seems to offer the participants an opportunity to not only take risks in front of others, but also to try out new ways of being with others (i.e. being more open, more emotionally vulnerable, etc.). In the same way that teen-agers at a two-week summer camp are able to "stretch their wings" away from the familiar constraints of family and friends, the participants in the training seem to relish the opportunity to push against their own boundaries and limitations as therapists in training as well as evolving individuals in this safe place that Violet's training represents. These themes of safety, personal risk-taking, and growth will be repeatedly highlighted by the participants during tomorrow's closing exercises.

From a curricular perspective, Thursday is the last day of the training for the participants. Tomorrow, Violet will not discuss any new information or topics regarding the practice of doing therapeutic work with children and adolescents. Instead, through various closing activities and exercises, Friday will serve as a way for the participants to reflect on their experience in the training over these past two weeks and share their thoughts and feelings to others in the group. As stated at the outset of this week's reflective notes, these eloquent comments — the voices of the participants themselves — will serve as the final set of reflective notes.

3	**Wednesday** **Clay** **Work**	Violet: "With your eyes closed, now that your clay has a lot of your energy in it, I'd like you to begin to form something"	Sabina: works with clay	Sabina: "I'm a baseball mitt. I catch things and I'm big"	Sabina: "which fits for me right now, I'm big and I hate it"
4	**Thursday** **Anger** **Drawing**	Violet: "find a time when something happened that made you feel angry"	Candice: draws with pastels, crayons	Candice: "This is me and my older brother and sister"	Candice: "you [uncle] were so awful to us all"
5	**Friday** **Music** **Process**	Violet: "experiment with them to hear the sounds they make"	Isabel: plays multiple musical instruments	Isabel: "Okay, let's play crazy"	Isabel: "I feel calm and good, not frenzied at all"

Table 9: Therapeutic Experiences with Adults, Week One

Types of Therapeutic Experiences ◀	Parts of the Therapeutic Experience	a. Imaginary Experience "Imagine it"	b. Sensory Experience ▼ "Make it"	c. Metaphoric/ Narrative Articulation "Be it"	d. Sense-making Application "Does it fit?"
1	Monday House, Tree, Person Drawing	Violet: "draw some scene that has a house, a tree and a person"	Elizabeth: draws with pastels, crayons	Violet: "This drawing, with all these large windows, tells me that you are a very open person"	Elizabeth: "This is true, but there are times when I feel very open, and other times when I do not"
2	Tuesday Safe Place drawing	Violet: "I want you to imagine that you can go to a safe place"	Lydia: draws with pastels, crayons	Lydia: "I'm this bed... cushioned and supportive"	Lydia: "maybe its Sonia... she's always there for me"

7	Tuesday **Medicine Cards**	Violet: "pick three cards to represent how you are, were, and will be"	Lark picks a butterfly card, a mouse card, and an owl card	Lark: "I just recognized what the butterfly does. It sort of lives its life really quickly"	Lark: "I guess I'm a bit... like the butterfly"
8	Thursday **Demon Drawing**	Violet: "think about one of your demons"	Beth: draws with pastels, crayons	Beth: "I'm the demon who can't let go of anything"	Beth: "its been so hard to let go of anything since my mother died"

Table 10: Therapeutic Experiences with Adults, Week Two

Types of Therapeutic Experiences	Parts of the Therapeutic Experience	a. Imaginary Experience "Imagine it"	b. Sensory Experience "Make it"	c. Metaphoric/ Narrative Articulation "Be it"	d. Sense-making Application "Does it fit?"
6 Monday Sand Tray Work		Violet: "I would like you to make a scene in the sand...It can be real or imaginary or like a dream"	Nicholas makes a sand tray scene which includes a white boat with a broken mast	Nicholas: "I am the boat, and I have a mast here that is not standing up...I need to get repaired"	Nicholas: "I need to take better care of myself, take more time for myself...Get repaired so I can continue on the journey"

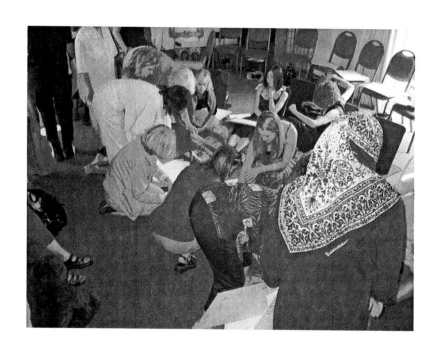

10

Day Ten: Friday
Closing Activities

"Draw your experience here"

One of the first things that happens on Friday morning, this last day of the training, is a spontaneous "group picture" where more than ten of the participant's cameras are used to take photographs of the whole group gathered together tightly in front of the room with Violet. A funny thing happens just after this "photo op" when one participant says, "Oh, somebody forgot their camera..." as she picks up my hand-held tape recorder from the chair next to her and, speaking loudly into the tape, says, "Let's see, there's no name on it. Oh! It's the tape recorder! I really thought it was a camera!"

After the laughter has receded, I use this moment as an opportunity to thank the participants for their willingness to be part of my research project on Violet's methods of training and therapy. I also gratefully think to myself that, other than this minor incident, my methods and technologies involved in documenting this training have become mostly invisible. These methods have included my note-taking, audio-recording, and occasionally video recording over the past two-weeks. I brought the video camera in only during the second week of the training so that it wouldn't be so intrusive for the participants as they were still "settling into" the experience during the first week. I audio-taped from the first day, after first securing the participants permission to do so. In the explanation of my project, I told the participants that the focus of the study was on Violet and her training methods and that participants could let me know if anything they were personally involved during the training was "off limits." Each of the participants signed a release form that gave me permission to use all that I have gathered in anonymous ways to write up this book. In fact, many of the participants told me the documentation of Violet's training was so important that I should get in touch with them after the training if there was anything they could do to help my work along.

Immediately following the group photos, Violet says, "All right, we're going to do a drawing, if you didn't know that." The drawing materials have once again been spread out in the middle of the floor of the room just as they were on the first morning of the training two weeks ago. In this way, the training ends in much the same way that it started, with the participants about to get their hands smudged by pastels as they silently work to depict their own particular images that come to mind after Violet gives them a prompt.

Before detailing Violet's prompt for this last drawing, I would like to highlight something about the first and the last drawings of the training. In the reflective notes at the end of the last chapter, I included a table of all the Therapeutic Experiences from the training. In that table I chose not to include either the very first drawing of the training (which was entitled "Draw yourself as a child") or this last drawing that the participants will make (which is entitled "Draw your experience here"). I excluded these two drawings from the Summary Tables in Chapter 9 for the reason that Violet does not intend for either of them to be examples of Therapeutic Experiences that she would regularly use with children. Since the first and the last drawing are intended primarily for the adult participants to first become engaged in the training and then to process the end of their experience in the training, Violet does not give examples of how she would use these two drawings with children in her practice.

That being said, Violet does tell the participants just before giving this last prompt that she often uses a similar type of "closing activity" to help a child process either the end of a significant life-event or the child's time with Violet in therapy. Additionally, it is also true that the Violet's prompt for the last drawing reflects the same four-step sequence that all the other Therapeutic Experiences have included. As transcribed below, the first paragraph of the Violet's prompt guides the participants through a couple of short relaxation exercises. In the second paragraph, she engages their imagination before asking them, in the third paragraph to draw that image on paper with the pastels and the crayons. Later, these images will serve as a basis of rich metaphoric and narrative meaning by which the participants will work to "make sense" of their time here in the training. In this way, I could have included this last drawing in the table in yesterday's reflective notes because it does have the same structure as the others. I chose not to, however, because it serves a different function in the training, with the focus being on the workshop participants themselves and not on the children or adolescents with whom they work.

When the participants have settled down on this early Friday morning, forming a circle around the room in their chairs and on the floor, Violet gives the following prompt for this last drawing of the training:

> What I'd like you to do is get into a relaxed position. And close your eyes. Go inside yourself. Notice how you are feeling inside your body. Your excitement or anything else you are feeling. Often when we're excited, we forget to breath, so let's take some deep breaths [sounds of inhaling and exhaling]. And I'm going to make the sound, and listen to the sound as long as you can (Violet rings the chime twice).
>
> I want you to think about the two weeks that you've been here. Think about the two weeks from the time you arrived. And remember what it was like when you first came into the room and didn't know anybody. Or you were worried about the language. And how everything evolved, the people you began to get to know and the things that we did, and your experiences in Santa Barbara. Just kind of run through that (10 second pause).
>
> And what I'm going to ask you to draw is something that relates to these two weeks. Maybe one thing has

stood out for you and you'd like to draw that, or maybe two or three things. Something that represents your experience here...again it could be in just lines, colors, or shapes. Whatever you want to draw. Don't worry about doing something wonderful and right. Just draw something that stood out for you. Or however you want to draw your experience here (25 second pause). And anytime you are ready, just begin drawing...

For a number of minutes there is an almost complete silence in the room as the participants intently focus on their drawings. These prolonged moments of silence have become a norm, a kind of ritual, within this group. Participants have now come to expect and seem to welcome this opportunity to silently and individually create something in the presence of the larger group. This is reflected in the calm but serious way that the participants use these minutes. There is obviously no rush to finish these final drawings. When individual participants have finished their drawings, they sit patiently waiting for all the others to finish, without moving around or talking. Perhaps especially today, these moments are savored, as it is clear that this last drawing is a way of saying goodbye to the group and the experiences everyone has had here.

Participant comments

After about ten minutes when everyone seems to have come close to completing their drawings, Violet says that she would like for each person, in no particular order, to share with the group what they have drawn and whatever comments they may have. Given the strong feelings shared by the participants during the next half hour, the training has obviously been quite a moving experience for most involved. Many participants express sadness at leaving this group in which they have shared so many of their intimate life details in the service of becoming better able to facilitate the therapeutic process with children and adolescents. These drawings and the comments that spring from them become a kind of evaluation of the participant's experience over the past two weeks. I have transcribed the comments of eleven participants that represent many of the themes and metaphors shared by most others in the training. Given Violet's focus on using imaginative and visual metaphors as a way of helping children "make sense" of their experiences, it is interesting to note the way that most of the adult participants use one or more metaphors to describe their own experience in the training:

> Peggy: The most important thing for me was the focus. To see the importance of the moment and to expand on it. Almost like this sun I have drawn. Also I tried to put a lot of colors in it, different colors in it, because of the richness, and the variety of this experience, and the many different people here that added to it.

> Candice: It felt wonderful to draw. The image that came was that of all of us sitting around the fire, alike, but very different. And the beach, and the water,

and the safety of the container. And the warmth of the sun. It struck me as a place where we can get together and tell each other our stories, it almost felt like it was from a very primitive time when people were very frightened of the wolves and the monsters outside so they would stay by the fire and comfort each other. I felt very much the same way here. Sitting around the fire of the moment and like Peggy said, the focus. Thank you all.

Joan: This is a picture of two people working with the clay. And they're surrounded by the unspoken things that are happening and the things that are coming out of the clay. I really learned about play, and using play, and more generally about expressive media.

Mary: There's so much wisdom in the universe. But there are very few people who know how to interpret that wisdom for others. In my drawing, each of us are stars. And the stars look so little from so far away. But the closer we get the brighter that star gets. And so I thank each of you. To know that all of us are stars and that we have so much to offer to the children that we go back to and that we work with. Because that wisdom has been interpreted for us by Violet.

Sheri: An important part for me has been to feel really safe. It's been awhile since I felt safe. I think that helped me grow more here than I have in awhile. That's been very important, to feel safe.

Camille: I believe in metaphors with all my heart. And when you offered the metaphor of the "Little Tree," I thought how that's something that I could use with every child that I work with. Or every person that I've ever met. That we are trees, and that there are times when storms come into life. And what you've given to me, Violet, is that you've shown me times that I think all of us have experienced, where certain limbs have been broken off. When you have had a son die, and when you were burned by boiling water, and how resilient your tree is. I know that there are so many other things that have broken. And to me you set an example that a tree can still flourish, and still have beauty and still go through the seasons and the changes. And for me... (long pause, she begins to cry and then references her own previously-mentioned, pending divorce)... I've just been through a scare, and I have so much faith that the tree will be there. And that there's a richness and a life in having some broken limbs.

Liz: What I took from this is probably not what you

wanted me to get from this. But I love working with kids, and love the idea of learning more about that. But as I watched everybody work, I decided that I'm going to do play therapy with adults! I don't think there should be any other kind of therapy. I think we are wasting our time until we go back and pick up that child piece. And the only way you could do it is to create a safe place, as Violet has done here, and go with it. My whole way I'm going to work from now on is different. So thank you for that. It feels good.

Juan Carlos: I drew a picture of a pier, like the one here in Santa Barbara. I like piers. They are a metaphor of a place to make contact with the world. On the pier Violet is sitting and working with a child. To me this was the best experience. In my country, we would never have been able to bring a child into this training. To see you work with children was wonderful because it helped me get in touch with me, with my own child inside me, as well as the children I work with.

Isabel: I'm aware of the fullness that I feel and the richness of this experience that Violet and each and every one of you has given to me. And the joy of this serious business of the work we do. And how much I've received and now it's my turn to try and pass it on.

Melanie: I feel that knowledge and stories go together so much. That the stories give knowledge and the knowledge is supported by the stories. Each of your stories has done this for me, and the stories that Violet shared.

Lindsey: I came in feeling self-contained. And having been with all of you for two weeks, I discovered that you have become my container. I have tremendous gratitude as well as great pride. I told my supervisor that I know the way I need to learn. I need to be somewhere for two weeks and in an intensive learning community. And my supervisor is a psychiatrist and quite traditional. I had no idea what his response would be. And his response was "Good for you for knowing how you learn." Thank you for giving me a model that I can conceptualize. The experiential part is, well, how I've grown. And the model is how I tell my head how the experiential part makes sense.

Closing the training

As the comments from participants come to a close, Violet says she would like to read a book to the group. She then reads Dr. Seuss' "Oh, The Places You'll Go!" (Seuss, 1990) which contains references to graduating and marching off into the world with a head full of steam, as well as references to the inevitable disappointments that each person faces in life.

After this reading, Violet makes some announcements about forms certain participants need in order to get continuing education credits for participating in this training (credits are available for California Marriage and Family Therapists and Psychologists). She also provides information about future workshops, including an advanced training that happens each year on President's weekend in February in Santa Barbara.

With all the participants smiling, laughing and humming "Pomp and Circumstance" in the background, Violet then ceremoniously hands out the certificates which allow the participants to receive credit hours toward their respective licenses. Many more photos are taken as each participant receives both a certificate and a hug from Violet.

Violet then reads another children's book to the participants. This one is called "Fairy Went A-Marketing" (Fyleman, 1992) and tells the story of a fairy who both acquires new and wonderful things ("she bought a winter gown all stitched about with gossamer and lined with thistle down"), but who also lets each of those things go or gives them away to someone else ("then she gave it to a frog to keep him warm at night"). After she has finished reading the book, Violet simply says, "This is a book about letting go." She then adds, "Since this particular group will never be together again in the same way, if there is anything anyone would like to say to someone else in the group, now is the time." For the next few minutes some heartfelt appreciations and comments are shared in the group, not only directed toward Violet, but also towards many of the other folks in the room. For example, one participant from California thanks all those in the group who came from different states and different countries and who added so much. She finishes with, "It really would not have been as rich an experience for me if you all hadn't been here."

After all such comments have come to a close, Violet refers to the musical instruments which have been spread out on the floor once again, and asks each participant to choose one instrument to play in a "closing exercise". After the clatter and cacophony of the participants choosing their instrument has subsided, Violet explains the exercise: she will start playing, to be followed after a few moments by the person sitting next to her. Then the two of them will play together for a few moments before being joined by the third participant. This progression will continue until everyone in the large circle around the room is playing together. Violet explains that at some point she will stop playing her instrument, to be followed after a few moments by the person sitting next to her. Eventually, only the last person in the circle will be playing alone, and when that person finishes, the whole piece will be ended.

A lot of noise erupts in the room as each participant joins the "playing circle," and soon Violet begins to move around the room dancing, followed by others. There is some hollering and whooping, punctuated by big drum sounds and a few folks banging on each other's instruments. Eventually, Violet sits back down and stops playing and soon the contagion of silenced instruments spreads until there is just one lonely whistle mournfully playing by itself at the end.

After this raucously non-verbal, unmelodious but fun closing exercise, there is a spontaneous and silent group circle formed for a few moments, with the participants wrapping their arms around one another, some crying softly. Finally, the day and the training end with lots of individual hugs and best wishes for safe journeys home.

Eventually, as the room empties, Violet and some helpers are left to sort, organize, remove, and load into cars all that remains: the bags of leftover clay, the clay tools, the boxes of musical instruments, the containers of pastels and crayons, the pads of drawing paper, the boxes of books, the bags of puppets, and some random sand-tray toys that are found under a pillow in the corner of the room. All of these objects now lie inert and lifeless, having only come to life when they were invested with so much energy, emotion, and meaning over the past ten days by the participants who now head for home.

11

Epilogue

Clay, Culture, and Age:
The Oaklander Approach in
South Africa

Introduction

As I mentioned in the introduction to this book, Windows to our
Children (Oaklander, 1978) is presently published or in the
process of being published in eleven languages – English,
Spanish, Portuguese, Italian, Serbo-Croatian, Croatian, Russian,
Chinese, Hebrew, Korean, and German. One result of these
international publications of her book is that Violet has been
regularly invited to do workshops or present keynotes in
countries around the world.

Another consequence of this international popularity is that
Violet has trained individuals in the U.S. or abroad who have
then trained others in their own country in the "Oaklander
approach." Because of this, there are places around the world
that have a surprising number of professionals who are both

aware of and trained in Violet's methods. Such is the case in South Africa, where one university professor from Johannesburg, having trained with Violet in Santa Barbara in the early nineties, returned home to train others. Years later, this same university professor invited Violet to come to South Africa to present at three workshops in three different cities.

In March, 2000, I accompanied Violet during her three South African trainings in Pretoria, Bloemfontein, and Cape Town. I traveled with Violet as an assistant in the trainings, but also as a researcher interested in exploring the cross-cultural relevance of her work. Essentially, my question was the same as it had been at the outset of my dissertation studies: I was curious to know what it was about Violet's work that appealed to practitioners in so many diverse cultural settings around the globe. In this chapter I report what I learned from South African child therapists and counselors about their experiences using the "Oaklander approach" in various cross-cultural settings.

First I give an overview of the content of the two-day workshops. Second, I highlight one South African woman's experience with the Clay work in much the same way that I highlighted Sabina's Clay work with Violet in Chapter Three. Third, I present seven cross-culturally relevant themes relating to Violet's approach that emerged from interviews of participants in small, lunch-time focus groups in the three cities that we visited. Lastly, I offer some concluding remarks for both the chapter and the book as a whole.

Overview of the South African workshops

As with most of Violet's shorter workshops and longer trainings that I have attended (over 20 in the past ten years), the three trainings in South Africa in March and April of 2000 were filled to capacity with therapists, social workers, teachers and academics. In Pretoria, nearly 300 participants came from all over the northeastern part of South Africa to attend the two-day training. Workshop organizers had expected 75 participants to enroll and were forced to change the venue of the workshop to a larger hall at the last minute because of the number of registrations. Each of the other two workshops in Bloemfontein and Cape Town were also full to overflowing with interested participants.

On the first day of each two-day workshop, Violet gave an overview of her working model with children and her ideas as to what brings children into therapy. These "mini-lectures" covered much of the same content that Violet presented during the first two days of her summer training (i.e. Chapters One and Two of this book). Violet then led the South African participants through a series of experiential drawing activities — including the Safe Place drawing as described in Chapter Two. During the last part of the afternoon she answered questions, heard comments, and engaged in dialogue with the workshop participants, sometimes through a translator.

On the morning of the second day of each South African workshop, participants had a "hands on" experience with Clay work. They arrived at their seats to find little plastic tubs filled with clay. This cream-colored clay had been collected from a streambed on the workshop organizer's property near Cape Town. Unlike the store-bought clay that Violet uses in the summer trainings, this natural South African clay was "unfiltered" and therefore contained bits of tiny rocks and sticks that were embedded in the otherwise smooth texture.

Soon after the participants arrived on the second day of the training, Violet had them open up their little tubs of clay and empty the contents onto the paper plates that were also provided for them. As she did in the summer training, Violet addressed concerns that clay is a messy and difficult material with which to work. Along with the comments that Violet had shared with the summer training participants, Violet also shared the following bits of information in the South African workshops:

I don't even take off my jewelry! You can put it on your face and give yourself a facial! It's a natural material. It comes out of the ground. In fact, this clay we are using today is from the banks of a stream that is in a farm here in South Africa. And clay is the most *versatile* of all the materials we use. You can do more with clay than with anything else.

After leading the workshop participants through both of the clay exercises that were outlined in Chapter Three (i.e. "getting to know the clay" and "making something with your eyes closed"), Violet then did a very brief demonstration session with a participant in the front of the auditorium. This demonstration session was intended to give the participants an idea of what to do with their own clay pieces when they shared what they had created with each other in small groups of three.

In each of the South African workshops, I also participated in the two clay exercises along with the participants in case I was needed to complete a group. In Cape Town, as the participants began grouping up, I was approached by Sima, a Black South African woman from Durban, who needed a partner. I learned that Sima was a mother of four and that she volunteered her time at a local Catholic church to work on weekends with children whose parents had died in the AIDS epidemic. I also learned that Sima was not a professionally-trained therapist, yet the church had paid her way so that she could come to the workshop. South Africa faces such complex social problems, as I came to understand during our stay there, that the efforts of all those willing to help are gratefully accepted. Sima knew I was working on a book about Violet's methods and agreed to my request that I tape record our work together.

Adult demonstration: Working with Sima

As she did in her summer training, Violet suggested that the small groups of participants do the following things with the pieces of clay that they had just created: First she asked the participants to alternate in roles of therapist, client, and observer. Then she encouraged the person in the role of the client to speak "as if" they were the object they had made, to "be the object" and give it a voice that was richly descriptive and detailed. Once the client had done this, the next task was to see if anything they had said made sense for their own lives. These prompts, following the initial imaginative and sensory aspects of the Clay work, align with the four-step sequence outlined in previous chapters.

In the following transcript, Sima shares her clay piece with me while I take on the role of therapist. Sima first describes some qualities of the clay "tennis ball" that she has created. She then poignantly identifies with some of the aspects of this object without any prompting from me — similarly to the way Sabina did with her clay "baseball mitt" in Chapter Three. Please note that my shorter interjections are placed in brackets within Sima's statements in the text below:

Peter: So, what did you make with the clay, Sima?

Sima: First I could mention that I started making something like a stone – a grinding stone [Ah ha] – like the kind we use to grind mealies...

Peter: Like corn? Sort of like corn?

Sima: Yeah, mealies is corn. So it broke...

Peter: It broke?

Sima: (laughing) Yeah...So I decided to make a ball – a tennis ball, okay? So it's a tennis ball. And after doing that, actually I like it! (laughs). Yeah...

Peter: So, could you speak as if you were that tennis ball?

Sima: Yeah...I'm a tennis ball. Um, I know that I am useful to a lot of people. They can play with it. They bounce it from here to there. But I think I don't feel *owned* by anybody. And I also think that as a ball I can't... just stand here. I usually roll over. So I need something to stand on [Mmm] in order not to roll off into places where I don't want to be (pause). Although I'm useful, and I feel I'm useful, sometimes I feel...that (pause) I'm being used [Mmm]. And being used, I can't really stand for myself (pause). Like when I'm rolling off into a place where perhaps I couldn't be found. Perhaps I could be found if somebody was interested in looking for me, they can find me. But if he's not interested, he can, you know, take another ball [Hmm]. So, that's how I feel as a ball and as a tennis ball. I can relate to this tennis ball, as a person [Uh huh]. Because sometimes, as a woman, you have to...Sometimes you find yourself in situations where you don't feel, where we feel that we don't have roots, or we don't have a stand. Or something like that. Not because you are not *able* to do that, but because you are a woman. And (long pause)...Mmm... yeah, I think that's it (laughs).

Peter: That's a very rich metaphor, isn't it?

Sima: Yeah, for myself. Yeah...(long pause, 10 seconds). For instance this morning, I...I was sitting at a table in the conference center...(voice shaking, tears welling up, long pause, 40 seconds)... [Hmm]...(two deep exhalations)...and a white gentleman came up to me and said that this was his place...and I had to move (long pause).

Peter: Hmm...(deep sigh)...So even this morning...

Sima: So, yes. So afterwards he came in to apologize [Mm mm]. He didn't hurt me that much when he said I must move. But after thinking about this, [Hmm] I think he was manipulating me...And that hurts.

Peter: Sorry?

Sima: That hurts.

Peter: And that hurts. (long pause)...I feel some...frustration or even anger myself when you tell me that. I'm sorry that happened to you.

Sima: (long pause, crying softly, sniffles) Mm mm, I think I felt he apologized, and I listened to that apology [Mm mm]. But the feeling was there [Mm mm]. So sometimes you're not responsible for feelings. You can *think* that it was all right [Mmm], but the feeling is there...So, I thought he was just on some (puts fingers to head, imitating a bull's horns)...like a bull...

Peter: Like a bull...

Sima: (laughs)...Aaaghh! (more laughing). Okay, I'm finished.

Peter: You know, I hope this isn't inappropriate, but I know that...it seems like that little example is an example of what the country is still dealing with in many ways [Mmm]. That sense of apology and people not being pushed around any more. I mean it's such a big issue here – I've been aware of that. We're dealing with it in the U.S. also. (Sigh, pause)...Would you like to stop, or do you have anything else you'd like to say?

Sima: Yeah. I'll just say that although I'm a ball, sometimes even a ball can have a stand (laughs). So, I can usually *bounce* back! (laughs) That's the positive side! I can always bounce back (more laughing). I think it's this way.

Peter: Mmm... Sima, thank you for being willing to share your piece.

I chose to show this piece of work with Sima for three reasons. The first reason is that I thought it was important to show an example of the Oaklander approach being facilitated by someone other than Violet. This is important because, as seen in Sima's work with me, it shows that the Oaklander approach in someone else's hands can still be effective and helpful. Though I make no claims of being able to facilitate this kind of work as effectively as Violet does, I think that Violet's relational and structural approach — upon which I was modeling my work with Sima — helped Sima bring important issues to the foreground for her to address. My point is that, while it is important to honor Violet as the "medium" of her message, there are important elements of her work, outlined in this book, that can and should be applied to the work of others in their own therapeutic practice. Violet herself will never be duplicated, but what she has discovered and created in her approach can certainly be extended.

The second reason I shared this example of Sima's work with clay is that it stands as a vivid example of the cross-cultural relevance of Violet's approach. Sima is a Black, South African woman living literally a hemisphere away from where Violet lives and works, yet the open and flexible qualities of Violet's Therapeutic Experience with clay allowed Sima to bring her own particular personal and cultural experiences to the foreground. Sima's example of working with the clay shows how Violet's approach to therapy allows the "here and now" experience of those involved to come forth, whether those individuals are in Santa Barbara or South Africa.

The third reason I chose to show this piece of work with Sima is that it not only shows the cross-cultural relevance, but also the cross-generational relevance of Violet's approach to therapy. Sima's work with the clay is one of many examples in this book that show how Violet's approach is relevant and helpful for adults as well as children and adolescents. Although the focus of Violet's approach is clearly on the application of her work with young people, throughout these chapters I have presented seven examples of adults finding benefit from engaging in Violet's Therapeutic Experiences. These six examples include: Lydia's work with her Safe Place drawing, Sabina's work with her clay piece, Candice and her Anger drawing, Isabel and the Music experience, Lark and the Medicine cards, Nicholas and his Sand tray, and Beth and her Demon drawing. Seen as a whole, these seven examples of Violet working with adults during the summer training, along with Sima's example of working with me in South

Africa, provide evidence that it is not just children and adolescents who are helped to make sense of their experience through Violet's approach to working.

Most adults have a tendency to use verbal language and numeric symbols as their dominant tools for making sense of the world. Such verbal and mathematical skills are highly valued in most adult cultures around the globe. In the United States, this is exemplified by the fact that the Graduate Record Exam (which most therapists must take to be admitted to graduate school) is organized around two dominant scores reflecting verbal and quantitative reasoning. Yet in all cultures across time and place, adults also make daily use of imagination, sensation, metaphor and narrative to process and make meaning of their experience (Werner, 1956, 1957). Violet's approach reaffirms these important modalities that are too often undervalued in adult experience.

Perhaps this is why Violet emphasizes the "experiential" aspect to such a degree in her trainings with adults. She not only wants the training participants to be able to be able to do themselves what they will ask children to do in therapy, but she also wants them to be reminded of how powerful these "sub-dominant" modes of understanding are for adults as well as children.

In this section I have highlighted some aspects of the cross-cultural as well as cross-generational strengths of Violet's approach to therapy. In the section that follows, I share comments from South African workshop participants that build on the theme of the cross-cultural relevance of the Oaklander approach in general and her method of Clay work in particular.

Cross-cultural relevance of the Oaklander Approach

In each of the three cities that Violet and I visited in South Africa, I asked for eight to ten volunteers who would be willing to meet with Violet and me at lunch to discuss the cross-cultural aspects of her approach to working with children. During each of these three focus groups, I recorded on audiotape the comments of participants as they addressed what they saw as the relevant aspects of Violet's approach to their work with children in South Africa. Because South Africa, like many African countries, is tragically facing an AIDS epidemic that has left many Black South African children orphaned and often homeless, most of the participants in the focus groups discussed their work with these grieving children in churches, children's homes, and community centers. What follows are seven themes that repeatedly emerged as relevant cross-cultural aspects of Violet's work during the focus groups. I have named each theme before briefly describing it. I have also supplied transcribed excerpts from the participants comments to illustrate the themes more fully.

1) Children talking indirectly to adults

Violet's therapeutic work with a child or an adolescent almost always involves a piece of clay, a sand tray scene, a puppet, or a drawing that the child has made. In this way, her work with children is usually mediated (Vygotsky, 1934) by some expressive medium. As I described in Chapter Two, the resulting object or form created by the child serves as a kind of "conversation piece" to help support the more verbal aspects of the therapeutic process.

Several South African workshop participants highlighted one important aspect of this "conversation piece" – that it gives both the child and the therapist something to look at during therapy and therefore to avoid prolonged and uncomfortable eye contact between the child and the adult. As Sima described it at lunch in Cape Town,

> In my culture, as a child you are taught not to look directly in eyes of an adult. It's across gender too, in that a woman can't look into the eyes of a man. We tend to look down or at something else. But in other cultures they do tend to look at the person when they are talking to them. So it's always a problem, like when we have a small child in school. Our children seem to look down when they talk to an adult person or a man. So in Violet's work, it is very helpful because the child always has something to look at, rather than talking directly with the therapist.

2) Working with client-interpreted symbols

As I have discussed throughout this book, one important aspect of Violet's work is that although she leaves plenty of room for the projective process to take place — through "being" the piece of clay, for example — she does not interpret the work of her clients for them. That is, the clients are free to create their own meaning out of the piece of clay rather than have the "therapist-as-expert" tell them what it means. We discovered in the focus groups that Violet's work is readily embraced by cultures within South Africa that make use of symbols culturally, but don't employ western interpretations of what those symbols might mean. Ette, an Afrikaans psychologist, spoke to this point in the Cape Town discussion in reference to her work with the Khosas, the people of Nelson Mandela's native tribe:

> I think there's a lot about psychological theory that is very foreign and also quite intrusive. So, I think working from the symbol is a much better place to come from. And I also think that at least the Khosa people – I can't speak for other cultural groups – already symbolize a lot, especially in illness. For example, a symbol of the tumor outside the body becomes something inside of you, and that thing inside of you lives outside of you too. So that is already a part of how they name illnesses and how they do already deal with the healing process.

3) Using media that cross language and class barriers

The use of expressive media such as clay to help facilitate work between people who speak differing languages was mentioned by many in the focus groups. Raime, a university lecturer and psychologist, spoke about the use of Violet's work in her own training of South African therapists:

I think the complexity at this stage is to train psychologists who are able to work cross-culturally. Previously, we had an elitist position as psychologists and now the whole new model we're developing focuses on becoming more contextualized. Specifically, we serve the Child Protection Unit for children that have been abused, and obviously, we work cross-culturally. We find the use of tactile media to be extremely effective — sand, clay, puppets, etc. — because it crosses the barrier of language that we often might have.

This focus on tactile media when working with children also takes the emphasis off the spoken word in another way, as described by Karen below. Karen described herself as "Colored" or "mixed race" and at the time of this interview was psychologist-in-training in Pretoria. She spoke about how, in a class-conscious society, clay and other media can help a child focus on language that signifies feeling rather than language that signifies class:

In relation to the language issue, I know, for example, that there was a time where being Colored and talking like a Colored person was an issue. Where if you spoke with a particularly *flat* accent, you were identified as being in the lower class. And if you rolled your R's more, you were of a higher class. So going to therapy and having to deal with that issue automatically puts you on guard. So how do you speak? What do you say? How do you say it? You watch what you're saying more than what you're actually *feeling*. So that's also an extra barrier of language. I think that with this use of clay and other media that kind of barrier is removed automatically and you can relate to the feeling and can connect much easier.

4) Expressing feelings visually — showing not telling

Throughout South Africa, native cultures share a constellation of deeply held values through the concept of "Ubuntu." Ubuntu reflects values placed on the individual's affiliation with and responsibility to the group. Individual identity is realized more through affiliation than through distinction: "People are people through other people" (South African Department of Welfare, 1997). In this way, Western psychology's predominant focus on the individual and the individual's feelings can run into conflict with deeply held cultural values in South Africa. Sarah, a therapist in Bloemfontein, described the influence of Ubuntu on the vocabulary of feeling in the Situ culture:

> You might ask a girl how she's feeling and she would describe the pain — "I'm hurt here" — but she wouldn't describe what she's really feeling inside. Situ families have certain rules. They don't speak easily about feelings. They are supposed to avoid such discussion. You can have the feelings, but you might not express it. You might *show* it, but you can't really talk about it, that's the rule. They actually have very few words to describe feelings.

They have a small vocabulary for feelings. The vocabulary is not there because the cultural rule holds down the verbal expression.

While respecting cultural traditions, many therapists described their efforts to address the emotional trauma that children had suffered by helping them express their experiences non-verbally. Many therapists in the focus groups, like Anna below, described their efforts to support the expression of feeling through the visual aspects of Violet's work:

I worked in a children's home in Durban with mainly African children. Out of 250 children, there were only about five White children. When I did my Master's in Play Therapy I was interested in looking at the use of play therapy and Gestalt with the African children that I worked with. And what I found was that they were very visual. I found that doing the fantasy play was really easy with them. And I think it's because as we discussed, culturally, they don't have many *words* to describe different types of feelings. So, when I'd ask the child, "Draw some anger for me," or "Draw your feeling of being mixed up," it comes out quite easily for them because their definition of an emotion is visual. They might say, "I don't know how to describe that I'm confused," but they can imagine that for you. It will come out through a vision.

Another social worker from Pretoria also described how the visual and metaphoric aspects of Violet's work helped her help children to express emotions:

> When I run my groups, they like to play with and make pictures with stones and sand and leaves and different pieces of nature. They'd rather use those than use crayons. And if I do exercises that include animal projections they can easily dialogue with those images and express emotions that way.

5) Expressing feelings actively and communally

Expressing feelings communally through enacted rites and rituals in a community setting is also a way that the values of "Ubuntu" are expressed in many native African cultures. A number of participants in the focus groups commented on how Violet's approach involves the use of the body to express feelings (through creative dramatics, pantomime, etc.) and how her work can be applied to group and family settings to match deeply held African values. Taba, a therapist and school counselor from Durban, stated:

> The support comes from family and community and neighbors. It's not a focus on the individual. And that might be why the language doesn't have words or why someone doesn't express *feeling* words, because there's always a ritual or a rite and you deal with it as a family, as a community. And the way they easily express their feelings is through dance and through the body. If they

are angry they are going to start singing or dancing or "toe-toeing." You know that something is happening through the body. Even when you have a meeting and it becomes *stuck* – you know, people do not know how to talk about it – they'll all jump up and start dancing and singing. And then they all sit down again and work it out.

I do a lot of group work and also a lot of children that have been sexually abused are referred to me. They come to me as individuals. They are referred by the schools or come on their own to come and talk to me about it. And then once we have worked through the situation of what has happened, they almost always ask to bring somebody from the family along, because they don't want to be alone with that situation. Because it's not something that happened to me alone, it's happened to my whole family also.

So, I have to work with the whole family. And that's the thing. You can use Oaklander's model to help the *group* to become reintegrated again. In so many cases the families are very disintegrated — most of the Black families because of their migration north. So what I've tried in my therapy with the family is to get them together again, to get them together as a priority — through enactment, or drawings, or whatever. And this serves the cultural value of Ubuntu, the collective values of the people. It's the collective consciousness — the set of principals that you need to follow and understand. It's a way of being, actually, a philosophy of life.

6) Settling emotions in the classroom

Another group of practitioners in the focus groups found Violet's approach to working with children relevant not only in a helping children express their emotions, but also in helping them become more "emotionally settled" in the classroom so that learning could happen. Rachel, who works in a children's home, shared this:

> Violet's book is like my Bible. I've read it word for word! And I've designed a program that I've shared with teachers in schools. The program is about communicating with children through the medium of clay. I've worked with primary school teachers and students ranging from the ages seven to about twelve years old. The response has been positive – they use a lot of fantasy play, a lot of visualization – to help settle the child in a classroom situation where there's *so* many children and the teachers are having difficulty with settling them emotionally. I know that Violet has spoken a lot about taking care of children's emotions before you can actually teach them. So, it's using that fantasy and that imagery and visualizations to help the child to be focused in the here and now. And once you've obtained that, then you move into the learning. Because once a child is present, or emotionally settled, then learning is more effective. So, that's been the whole *aim* of the program. And it's working quite well. So this is not only a

cross-cultural example of her work, but also cross-disciplinary as well.

7) Regaining a lost experience of childhood

One workshop participant had a particularly powerful personal experience with the clay during the training in Bloemfontein that led her to speak at length about certain cross-cultural benefits of Violet's approach to working with clay. Her comments were also supported and picked up by many other participants in the discussion that followed. Jala spoke poignantly about two themes during the focus-group lunch in Bloemfontein. The first theme, presented in her story below, is about how as an adult, the clay helped her recapture part of her own childhood experience. The second theme is about how she sees this way of working with clay as helping children experience their own childhood, a childhood that may be lost to them otherwise.

> I am Jala. I work as a counseling psychologist in private practice. I also work in a student-counseling unit at a local school. I'm actually the director of the student-counseling unit there. I see quite a few of sexually-abused children and other emotionally-traumatized children.
>
> I'd like to go back to the moment when Violet introduced us to her theory of working with clay. What came to my mind was the existential baseline that is tied to the theory itself. In other words, how her way of

working with clay pertains to the everyday life world of children. Children are accustomed to working with *mud*, and enjoy working with *mud*. They are getting dirty and messed up. I didn't really pay attention to this idea when Violet was talking. It was only when Violet actually asked us to work with the clay, to feel it, manipulate it, and then begin to make something while our eyes were closed. That's when I thought, "Oh my gosh! When did I last make something with my hands, especially with clay?" And then I remembered my own experience as a child.

I grew up in a rural area. As children we would actually stray away from home looking for wet areas where water was, or where the river was, looking for clay, so that we could just make up *things*. You know, in the rural area down there in Kwa Zulu Natal, we found dark, *very* good clay, out of which very good African pots are made. The very expensive African pots that you will find in curio shops. So we used that clay to make cows, mud huts, African pots, babies, families, and everything. So when I was working with the clay this morning, my whole childhood experience with clay just came back to my mind.

And I thought about the sexually-abused children I work with now. How the whole environment, the whole social world of children is changing so much. They are such traumatized children because the whole environment is so insecure, it's so dangerous. It is so dangerous that children have got to stay within their community – within the premises of their homes. They can't play as freely as we used to. We used to go to forests and to bushes to look for wild fruits and all sorts of things, but they *can't* do that anymore. They've got to stay within the premises because the moment they wander about, they get sexually molested. They are molested within the families, they are molested at preschools, and they are molested when they walk on their own. It's very much unsafe for children out there. They are now in urban areas. So it's not safe for them any more to stray away from homes and be looking for mud and things.

I find that this kind of experience is actually lost to them, because you won't find mud or clay, you know, within the premises of your home. I can't even say they've lost it. I don't even know that they *know* or that they've had this experience before. So, clay therapy, with the mud, can restore them to, or help them to discover a new world of childhood. It is an experience with which they might still get accustomed to or make use of the clay to deal with their angers and anxieties and any other traumas that they have experienced. I find that this experience with clay helps them relate to their own child within.

Concluding thoughts on the Oaklander approach

One's culture is embodied in one's individual artistic

expressions. An individual's rich cultural heritage is reflected in symbols that are used, in words that are chosen, in the references to familial and cultural customs that a creative piece necessarily reflects. Artistic expression is therefore a personal vehicle for embodying culture and, conversely, the repression or devaluing of individual artistic expression is a way in which an individual's cultural context and reality can be denied or ignored. Music, clay, drawing, and story each have deep roots as expressive and artistic media in every culture around the world (Brown, D., 1991). These amazingly flexible media of expression are malleable enough to reflect an infinitely rich diversity of both individual and cultural values and aesthetics. As reflected in the voices of the South African training participants quoted above, to use such media in the service of therapeutic work with children honors both the personal and cultural realities of the children with whom we work.

It is also true that the spoken word is a powerful expressive medium that can carry much cultural and personal meaning (Bruner, 1990). But to use only words in a rational exchange of ideas in the counseling context, particularly with children, reflects a limited palette for both personal and cultural expression. Children and adolescents around the world are not yet master wordsmiths like the adults are who work with them are. To question the tyranny of words that most counseling practices employ is to challenge a bias that is deeply held by both adults in general and white, western adults in particular (Heath, 1986). The use of clay and other expressive media in the counseling context with children honors both individual and cultural expression— through the body and senses — in a manner that words alone can never convey. In this way, Violet's creative approach to therapy both "speaks to" diverse cultural groups as it also allows individuals within those cultural settings to "speak through" the media that she employs.

In closing both this chapter and this book, I want broaden this discussion of cross-cultural relevance a bit. To do so, I want to emphasize that there are important links between the particular values of the various Black South African cultures described by the workshop participants and what we know to be developmentally appropriate practice for all children around the world. In other words, there are universal lessons to be learned from the culturally-specific experience of the South African workshop participants. As Maya Angelou states: "I note the obvious differences between each sort and type, but we are more alike, my friends, than we are unalike" (Angelou, 1990).

So how does Violet's therapeutic approach with children speak to the ways in which we are all alike, in South Africa as well as Santa Barbara and elsewhere? Regardless of culture or class, children the world over use sensory information as a primary way to process and make sense of the confusing world around and inside of them (Piaget, 1962). Additionally, the ability to use one thing (e.g. a piece of clay) to describe another thing (e.g. what I am feeling today) reflects an ability to think metaphorically that is one of the earliest developing cognitive skills in children the world over (MacCormac, 1990). The early development of narrative thinking, the ability to derive meaning from creating and hearing stories, is also a basic human function shared by both children and adults around the globe (Bruner, 1990). Lastly, Violet's often-repeated prompt to "use your imagination" in order to make something out of clay or some other medium of expression reflects another universal strength of childhood: the ability to think imaginatively — literally, in images — before having to put those imagined thoughts and feelings into words (Vygotsky, 1978).

In these ways, Violet's work with children and adolescents in the therapeutic context can be seen as building on core, universal strengths of childhood. These strengths of childhood — imagination, sensation, and the figurative languages of metaphor and narrative — all support a child's ability to make sense of the world, to address problems, and to be resilient. Put in Violet's language of Gestalt theory, these core strengths of childhood support organismic self-regulation, and the ability of a child to address and gain closure on troubling experiences.

In the end, perhaps Violet's approach to child therapy is so universally appreciated and adapted because these core strengths are found not only in the children of South Africa and California — the settings of this book – but in children from every country and culture around the world. Similarly, Violet's approach to working with adults in the two-week summer training in Santa Barbara may be so popular with practitioners from around the world for two related reasons. In her trainings, Violet gives adults a "window" into fundamental, experiential, and universal world of childhood while also helping those adults remember how to speak and understand the languages — both verbal and non-verbal — that children know best.

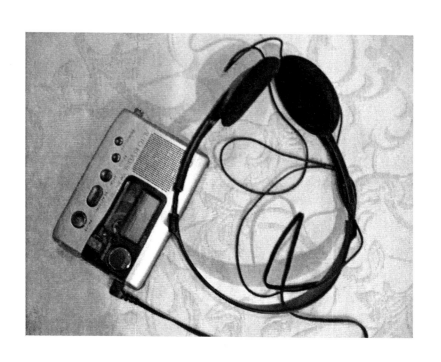

12

Afterword

Background and Methods

of the Study

In this chapter on the background and methods of this study, I tell the story of the "journey of inquiry" that I took and the methods of investigation that I used to study Violet's work and, ultimately, to write this book. I describe the path that I took in this process of research and documentation for two reasons: 1) to provide the reader with a clearer understanding of my relationship to Violet and my stance as the author of this text; and, 2) to provide the interested reader with more information about the theoretical and methodological ground upon which this book rests.

Initial steps

Having been a teacher and counselor of children and adolescents for much of my twenties, I entered a graduate program in 1988 that helped me bring into focus what continues to be one of my primary professional interests: the relationship of thinking, feeling and experience in the learning process. The program was at the University of California, Santa Barbara and was called Confluent Education. One of the programs founders, George I. Brown, described the underpinnings of this program in his 1971 text Human Teaching for Human Learning :

> Confluent Education is a philosophy and a process of teaching and learning in which the affective domain and the cognitive domain flow together, like two streams merging into one river, and are thus integrated in individual and group learning. (Brown, G., 1971)

The idea of bringing together the cognitive, affective and experiential domains in the learning process had already been a keen interest of mine in my work with children and adolescents as a teacher and a counselor. What was particularly fascinating about the Confluent Education program was that my professors were taking this idea of an integrated approach to learning that addressed cognitive, emotional and experiential domains and applying it to adult as well as child or adolescent education. For example, when we as Confluent Education students were struggling to understand some of the more complex aspects of the Gestalt theory being presented in our classes, our professors would have us break into pairs and do exercises geared to help us emotionally experience some of the abstract cognitive concepts such as the "I/Thou relationship" and "organismic self regulation".

It was during my introductory year in the Confluent Education program that I first read Violet's book Windows to our Children (Oaklander, 1978). Intrigued by her approach, I soon began to attend as many of Violet's trainings as I could. I also began to use her approach to working with children in my role as counselor and art director at Laurel Springs, a performing arts center and camp for children and adolescents in the Mountains above Santa Barbara, California that was owned and run by actress Jane Fonda. During my three years working at Laurel Springs, I experienced first-hand the power of Violet's method of incorporating the expressive arts in working with children and adolescents. I watched, for example, as fifty teenagers from inner-city Los Angeles used the expressive and performing arts to tell their story of struggling to make sense of the presence of gangs and AIDS in their communities, creating death masks, painting backdrops of ghetto scenes, and performing plays that they had written themselves.

The first book I intended to write, in fact, was meant to be a documentation of Jane Fonda's unique performing arts camp with an introductory chapter written by Violet. Laurel Springs closed down, however, when Jane Fonda married media entrepreneur Ted Turner and moved away. I gave up the idea of a book for the time being, but I continued to attend Violet's trainings and eventually decided to further my education by getting my license as a school psychologist and by subsequently enrolling in a doctoral program.

In the Educational Psychology program at UCSB, I was excited to learn that there were research methods that could help me address my continuing interest in Violet's approach to training adults to work therapeutically with children and adolescents. By this time, in the mid 1990s, I was regularly attending her summer training as both a participant and as an assistant. I decided at that time that I would focus my dissertation efforts on a study of Violet's trainings methods and that I would use a combination of anthropological and linguistic methods to help me do it. I had found that anthropological ethnography (Hammersley Atkinson, 1983; Spradley, 1979, 1980) could help me describe and analyze the kind of rich "culture of learning" that Violet constructed over the time she spent with her participants in her trainings. I also found that discourse and narrative analysis, borrowed from the broader field of linguistics (Capps and Ochs, 1995; Labov and Fanshel, 1977; and Tannen, 1993), could help me analyze and understand the subtle verbal and non-verbal interactions that took place between both adults and children in Violet's trainings.

As I will outline below, the "wide angle lens" of ethnography and the "zoom lenses" of discourse and narrative analysis provided me with a coherent way to frame and to understand how Violet trained adults to do therapeutic work with children and how she integrated cognitive and affective elements of experience in that training process. In the section that follows, I give an overview of what others have described as the "ethnographic journey" (Atkinson, 1990) and I detail my own journey as a qualitative researcher using both "wide angle" and "zoom" lenses to better understand Violet's work.

The ethnographer's journey

A common theme that ties together all methods of research is the effort to discover and make known that which is unknown. In this way, the process of research can be described as a journey in which the researcher leaves "home," or that which is known, to explore parts of the world that are new and different. The end goal of this journey is to bring back important and new information when the journey is done in order to share it with others. Atkinson (1990) describes the "ethnographer's journey" as having the "features of a quest ...a voyage of search, adventure and exploration" (p. 106).

While most anthropological studies are assumed to take place in far-flung locations, my study was to take place not far from my own home. My goal was to study the unique "culture" of Violet's trainings in Santa Barbara and see if I could write about this setting in a way that was helpful to others who were interested in her work. At the beginning of my quest to understand what made Violet's methods of training and therapy so interesting to so many practitioners world-wide, I had the feeling of setting off on an adventure. Here was a woman whose approach to working with children and adolescents was known and utilized around the world and yet no serious study of her methods of therapy or training had been undertaken. I was excited by the possibilities of what I might find in such a study, yet I also felt daunted by the project and full of questions: how would I identify and describe what is centrally relevant to Violet's work with both children in therapy and adults in training? How would I frame a dissertation around this study using respectful and non-invasive methods that were also theoretically rigorous and able to yield meaningful and practical results?

I learned that in qualitative research, these types of questions and concerns are common at the beginning of a project. The first phase of the ethnographic journey of exploration often requires quite a bit of "mucking around" in new environments without clear direction before one can determine methods and approaches that will lead to real understanding. At the beginning of my study of Violet's trainings, for example, I felt as if I had entered a rich and engaging culture but did not have any way of distinguishing what events or rituals within that culture had meaning and significance. As a researcher, I knew that I needed tools to help me gain some understanding of both the structural and functional aspects of the culture and environment that I was studying. I wanted these tools to help me describe the "shape" and "rhythm" of a particular day in Violet's training, for example, but also to help me identify important events that recurred or evolved over the course of the whole training as well.

From an anthropological perspective, Spradley (1980) suggests that researchers at this stage of a study need tools to help them make "grand tour" observations to document the "major features" of the research setting. As I will detail below, my first steps in studying and documenting Violet's trainings were to use such tools with which to observe and write up the major features of her trainings. The use of these tools involved documenting what things happened when in the training, how long they took, and who was involved.

Spradley (1980) describes the next step of the research process in which, after a researcher spends some time immersed in a research setting, salient features of the environment become clearer and the researcher then switches to a more focused set of lenses to document those particular features. Spradley describes this analytic process as "changes in the scope of the observation." The graphic in Figure 14 details this process as it occurs over the course of a research study:

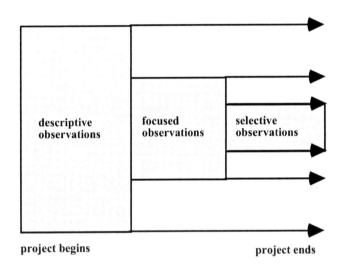

Figure 14: Spradley's "Changes in the Scope of Observation"

Similarly, researchers Hammersley and Atkinson (1983) use a "funnel" metaphor to describe the ethnographic research process as one moves from the more general to the more specific. They also describe that through this process, the researcher may discover a new point of focus for the study:

Ethnographic research has a characteristic "funnel" structure, being progressively focused over its course.

Progressive focusing has two analytically distinct components. First, over time the research problem is developed or transformed, and eventually its scope is clarified and delimited and its internal structure explored. In this sense, it is frequently only over the course of the research that one discovers what the research is really "about," and it is not uncommon for it to turn out to be about something quite remote from the initial foreshadowed problems. (p.175)

In the following sections, I will describe and detail the specific steps and particular methods of qualitative research that I used in my study of Violet's trainings. My methods parallel the "ethnographic journey" described above by Spradley, Hammersley and Atkinson. That is, my work became progressively focused over the course of the study, starting out more broadly focused and less-defined at the beginning and ending up with a tight focus and new sense of what my research project was really "about" as the study drew to a close.

Phase one: The pilot study

For a two-year period of time, from April 1995, through April 1997, I attended seven of Violet's workshops and trainings, which varied in terms of length and focus. Three of the workshops were a day long and focused on particular themes such as working with adolescents or working with children and grief. I also attended two of Violet's two-week summer trainings during this period, each of which were ten days long, as well as two "advanced trainings" which were each two days long. All of the workshops and trainings shared the common goal of training adults to work therapeutically with children and adolescents using the "Oaklander approach."

During this first phase of my study, I collected data as if I were looking through a "wide angle lens." That is, I worked to document the trainings as broadly and descriptively as possible. To accomplish this, I used a number of specific methods and techniques. For example, I wrote up detailed field notes describing the moment-to-moment interactions and events of the trainings. I also conducted interviews with Violet that enabled me to clarify some of the events and interactions that I had written about in my field notes. At the same time, I recorded all of the trainings on audiotape and I recorded much of the 1996 summer training on videotape. Additionally, I collected "artifacts" from the trainings that provided specific examples of events and activities. For example, I collected drawings created by some participants and took photos of Violet and the participants as they engaged in various activities throughout the trainings.

All of my research efforts during the pilot study were focused on the intention of answering a broadly framed and descriptively focused ethnographic question: "What is happening in these trainings?" In the next section, I detail how I worked to answer this question by composing a narrative description of one specific type of Violet's trainings.

Phase two: Writing a narrative account

The findings from my pilot study made it clear that the "full palette" of Violet's training methods could best be best seen in her two-week intensive summer trainings. Therefore, in Phase Two of the study, I focused on a two-week training that took place during July of 1997. During this phase of the project, I collected ethnographic data through the same methods that I have described, yet my focus was more clearly directed on documenting and analyzing a single training as it unfolded rather than multiple trainings across time.

In the months following the July 1997 training, I composed a narrative account of that two-week summer training. To write this story, I drew upon all of the data that I had collected over the two weeks of the July training. The intent of this narrative account was to represent the events of the training as descriptively and coherently as possible. This move to document the training in a narrative, descriptive form should also be seen however, as an analytical step that was informed by theory. As Hammersley and Atkinson (1983) argue, one must acknowledge through "reflexivity" that the act of writing a narrative account is, in itself, a kind of analysis:

> There can be no hard-and-fast distinction between "writing" and "analysis" ...The "analyses" that ethnographies embody are often embedded in, and constituted by, their very organization as texts, their "style," the choice of language, and so on... It is no good

being reflexive in the course of planning and executing a piece of research if one is only to abandon that reflexivity when it comes to writing about it. Likewise, one is guilty of a dangerous double standard if research is conducted under the auspices of an interest in meaning and language, and the language and meaning of one's own products are not also scrutinized. (p. 209)

To be reflexive on my own writing, it is necessary for me to make explicit the analytic choices I made in representing the two-week training in narrative form. These analytic choices and embedded assumptions are as described in the following paragraphs.

Perhaps the main reason I chose to write up a narrative account of Violet's summer training was to provide a "window" into a world to which I had access and to which other's (i.e. counselors, therapists, teachers, parents) may also benefit from having access: "Such accounts," state Hammersley and Atkinson (1983), "can be of great value. They may provide us with knowledge of ways of life hitherto unknown and thereby shake our assumptions...or challenge our stereotypes" (p. 176).

This apt quotation touches upon three other reasons why I was so interested in providing a window into Violet's summer training: first, I knew that Violet's work, while being extremely popular world-wide with many practitioners, was not highly regarded in the academic mainstream of child psychology. Therefore, I knew that documenting her particular approach to training adults (and to doing therapy with children) would provide a unique account of such work being done in the field and perhaps, in so doing, "challenge some stereotypes" or "shake some assumptions." Second, I knew that there was a greater demand for attendance at the summer training that Violet offered than she was able to provide for. That is, each year many people were not able to attend the summer training because of time, travel, or financial constraints. Finally, it was not clear how many more years Violet would continue to offer the training and therefore I wanted to be able to provide a lasting record of her unique way of working with both children and adults.

I also chose to create a narrative account of the summer training in order to have a foundation upon which I could later add more explicit analysis of Violet's therapeutic and training methods. Davis (1974) states: "I do think it is essential that you...find some kind of story which will give you an opening, a beginning working stratagem with respect to the data" (pg 434). The narrative core that I composed documenting Violet's 1997 summer training became not only the centerpiece of my dissertation, but also serves as the foundation for each of the previous chapters of this book.

Although I worked to be as descriptive as possible in writing the narrative account, Hammersley and Atkinson (1983) state that such portrayals are "in no sense pure descriptions, they are constructions involving selection and interpretation, not mere unedited recordings of sound and movements" (p. 176). One way that I worked to address this fact that a story is also an interpretation of events was that I made explicit in the narrative account when I included my personal reactions, comments, and interpretations. I chose to include personal responses in the writing because the training itself was so experiential in nature that I felt that I would be remiss if I didn't include notes on how I felt as a participant in the room when another participant screamed at the top of her lungs while working with Violet, for example, or when the room suddenly got so quiet that I could hear the sounds of crayons scratching on paper. I also made the decision to include visual images (photos and figures) within the narrative text so that I could in some way represent the strong visual element of the training that was so clearly present throughout the two weeks.

Such a personal account of any event is clearly biased by the writer's point of view. In order to address this fundamental issue of any qualitative study (or any quantitative study, for that matter) I worked hard to include multiple points of "triangulation" in the process of writing up the narrative. Hammersley and Atkinson (1983) describe the term triangulation as being derived from a loose analogy with surveying and navigation. In both surveying and navigation, as well as in qualitative research, one seeks confirmation of data points from more than one source. In my case, I used interview data with training participants to confirm my views of the events of the training, and, at times, included their remarks verbatim in my narrative account. I also worked closely with Violet in the process of writing up the narrative. In this way, Violet was able to clarify some of her actions and motivations that were represented in the text as well as some of the concepts that I had described incompletely. Additionally, I had help from research colleagues who served as "reflective readers" of my narrative of the training. From their comments I learned, for example, that I could summarize certain events or scenes without compromising the story as a whole.

Phase three: Constructing and analyzing Event Maps

I completed the narrative account of Violet's training in the Fall of 1997 and, in doing so, culminated more than two years of work documenting her methods of training adults to do therapy with children and adolescents. Having this much experience studying her work under my belt, I began to see recognizable patterns in the way that Violet structured the summer trainings. As Spradley (1980) states, "With repeated observations, individual acts begin to fall into recognizable patterns of activity...Sometimes sets of activities are linked together into larger patterns called events" (p. 41). These "events" that Spradley describes have also been described by classroom researchers Collins and Green (1992) who state: "One way to examine the continuity of experience is to identify cycles of activity that form the substructure of classroom life" (p. 67). Through careful examination of my field notes and audio recordings, it became clear that the manner in which Violet organized time in the training could be documented and analyzed by noting obvious changes in events and focus. For example, Figure 15 contains an excerpt from my field notes from the first morning of the 1997 summer training that shows the manner in which I kept note of the changing events of the training over time.

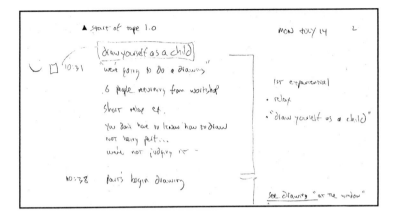

Figure 15: Excerpt From Field Notes

In this excerpt, I note the time (10:31 a.m.) that Violet introduced what I identified at that time as the "1st experiential," and the time (10:38 a.m.) that Violet asked participants to begin to "draw yourself as a child." Building on this close examination of my field notes, I constructed "Event Maps" for each day of the training. An excerpt of the Event Map for the first morning of the training on July 14, 1997 is detailed in Figure 16. Although I constructed one complete Event Map for each day, this excerpt shows only the first four and half hours of the "morning session" of Day One.

In the Event Maps for each day of the training, I had a particular function in mind for each of the columns. In column one, I categorized and named each event using "folk terms" (Spradley, 1980) whenever possible. That is, I used Violet's own descriptors of events rather than coming up with my own terms, thereby avoiding interpreting the events rather than simply describing them. As Figure 16 shows, after spending 70 minutes on introductions and basic business items, Violet then spent 55 minutes later in the morning having the participants engage in an opening exercise where they were asked to "draw themselves as a child." I identified this event as "Exercise #1" in column one. After this drawing activity, Violet spent two hours and twenty-five minutes presenting on theory and issues regarding "what brings kids into therapy." I identified this event in the first column as "Topic #1." In column two, I noted the times at which clear changes in the action or focus of the training took place.

In column three of the Event Maps, I focused on Violet's actions in the training. Through a review of my pilot study data, I was able to determine that Violet generally took on one of two roles in the training: she either spent her time "presenting" information, case examples, and theory, or she engaged in "demonstrating" the kind of therapeutic work that she does with children and adolescents (within both of these modes, there were also many dialogues and question/answer discussions as well). These two modes of activity were clearly linked in that her presentations generally served to explain the theory behind her demonstrations. The demonstrations also conversely served to give concrete examples of the theoretical aspects of her work.

In column four of the Event Maps, I focused on the actions of the participants in the training. This focus on the participants' activities lead me to a key discovery that then informed the next step of my research.

Events	Time	Violet's Actions	Participant's Actions
Opening	9:05 – 10:15	Presentation: introductions and general business	each person introduces themselves
Break	10:15 – 10:30		
Exercise #1 "draw yourself as a child"	10:30 – 10:38	Demonstration: verbally prompts relaxation, visualization, and drawing	non-verbal/fantasy experien participants draw childhood scene using "messy" pastels
	10:38 – 10:55	makes herself availa for questions	verbal articulation of experience: participants sha drawing in groups of five
	11:20 – 11:25	asks for comments o exercise	verbal articulation of experience: participants sha comments in large group
Topic #1 "what brings kids into therapy"	11:25 – 12:05	Presentation (theory emphasizes "using a the modalities and senses of the organis	participants listen, take note ask questions, make comme
Lunch	12:05 – 1:30		

Figure 16: Event Map for First Morning of the Training - Day One: Monday, July 14, 1997

Phase four: Constructing typologies

In the process of constructing the Event Maps of the 1997 summer training, it became clear that Violet spent a large percentage of time in the training — nearly 50% over the two-week period — engaging the training participants in experiential exercises that modeled the kind of therapeutic work that she did with children. In consultation with Violet, I decided to call these experiential exercises "Therapeutic Experiences" because of both the experiential and the therapeutic focus of each of them. An example of one of these Therapeutic Experiences happens on day two of the summer training and involves the participants drawing a picture of a safe place in their lives. As described in Chapter Two, this is the same activity that Violet may ask a child to do in the therapeutic setting. In this way, each of the Therapeutic Experiences in the summer training are "hands on" examples for the participants of the kind of work that Violet does with children and adolescents in the therapeutic setting.

Having identified that the Therapeutic Experiences played a key role in the summer training, I once again relied on theory to help inform my next analytical move in the study. I found the writings of Hammersley and Atkinson (1983) helpful at this point in regards to their theoretical and practical conceptualizations of "typologies." These authors describe the construction of typologies as "one of the major way stations on the road to theoretical models in ethnographic work" (p. 181). They go on to describe the construction of typologies as the process by which "a set of phenomena is identified that represents sub-types of some more general category" (p. 181). From this description, it was clear that it would be helpful to conceptualize Violet's Therapeutic Experiences as a kind of typology in that each of them was unique in itself, yet could also clearly be identified as part of a larger category of items.

My first step in creating a typological analysis of the general category of Therapeutic Experiences was to ask the question "What are all the examples of Therapeutic Experiences in the training?" In answer to this question, I created a list of each instance of a Therapeutic Experience that took place over the two-week period, ordering them chronologically. I detailed the resulting list is Table 1 in Chapter Three, showing that Violet introduced a specific example of a Therapeutic Experience on most days of the training.

After having identified this set of Therapeutic Experiences as a kind of typology, I next needed to figure out how these examples were both similar to and different from each other. Spradley (1980) suggests asking "structural questions" to identify similarities and differences. Therefore, I next asked, "What are the parts of each Therapeutic Experience in the typology?" I also asked, "How are each of these examples of Therapeutic Experiences related to the training as a whole?"

The answers to these questions were significant in terms of identifying meaningful, structural aspects of Violet's training and the findings serve as a centerpiece to the "reflective notes" that conclude many of the chapters of this book. In those reflective notes, I discussed how the each of the Therapeutic Experiences in the training are almost identical to each other in terms of structure, but also that they serve very different functions when they appear at different points in the training. In other words, Violet uses a "type" or "kind" of exercise that has a recognizable structure, yet she uses these exercises in progressively differentiated ways in the unfolding process of training adults or of doing therapy with children.

Phase Five: Discourse and narrative analysis

When I started "zooming in" on and taking a close look at the structure and function of the Therapeutic Experiences, I discovered that one important thing they all had in common was narrative and metaphor. As described initially in Chapter Three, in each case where Violet used a Therapeutic Experience in the training, she included a prompt for the person she was working with to create a story or a metaphor. For example, after having the participants work with sand trays on the sixth day of the training, Violet had the participants tell a story that described the scene they had created in the sand.

After observing that stories and metaphors formed the heart of each of the Therapeutic Experiences, I realized that to understand Violet's work, I would need to understand these discursive elements better. Luckily, at that point in my research a class was offered at UCSB for the first time called "Discourse and Narrative Analysis." I immediately signed up and learned that discourse analysis, of which narrative analysis is a subset, is defined as the analysis of strings of verbal utterances that are longer than one sentence (Stubbs, 1983). I also learned that with discourse analysis I could analyze "chunks" of language, such as the dialogues inherent in therapeutic contexts. Those who work in discourse analysis are mainly concerned with the way in which language is used to help individuals construct personal meaning in the midst of social contexts (Cook-Gumperz, 1986; Kyratzis and Green, 1997). As Bahktin (1986) describes, "the unique speech experience of each individual is shaped and developed in continuous and constant interaction with other's individual utterances."

Importantly, the "zoom lens" of discourse analysis enabled me to focus on the language used between Violet and those with whom she worked in the training in a helpful and meaningful way. Specifically, discourse analysis helped me do two things: 1) to understand better the role that narratives and metaphors played in the Therapeutic Experiences, and, 2) to understand better the role that Violet played in helping others "make sense" of their experience through these narratives and metaphors in both the training and therapeutic context.

Chapter Seven of this book was devoted to a "zoom lens" viewing of one particular discursive exchange that took place in the training, a dialogue that is full of rich examples of both narrative and metaphors. In that exchange, Violet works with a child guest, Elisa, and helps her to make sense of some significant trouble that she has faced in her life. I chose to focus on this particular exchange not only because it was such a clear example of Violet's approach to working with a child, but also because it served as an example of how Violet demonstrated her approach to working with Therapeutic Experiences to the adults in the training.

Parallels between qualitative methods and Gestalt approaches

I started out my study of Violet's trainings using the "wide angle" lens of ethnographic observation to discover what was generally happening in the trainings. As the study progressed, my methods of data collection and analysis (i.e. Event Maps and typologies) led me to an increasingly focused examination of Violet's Therapeutic Experiences and to an examination of the role of narrative and metaphor within each of them (Mortola, 1999a, 1999b). In this way, my study moved in a progressively more focused manner from beginning to end — as described by Hammersley and Atkinson (1983) — from a broad look at the structure of the training to a very tightly focused look at the Therapeutic Experiences and at narratives and metaphors in particular.

In this chapter, I have made explicit the theoretical assumptions that guided my research methods as well as outlining the practical steps that I took in collecting and analyzing the data in this qualitative study. Although qualitative studies are still the exception in the larger field of psychology, that is starting to change. Carey and Wilson (1995) argue that a better relationship between researchers and practitioners could be achieved by:

> ...examining and modifying the view that research is generated only in formal settings using standard procedures and statistical analyses. Those in Academe

might consider expanding the repertoire of acceptable techniques to include qualitative methodology and clinical expertise. This shift would allow practitioners to contribute more fully to the expert base of knowledge and to more readily assimilate research-based knowledge into their practices. (p. 175)

My hope is that the study that has filled the pages of this book will make a contribution to: 1) practitioners who may benefit from the methods of training and therapy it describes, documents and analyzes, and, 2) researchers in the field of psychology and education who may benefit from seeing a rigorous qualitative approach applied to a field that has traditionally and predominantly employed quantitative research methods.

Throughout this book, I have paid great attention to the theme of "parallels and congruence." I highlighted the parallels and congruence between the way that Violet trains adults and the way that she works with children in therapy, for example. I also "foregrounded" the parallels and congruence between her Gestalt theory base and how that theory informs the practical moves that she makes in her work with children and adults. During the writing of this book, I was excited to discover that there were also "parallels and congruence" between the "how" of this book and the "what" of this book. That is, as I was conducting this study, I became aware of a number of parallels between the theoretical and practical foundations of Violet's Gestalt approach to therapy and the theoretical and practical foundations of my own qualitative approach to researching her work. I have identified four important ways that Gestalt therapy theory and qualitative research theory are parallel and congruent in that they share an emphasis on: 1) A respectful and non-hierarchical relationship, 2) A process orientation, 3) A reflective process, and, 4) A stance of authentic participation. I detail and describe these parallels further in the paragraphs below.

1) A respectful and non-hierarchical relationship

Both Gestalt therapy theory and qualitative research theory assume that productive work can only take place when there is a respectful and non-hierarchical relationship in place between the parties involved (i.e. between the therapist and the client or between the researcher and the informant). In other words, Martin Buber's (1958) description of the I/thou relationship is relevant to both Gestalt therapy as well as qualitative research.

2) A process orientation

Both Gestalt therapy theory and qualitative research theory are process oriented as opposed to being goal directed. This means that both orientations allow for and encourage the identification and exploration of emergent themes rather than previously held assumptions or models. In her Gestalt orientation to practice, this means that Violet patiently waits for themes to emerge in her work with children and adults. In my qualitative approach to research, it meant that I went into the Violet's training not to test hypotheses, but rather to see what important themes emerged in the culture of her training over time.

3) A reflective process

The practice of both Gestalt therapy and qualitative research methods require a consistent and thorough reflective process on the part of the practitioner. That is, both Gestalt therapists and qualitative researchers go through a training process in which they learn to consistently pay attention to the affect that their own assumptions, biases, and personal processes are having on their work. Moreover, they both take the firm stance that the person of the therapist or researcher necessarily impacts the work undertaken and that this influence is best monitored by making it explicit.

4) A stance of authentic participation

Linked to this third point, the last parallel I found between Gestalt therapy and qualitative research methods is that both approaches also require that the practitioner must take a stance of authentic participation in the process rather than assuming a stance of false objectivity. To this end, neither a Gestalt therapist nor a qualitative researcher is able to hide behind a pre-determined role and must instead engage him or herself in the therapeutic or research process in an authentic participatory role.

Given these parallels between Gestalt therapy theory and qualitative research theory and methods, perhaps it is not a coincidence that I should have chosen the one to study the other. The fact is, I already had years of Gestalt therapy training and practice before learning about qualitative research design. I felt a deep kinship to Gestalt therapy theory as a helpful way of approaching and working with people. Given the fact that my theory and practice base was already substantially rooted in Gestalt therapy theory, and given the deep theoretical linkages between Gestalt therapy theory and qualitative research theory, perhaps my choice is not surprising when it was time for me to settle into a theoretical orientation as a researcher.

If anything, I think these parallels between the content of my study (i.e. Violet's Gestalt-based approach to therapy and training) and the methods of my study (i.e. qualitative methods and approaches) have helped me to create a more sympathetic and respectful record of Violet's work in this book. By this I mean that my methods of study allowed me to address and document Violet's work from a distinct but related perspective. In Gestalt terminology, my qualitative research methods helped me to have good boundaries, to make good contact, and to make meaning of my project in a clearly relational way. "All real living is meeting," said Martin Buber (1958), and I have certainly been enriched and am grateful for all the meetings that this book represents.

References

Angelou, M. (1990). *I shall not be moved*. NY: Random House.

Atkinson, P. (1990). *The ethnographic imagination: Textual constructions of reality*. NY: Routledge.

Bakhtin, M. M. (1986). *Speech genres and other late essays*. Austin, TX: University of Texas Press.

Baylor, B. (1974). *Everybody needs a rock*. NY: Macmillan Publishing Company.

Bowlby, J. (1988). *A secure base*. NY: Basic Books.

Brown, D. E. (1991). *Human universals*. NY: Mcgraw-Hill, Inc.

Brown, G. I. (1971). *Human teaching for human learning: An introduction to Confluent Education*. NY: The Viking Press.

Brown, L., Brown, M. (1988). *Dinosaur's divorce: A guide to changing families*. NY: Little Brown and Company.

Bruner, J. (1990). *Acts of meaning*. Cambridge, MA: Harvard University Press.

Bruner, J., Lucariello, J. (1989). Monologues as narrative representation of reality. In K. Nelson (Ed.), *Narratives from the crib* (pp.). Cambridge, MA: Harvard University Press.

Buber, M. (1958). *I and thou*. NY: Scribner.

Capps, L., Ochs, E. (1995). *Constructing panic: The discourse of agoraphobia*. Cambridge, MA: Harvard University Press.

Carey, K. T., Wilson, M. S. (1995). *Training school psychologists*. In A. Thomas, and J. Grimes (Eds.), *Best practices in school psychology*. Washington, DC: National Association of School Psychologists.

Carlson, J., Keat, D.B., Oaklander, V. (2002). *Gestalt therapy with Violet Oaklander: Child therapy with the experts* (video). NY: Allyn Bacon

Collins, E., and Green. J. (1992). Learning in classroom settings: Making or breaking a culture. In H. Marshall (Ed.), *Redefining learning: Roots of educational restructuring* (pp. 59-86). Norwood, NJ: Ablex.

Cook-Gumperz, J. (1986). *The social construction of literacy*. Cambridge: Cambridge University Press.

Csikszentmihalyi, M. (1991). *Flow: The psychology of optimal experience.* NY: Harper Perennial.

Davis, N.J. (1974). *The abortion consumer: Making it through the network.* Urban Life and Culture, 2(4):432-59.

De Mille, R. (1997, 1955). *Put your mother on the ceiling: Children's imagination games.* Highland, NY: The Gestalt Journal Press, Inc.

Freud, S. (1957). *A general selection from the works of Sigmund Freud.* NY: Doubleday.

Freud, S. (1959). *Inhibitions, symptoms, and anxiety.* NY: W.W. Norton and Company.

Fyleman, R. (1992). *Fairy went a-marketing.* NY: E.P. Dutton.

Gardner, R. (1971). *Therapeutic communication with children: The mutual storytelling technique.* NY: Science House Inc.

Goodman, L. (1985). *Linda Goodman's sun signs.* NY: Bantam Books.

Hammersley, M., Atkinson, P. (1983). *Ethnography: Principles in practice.* NY: Routledge.

Handford, M. (1997). *Where's Waldo?* NY: Candlewick Press.

Heath, S. B. (1986). Taking a cross-cultural look at narratives. *Topics in Language Disorders* 7(1):84-94.

Hindman, J. (1983). *A very touching book...for little people and big people.* NY: Alexandria Association.

Jolles, I. (1964). A catalog for the qualitative interpretation of the House-Tree-Person (H-T-P). L.A., CA: Western Psychological services.

Kyratzis, A., Green, J. (1997). Jointly constructed narratives in classrooms: Co-construction of friendship and community through language. *Teaching and Teacher Education* 13(1):1-21.

La Chapelle, R. (1975). *Demons.* NY: Pure Diamond Press.

Labov, W., Fanshel, D. (1977). *Therapeutic discourse: Psychotherapy as conversation.* NY: Academic Press, Inc.

Lakoff, G., Johnson, M. (1980). *Metaphors we live by.* Chicago, IL: University of Chicago Press.

Latner, J. (1973). *The Gestalt therapy book: A holistic guide to the theories, principles, and techniques of Gestalt therapy developed by Frederick S. Perls and others.* NY: The Gestalt Journal.

Luscher, M. (1980). *Luscher color test*. NY: Random Library.

MacCormac, E. R. (1990). *A cognitive theory of metaphor*. Cambridge, MA: MIT Press.

Mills, J.C. (1992) *Little tree*. Washington, DC: Magination Press.

Morrison, T. (1993) Nobel prize acceptance speech. [on line] http://nobelprize.org/literature/laureates/1993/morrison-lecture.html

Mortola, P. (1999a). Giving Voice: Undoing negative body images and introjects. *Australian Gestalt Journal*, 3:85-93.

Mortola, P. (1999b). Narrative formation and gestalt closure: Helping clients make sense of "disequilibrium" through stories in the therapeutic setting. *The Gestalt Review*, 3(4):308-230.

Murray, L. (1943). *Thematic Apperception Test*. MA: Harvard University Press.

Nevis, E. (1992). *Gestalt therapy: Perspectives and applications*. Cambridge, MA: GestaltPress.

Oaklander, V. (1978). *Windows to our children: A gestalt therapy approach to children and adolescents*. Highland, NY: The Gestalt Journal Press.

Oaklander, V. (1999). *Group* play therapy from a gestalt perspective. In D.S. Sweeney and L.E. Homeyer (Eds.), *The handbook of group play therapy: How to do it, how it works, whom its best for* (pp. 162-175). NY: Jossey-Bass.

Perls, F. (1947). *Ego, hunger, and aggression*. London: Allan and Unwin.

Perls, F., Hefferline, R., Goodman, P. (1951). *Gestalt Therapy: Excitement and growth in the human personality*. NY: Dell Publishing Company.

Perls, L. (1992). *Living at the boundary*. J. Wysong (Ed.). Highland, NY: The Gestalt Journal.

Piaget, J. (1962). *Play, dreams and imitation in childhood*. NY: W.W. Norton and Co.

Piaget, J. (1971). *Biology and knowledge: An essay on the relations between organic regulations and cognitive processes*. Chicago, IL: The University of Chicago Press.

Piaget, J. (1977). *The development of thought: Equilibration of cognitive structures*. NY: Viking Press.

Polkinghorne, D. (1988) *Narrative knowing and the human sciences.* Albany, NY: State University of New York Press.

Polster, E., Polster, M. (1973). *Gestalt therapy integrated: Contours of theory and practice.* NY: Vintage Books.

Potter, B. (1902). *The tale of Peter Rabbit.* London: Penguin Group.

Preston, E. (1969) *The Temper Tantrum Book.* NY: Viking.

Propp, V. (1968, 1928). *Morphology of the Russian folktale.* Austin, TX: University of Texas Press.

Rhyne, J. (1973). *The Gestalt art experience.* Belmont, CA: Wadworth Publishing Company.

Sams, J. Carson, D. (1988). *Medicine cards: The discovery of power through the ways of animals.* Santa Fe, NM: Bear and Company.

Seuss, D. (1990). *Oh, the places you'll go!* NY: Random House.

Spradley, J. P. (1979). *The ethnographic interview.* Fort Worth. TX: Holt, Rinehart and Winston, Inc.

Spradley, J. P. (1980). *Participant observation.* NY: Harcourt Brace Jovanovich College Publishers.

South African Department of Welfare, (1997). White paper for social welfare: Principles, guidelines, recommendations, proposed policies and programmes for developmental social welfare in South Africa. [online] http://www.gov.za/dept/welfare/docs/1997/soswel97.html

Stock, G. (1987). *Book of Questions.* NY: Workman Publishing Company.

Stubbs, M. (1983). *Discourse Analysis.* Chicago: University of Chicago Press.

Sutton-Smith, B. (1979). *Play and learning.* NY: Gardner.

Tannen, D. (1989). *Talking voices: Repetition, dialogue, and imagery in conversational discourse.* Cambridge. NY: Cambridge University Press.

Tannen, D. (1993). What's in a frame? Surface evidence for underlying expectations. In D. Tannen (Ed.), *Framing in discourse* (pp. 14-56). NY: Oxford University Press.

Viorst, J. (1972) *Alexander's terrible, horrible, bad day.* NY: Simon Schuster.

Vygotsky, L. S. (1962,1934). *Thought and language*. Cambridge, MA: MIT Press.

Vygotsky, L. S. (1978). *Mind in society: The development of higher psychological processes*. Cambridge, MA: Harvard University Press.

Werner, H. (1957). The concept of development from a comparative and organismic point of view. In D. B. Harris (Ed.), *The concept of development* (pp. 140-163). Minneapolis, MN: University of Minnesota Press.

Werner, H., Kaplan, B. (1956). The developmental approach to cognition: Its relevance to the psychological interpretation of anthropological and ethnolinguistic data. *American Anthropologist*, 58:866-880

Wheeler, G. (1991). *Gestalt reconsidered: A new approach to contact and resistance*. NY: Gardner Press.

Wheeler, G. (2000). *Beyond individualism: Toward a new understanding of self, relationship, and experience*. Hillsdale, NJ: The Analytic Press/GestaltPress

Wheeler, G. (2005) Spirit and shadow: Esalen and the Gestalt model. In J. Kripal, (Ed.), *On the edge of the future: Esalen and American religious culture* (pp. 165-196). Bloomington: Indiana University Press

Winter, P. (1978). *Common Ground*. [CD]. NY: Living Music.

Wood, A. (1988) *Elbert's bad word*. NY: Harcourt Brace Co.

Young, G. R., Wagner, E. E. (1999). *The hand test: Advances in applications and research*. NY: Krieger Publishing Company.

Selected Titles from GestaltPress